S0-AAC-258

Documentary Superstars

How Today's Filmmakers Are Reinventing the Form

By Marsha McCreadie

© 2008 Marsha McCreadie

All rights reserved. Copyright under Berne Copyright Convention, Universal Copyright Convention, and Pan-American Copyright Convention. No part of this book may be reproduced, stored in a retrieval system, or transmitted in any form, or by any means, electronic, mechanical, photocopying, recording, or otherwise, without prior permission of the publisher.

12   11   10   09   08   5   4   3   2   1

Published by Allworth Press
An imprint of Allworth Communications, Inc.
10 East 23rd Street, New York, NY 10010

Cover design by Derek Bacchus
Interior design by Kristina Critchlow
Page composition/typography by Integra Software Services, Pvt., Ltd., Puducherry, India

ISBN-13: 978-1-58115-508-2
ISBN-10: 1-58115-508-5

Library of Congress Cataloging-in-Publication Data:
McCreadie, Marsha.
    Documentary superstars : how today's filmmakers are reinventing the form / Marsha McCreadie.
    p. cm.
    Includes bibliographical references and index.
    ISBN-13: 978-1-58115-508-2
    ISBN-10: 1-58115-508-5
    1. Documentary films—History and criticism.   2. Motion picture producers and directors—
    Interviews.   I. Title.
    PN1995.9.D6M375 2008
    070.1'8—dc22

                                                                                2008029168
Printed in the United States of America

Very interesting if true.

—Gertrude Stein

TABLE OF CONTENTS

· · · · · · · · · ·

ACKNOWLEDGMENTS

· · · · · · · · · ·

Thanks to the staff at Lincoln Center's Billy Rose Theatre Collection for, as ever, their unfailing and gracious efforts in researching materials. Much appreciation to my students in our documentary film class at Fordham University's Lincoln Center Campus in the fall of 2006. Especially Adam Benic for his unflagging intellectual curiosity, which pushed at me in a good way, and Casey Michael McGarry for his fascination with the spiritual impact of movie music, both qualities that can get lost along the way in the professional or academic practice of film criticism.

And so came the inspiration for this book and a new group of students of sorts—readers—for the ideas germinated in that class.

Also, appreciation to the Faculty Technology Center at Fordham University, especially Jay Savage and Rien Chy, who untied some of the knots I got tangled up in when computers and the new technology sometimes seemed an obstacle, not an aid. The Authors Guild provided a loan to help me complete the manuscript by relieving some financial anxieties. And thanks to Nicole Potter-Talling, an acquisitions editor who took a chance on a new angle on film studies.

I am grateful for the help of Professor Jeff Jaeckle, whose paper on spoof films, "Allow Myself to Introduce Myself" (an Austin Powers line), led to his uncommonly generous sharing of references for critical theory on the spoof subgenre. Professor Emeritus Jim Welsh always communicates support and has been unusually creative in looking at genre, and film, in pioneering ways. The enterprising Ruth Benedict of Syracuse University's Office of Development was the first to connect me with a master documentary filmmaker, Al Maysles, a graduate of Syracuse.

Of course, I am most indebted to those documentary filmmakers who gave me their time and thoughts; especially those who straightened me out on a number of misconceptions I had about their own work, and the documentary form as well. Those gentle, if occasionally pointed, instructors were Albert Maysles, Henry Corra, Aviva Slesin, Mark Wexler, to mention just a few.

And a brief disclaimer. It is bound to come up that I did not treat or interview D.A. Pennebaker, a major documentary filmmaker living in New York City. I have no reason to offer, just as I have no good answer to give to those who might complain that their favorite filmmaker has not been given space. This has already come up a few times socially, as in, "You mean you didn't talk to X? She/he started the whole thing." On the plus side, to me this just shows how incredibly important the doc form has become to our time, when people have such passionate opinions about it.

—May, 2008

INTRODUCTION
· · · · · · · · · ·

If Jane Austen were in Hollywood—which, of course, she is—she would observe that it is a truth universally acknowledged that most mainstream Hollywood films are in want of a rich corporate husband with a committee mentality to insure against money loss. And that even many of the smaller independent films have now taken on the character of Indiewood: a cottage industry, if you will, but—if successful—organized around a business model more frequently than not.

Instead it has fallen to a different genre to revive and let loose the rivulet of creativity, innovation, and—may as well put it out there—star power that used to, and is used to, drive movies. Ironically, it came from the least likely source: the homely little documentary, formerly considered—at times—dull or even dreary.

No longer. In fact, the form is now so exciting that it has spun off all kinds of new and interesting subgenres. Protean-like, the doc now incorporates personal filmmaking, documentaries and rockumentaries, socially conscious docs (nothing new there), old-fashioned talking heads information docs, and docs with an inserted narrator starring him- or herself. The documentary is turning out to be a kind of pluripotent stem cell that can develop into many new forms; like stem cell research, it has a lot of controversy surrounding it.

Another explanation for the doc's popularity is that the studio system, which—despite its numerous flaws—produced literate and highly entertaining scripts and films, is broken. Documentaries instead are filling the need for intelligent entertainment.

Still other proponents of the thrilling documentaries around today remind us that documentaries have always been one (ignored) branch of filmmaking and that feature films, while they had their day, are now yielding the forefront again to documentaries: simply put, films taken from fact, not from narrative.

The two diverging streams of film. Vertov versus Eisenstein. The Lumiere Brothers versus Melies. You know the drill.

Yet this doesn't entirely take into account the vigor with which some filmmakers are constructing their films, and their boundary-pushing efforts in appropriating all approaches for their purposes. And some of the most energetic practitioners are constantly making statements about reworking the older format of the television-influenced straightforward documentaries, citing even earlier films and formats that may have been underground or unheard of for a while.

This contemporary viewer is old enough to remember a time when documentaries were fact-filled, earnest and well-meaning movies that prefaced a main feature, or nature shows on television with embarrassing or comic sex scenes (depending on whom you were watching the movie with), or—a bit later in one's career—something you had to make excuses for not attending when more right-thinking colleagues would be trying to gather a group for screenings of little-seen Oscar-nominated docs.

Now, Fortuna's wheel has turned and everyone is trying to grab on, riding the wheel to the top of documentary viewing, if not stardom.

It is the province of this book to determine how this has happened, mainly (though not entirely) by talking to some of the practitioners and promulgators of the new docs.

For it cannot be denied: Documentaries with a point of view, and a creative mix of fact and fiction, have become the place to be. And if that means starring yourself in your own film, so be it. In fact, be it better.

chapter one

TRANSFORMING THE IMAGE OF TRUTH
· · · · · · · · · ·

There are many names we could assign to this new mélange, from "meta-docs" to the "shaped documentary" to "mockumentary" (one of the first in this mode being *This Is Spinal Tap*, by Rob Reiner and Christopher Guest) to the spectacularly successful "stunt doc" *Super Size Me*, by Morgan Spurlock.

But labels, while cute, can be misleading. The documentary did start out as fact-based, and most historians seem to agree that the term came from the French word *documentaire* (to travel to strange places, to observe, and, perhaps, to instruct).

A short timeline through the twentieth century takes the documentary from its early phase of going to foreign places to explore, record, and learn, through an expressive and poetic phase of cine clubs, to the Grierson-influenced school of socially impactful documentaries occasioned by the Depression, up through their natural child, guerilla docs of the 1960s, with their frequently upending cinéma vérité, to the purer Direct Cinema of observational documentaries. The personal and autobiographical film of the 1970s and 1980s emerged with roots in the expressive formats of the Vertov school of filmmaking, but in many places made parallels between the self and society, much like the Gonzo journalism of its era.

And it is a tree that has produced many strange fruits, such as Michael Moore's donning an orange sheet in *Roger and Me* to determine if he's a "spring," helping out a friend who is turning to color analysis as a career alternative in economically depressed Flint, Michigan.

One working definition of documentary was formed in the 1930s and it is a theory against which subsequent ideas have been in reaction. Paul Rotha, in his classic book *Documentary Film*, called the documentary "the first real attempt to use cinema for purposes more important than entertainment." He broke down the various strains into the naturalistic (or outdoor, frequently American), realistic (or city, mainly European), and newsreel and propagandist (mostly British and Russian). In many ways, these categories still apply, and he even set forth some issues, which run throughout this book. For instance, Rotha's take on Robert Flaherty, a kind of D.W. Griffith of the documentary: "Flaherty serves us well to demonstrate the elementary demands of documentary. He asks an observation of natural material on its actual location, from which the theme might arise . . . and [emphasis mine] *he prefers the inclusion of a slight narrative, not fictional incident or interpolated 'cameos,' but the daily routine of his native people.*"[1]

How Literal is Reality?

The first use of the term documentary in professional reviewing was by John Grierson (signed "anon." at the time), covering Flaherty's film *Moana* for the *New York Sun* in 1926. Grierson was first known for being the head of a British government agency, the Empire Marketing Board, in the late 1920s and 1930s, producing socially aware films about pressing social issues such as Britain's food supplies. (Today, following current trends swirling around the neo-doc, revisionists are pointing out that even Grierson was known to occasionally use narration and point of view in his films.)

Real or not real was no big deal for earlier British audiences, who, according to Rachael Low, had "a certain lack of sophistication, a certain indifference to whether what they saw on the screen was real or merely a reconstruction, or even a topical allusion."[2] The British producer James Williamson shot his 1898 *Attack on a Chinese Mission Station* in his backyard, and some of his Boer War scenes on a golf course. And in the US, there was faked war footage in *The Battle of Manila Bay* (1898) and *Raising Old Glory Over Morro Castle* (1899). With what appears to have been full cooperation of the warring factions, filmmakers also photographed faked footage of the Chinese Boxer Uprising of 1898–1900, the Russo-Japanese War of 1904–05, and the Mexican Revolution of 1910–11.

Nevertheless, socially aware, Grierson-influenced realism had taken over in docs in the intervening years, so by the time the world's most famous female documentarian Leni Riefenstahl came along, she took some criticism for altering chronology, particularly in her propagandistic doc *Triumph of the Will*; her Nazi associations didn't help either. Though for a while she denied altering reality and chronology, the matter has since been settled: She did. The speeches delivered from the podium at the opening of the rally were not sequential on that day, as the film indicates, but were excerpts from speeches made on five different days; shots of Hess and others leaving the scene of the folk parade were edited in later, and not taken at the same time or place.[3] And when the pendulum started to swing away from the representation of literal reality, perhaps the clever witch Riefenstahl prophesied this, admitting to her rearrangements. "In *Triumph of the Will*, for example, I wanted to bring certain elements into the foreground and put others into the background. . . . There is, first of all, the plan (which is somehow the abstract, the précis of the construction); the rest is the melody. The rest is melody."[4] Not only is she commenting on dramatic structure, but she is moving toward an "art for art's sake" stance (read: non-Nazi propaganda).

Leaving Literalism Behind

Some of the insistence on literal reality was underscored by the newsreel branch of documentary, updated by the ubiquity of television, and influenced by editor turned documentarian Robert Drew and his acolytes, including the Maysles, Frederick Wiseman, and others newly working in that stricter mode. As Stella Bruzzi points out in the introduction to her book *New Documentary: A Critical Introduction*, a clever argument ultimately promoting the softening of the form, even Grierson was more relaxed than we have become: "Worries over authenticity and the evolution of documentary are frequently linked to the increasing sophistication of audio-visual technology."[5]

Things might have ended there, but in a postmodern age, when truth is indeed stranger or in some cases caused by fiction, the humble little documentary is bringing up even more exciting questions about its own form, and its writers, directors, and stars (sometimes the same thing). And if we ever doubted it, ask the French again, who came up with the term *cinéma vérité* for films that had a designed social purpose, or were intended to agitate, reflecting both the temper of the times (the late '60s and '70s) and the guerilla tactics made possible by the very portable equipment which was also useful for the generally objective television. Even here there is a bit of a controversy; according to Richard Meran Barsam in his book *The New Nonfiction Film*, "It is argued that Jean Rouch, not Edgar Morin, coined the *cinéma vérité* label."[6]

To confuse things a bit more, documentary has been the term used for nonfiction film in general, the more objective fly-on-the-wall type, even for polished PBS documentaries. Compare to the more spontaneous kind of filmmaking Ross McElwee has said inspired him to make his own brand of personal films in the 1960s and 1970s—films that still use the term "documentary." The emergence of personal filmmaking brought up matters which hadn't been heard about for a while and are once again in our new century deemed highly significant, up for discussion, and even controversial. This includes the ethics of constructing footage or rearranging timelines and chronology, whether participants should ever be paid, how far the film and its form is to be shaped, and what, if any, is the proportionate mix of fact and fiction. And of course, if or how much of the director, sometimes the narrator, should be seen: whether to be a "fly on the wall" in the sometimes overused phrase, or to present a point of view and announce the filmmaker's intent.

To Reconstruct or Not

Compared to today's stunt docs, or films which unabashedly admit to changing chronology and sometimes even facts to reach a higher truth or better purpose, some earlier adaptations seem tame. For instance, complaints about Flaherty's reconstructions in *Nanook of the North* started as early as the 1930s, when Grierson, the aforementioned head of the British Film unit who eventually came to the US under a Rockefeller grant to work with Flaherty, declared Flaherty's work "the creative treatment of actuality." In the context of today's frequent recasting and citing of *Nanook of the North* as a forecaster of the subjective documentary, these comments put things in perspective.

These days, one can't help but wonder what Grierson would make of Michael Moore, whose *Fahrenheit 9/11* is one of the highest grossing documentaries of all time. Or what he would have thought of Werner Herzog's *Grizzly Man*, which tells us not only what motivated Timothy Treadwell to go live in the wilderness among a threatened species, and die in the process, but what he, Herzog, the film's writer-director, thinks about the enterprise. And life. Or Morgan Spurlock's *Super Size Me*, which would be easy for purists to dismiss as a prank, except that it achieved an incredible goal: forcing McDonald's to drop its obesity-producing Super Size portions, and causing other chains to do the same thing with more healthy menus. *Super Size Me* was the eighth largest grossing documentary ever when I interviewed Spurlock in the fall of 2007 (and even he cautioned that these figures change rapidly; he wasn't sure of the exact rating at the time).

In *An Inconvenient Truth*, the transformative qualities of the documentary renovated and made glamorous the persona of former Vice

President Al Gore, making global warming a recognized reality rather than an easily dismissible complaint.

Not bad for a genre which used to be relegated to the backwater of public television, shown late at night or early in the morning.

More about *An Inconvenient Truth* and other highly impactful films and filmmakers will follow in subsequent chapters, wherein preeminent documentarians of our time talk about getting their films made. Along the way, they changed the form of the documentary, and sometimes the world too.

Social-Purpose Docs Give Birth to Superstars

Our acceptance of the documentarian as star/auteur is now so ingrained that very little about their behavior surprises us anymore. Even Robert Flaherty, whom film scholars probably never saw as pure, is being more and more revised as the Big Daddy of documentary studies. Now when Flaherty is mentioned, or studied, it's with an eye showing how much he is in the film, how he shaped the igloos as well as the storyline. And, of course, how he directed and affected Nanook and Nanook's little family.

Still, nobody has thrown the baby out with the bathwater. Many of the traditional elements of the documentary—such as going to a foreign place to look; the use of maps, charts, and statistics; collecting historical and sociological data—have been incorporated in the new model. So has social intent, and sometimes even the dirty word "propaganda." And whatever you think of *Roger and Me, Bowling for Columbine, Super Size Me*, or a host of other documentaries made by filmmakers such as Michael Moore and Morgan Spurlock, the importance of the director—hell, let's put it out there, often the star—goes unchallenged.

But it wasn't always so. Al Maysles, a living legend, seems to be everywhere these days, reminding us of the pure documentary as he started to practice the mode in the late 1950s: an entirely observational approach. This is the method that Maysles has insisted on in his long and distinguished career as a documentary filmmaker, a career he established with his brother David when they set up together as a documentary filmmaking team. "Direct Cinema" is Maysles' preferred term, and he believes now, as always, that no point of view should be imposed on a film, but rather that one should emerge gradually from the material itself.

In the documentary as we have come to know it today, the prominent film historian Bill Nichols (in his books on the documentary) originally found four types: the didactic, observational, interactive, and reflexive modes. His latest addition and adjustment, with clear acknowledgment of Michael Moore and others, is the performative category.[7]

All unconcluded if interesting controversies, but here's a thought. As unique and interesting as Michael Moore may be, and as we've gotten used to him, here is something quite ironic: In the early twentieth century, Indian director Abdullay Esoofally provided entertainment for audiences in Southeast Asia. He recalled: "When I started my bioscope shows in Singapore in 1901, little documentary films I got from London helped me a lot in attracting people. For instance, a documentary about Queen Victoria's funeral, or famous figures of the Boer War in action."[8] During these shows, speakers would stand beside the moving picture and narrate the events on screen. At times they misbehaved, turning up for work drunk or dissolute.

They were called *benshi*.

I guess you might see Michael Moore as a kind of comic, scruffy, overweight, Westernized *benshi*, entertaining and enlightening us.

Only somehow he slipped inside the frame.

Everything Old is New Again

There have been intimations of the inserted filmmaker before, even in what you might call the modern era (and we make a distinction between the self-inclusion of documentarians and cameos by directors like Hitchcock, who employed visual IDs as a signature more than a statement). Haskell Wexler's *Medium Cool* was a film that stirred things up with its political statements about police beatings and harassment during the then contemporary Chicago convention of 1968. The film was not a documentary, but it intercut some footage of real events with a fictionalized line about a reporter who falls in love with a "cracker" living in the projects just north of Chicago. Today, Wexler summarizes the approach in *Medium Cool* as "the mixture of fiction and so-called reality."

Wexler turns the camera on himself at the end of the movie, demonstrating that "the whole world is watching" (the repeated slogan of the film). It's not just an inadvertent shot of the cinematographer/director, for he fills the entire frame.

In fact, *Medium Cool* might be taken for one of the hybrids of today such as *The Last King of Scotland*, which combines real life and documentary footage in a novelistic context.

Medium Cool brings up the interesting aesthetic and philosophical question which has bugged documentarians from time immemorial: Should the order of narrative events be played with? (And its correlative questions: How much footage—if any—should be faked?) While the majority of by-the-book documentary filmmakers eschew such practices and claim to abhor the idea of hiring actors or rehearsing scenes, this is not seen infrequently nowadays.

Haskell Wexler: On the Scene

"Kennedy was killed a couple of weeks before we were due to start shooting, so I got a small crew together along with my two principal actors and we all went to the funeral in Washington, D.C. to shoot scenes that I thought would have a use in the final film," Wexler says, explaining the chronology of events which helped germinate *Medium Cool*. "We also went to watch the Illinois National Guard, who were preparing for the expected troubles in Chicago later that summer, and got some great footage of them training. The troops were split into two sides and groups from each unit would dress up as hippies and protesters while the rest of the soldiers would be instructed in how to deal with these so-called deviants."

Wexler's first-draft screenplay even contained scenes of protests and disturbances at the Chicago convention that hadn't even taken place yet. "Of course the script didn't specify exact shots," Wexler explains, "but we all knew months before that there would be clashes between the protesters and the establishment. What surprised us all more than anything was the extent of those clashes. For my film I had planned to hire extras and dress them up as Chicago policemen, but in the end Mayor Richard Daley provided us with all the extras we needed."

The director threw Verna Bloom into what the official report was later to call the "police riots" in the parks around the Convention Hall, and though she made her way through the battered and bloodied crowds without mishap, Wexler and his crew were tear-gassed. As the canister comes flying toward the camera, a voice on the soundtrack exclaims, "Look out, Haskell, it's real!"

Medium Cool stars two professional actors (Robert Forster and Bloom), one of whom plays a Chicago reporter (another intricate layer here) who ends up covering the riots. And when real-life events cooperated by providing convention-related violence in the streets, Wexler was there and able to place his actors in those scenes. As his friend Studs Terkel said about *Medium Cool* (in an interview given to Mark Wexler for his 2005 documentary about his father, *Tell Them Who You Are*), "*Medium Cool* is a documentary, though there are a few actors in it."

Herzog: High Priest of the New Form

Well, so what, you say. So it's got documentary elements; it's still not a "real" documentary.

In fact, this signals many of the issues that today's documentary filmmakers have been talking about in panels and at festivals which cover the globe. It is the kind of thing doc filmmaker Werner Herzog has been espousing for decades, even saying that for one of his films, *Bells from the Deep*, he hired local drunks to play meditating monks looking into the frozen-over sea; one of the most effective shots came about when one of said drunks actually passed out on the ice. No self-respecting documentary filmmaker would have admitted this kind of thing in years past, but these days Herzog brags about it, just one of many anecdotes staking out his turf as the primary creator of the new documentary.

"I have always been a fierce opponent of cinéma vérité, the accountant's truth. And in any case, there already is a momentous onslaught on our sense of reality. Virtual reality on the Internet, computer games, all artificially created. Even Photoshop. Photographers aren't believed anymore, because Photoshop can manipulate reality. We must be like medieval knights doing combat," he said at Goethe House in New York in the spring of 2007, referring to his messianic stance.

This spiel was part of his introduction to clips of his latest film, about Antarctica, made for the Discovery Channel, and supported by the National Science Foundation. Even the NSF has bought in, declaring on its Web page that Herzog will "find the poetic truth in Antarctica," in the film *Encounters at the End of the World*. Herzog is no *arriviste* to this way of thinking. For decades now, whenever he gets a chance Herzog says he wishes to "murder vérité." He is so well known for promoting his philosophy of ecstatic truth, in fact, that independent filmmaker Henry Corra says, "I think Werner was born spouting the phrase 'ecstatic truth.'"

"It's no *Happy Feet*," Herzog says ironically, referring to the cheerful penguins of a contemporaneous movie. "I have done the film in a way which borders the surreal." Indeed, the clips of the movie he showed to the enthusiastic crowd at Goethe House juxtapose images of a soft-serve ice-cream machine named Frosty Boy (worshiped by the locals with a nearly religious fervor) with archival footage of the Shackleton team which explored Antarctica years ago.

Taking it down a notch, the maker of more than fifty-five documentaries says, "In these last films, it's more my point of view." You couldn't argue with that.

Not making social issue documentaries in the fashion of a Grierson, a Peter Davis, or a Michael Moore, Herzog may also be seen as in the expressionistic tradition of Vertov, though unquestionably he is his own man, his own voice.

"*The Man With the Movie Camera* [the 1929 film that showed numerous brand-new film technical devices, including freeze frame, fast and slow motion] involves staging and contrivance to an extent previously rejected by [Russian director] Vertov.... The artificiality is deliberate; an avant-garde determination to suppress illusion in favor of a heightened awareness. The film is an essay on filmed truth, crammed with tantalizing ironies. But what did it finally mean for audiences? Had Vertov demonstrated the importance of the reporter as documentarist? Or had his barrage of film tricks suggested—intentionally? unintentionally?—that no documentary could be trusted?" wonders Erik Barnouw.[9]

Expressionism Branches Out

Perhaps Herzog, a European, is closer to his expressionistic roots than American filmmakers. But when American filmmakers caught up with him, the results were spectacular. In the United States, starting with *Roger and Me*, Michael Moore created a similarly impassioned swirl of fact, fiction, and opinion (his own). One may consider himself a poet, the other a journalist. But they both define themselves as documentary filmmakers.

No, Moore did not hire people to be in his films, as far as we know. But within the travel and information-gathering aspect of the documentary tradition, he did break form in a number of significant ways, most notably by inserting himself as hero/interviewer. He made his persona, his background, his birth city not just part of the story, but the story itself. He sometimes becomes an emblem of a tale, or uses friends he grew up with to signify this.

Moore plays with timelines (more on this later), and his editing techniques have now become a serio-comic cinematic model for American audiences and other directors: juxtaposing footage from other films, using emotive music, cross-cutting in a radical manner, and even inserting comic book images. As it turns out, Peter Davis's 1975 *Hearts and Minds*, a film so critical of the war in Vietnam that some called it didactic, was a stylistic model of sorts. But Moore is in his movies, whereas Davis is not.

Even more outrageously, Moore set up scenes, such as the opening of a bank account (in *Bowling for Columbine*) at a bank which was giving away free guns to new customers. It's clear from even a casual glimpse of the film that the bank employees knew who Moore and company were.

As acclaimed documentarian Frederick Wiseman says critically about this kind of practice in chapter 2, viewers know when they are being conned. But for the most part, with Moore's first efforts anyway, audiences did not seem to mind a little obvious artifice.

The Gonzo director also made book on the "accidental" disaster of his inability to interview the chairman of General Motors. The excitement came in the casting of himself, the narrator/interviewer, as a major character in the film. Still, much more than Werner Herzog, Moore has a social purpose to his films—he wishes to right a wrong, whether it is about his hometown, violence and gun abuse in America, or the health care crisis. In this way, he is firmly within the tradition of socially-conscious documentarians, a kind of Falstaffian bastard child of the grim and serious Grierson.

But What About Me, the Filmmaker?

The stylistic method, apparently, was catching. Or maybe it was simultaneous, as often seems to happen with a new idea or movement. In 1988, for instance, documentarian Nick Broomfield went this route in his movie *Driving Me Crazy*. The then *New York Times* film critic Janet Maslin describes the making and shaping of the new syndrome: "As Michael Moore has lately demonstrated and Nick Broomfield now reaffirms, sometimes the best thing that can happen to a documentary filmmaker is for everything to go wrong. Roger Smith, the chairman of General Motors, gave Mr. Moore the lucky break of a lifetime by refusing to have anything to do with him, and in *Driving Me Crazy*, Mr. Bloomfield is similarly favored by everyone who insults him, ignores him, threatens to cut off his financing, and uses him as a sounding board."[10]

The film had originally been planned as a companion piece to an all-black musical revue, but budgetary cuts and "creative differences" led to such acrimony that Broomfield even includes a sequence of one of his nightmares to show how bad things got. In his dream, Broomfield and a contentious screenwriter he is working with become Siamese twins, with the screenwriter growing out of his shoulder—an image worthy of the Gothic imagination of a Herzog.

To read more about Broomfield's own description of his creative breakthrough, check out his Web site, which declares: "Nick was originally influenced by the observational style of Fred Wiseman, and Robert Leacock and Pennebaker, before moving on largely by accident to the more idiosyncratic style for which he is better known. While making *Driving Me Crazy*, a film project hopelessly out of control, Nick decided to place himself and the producer of the film in the story, as a way of making sense of the event."[11]

The New Paradigm

But the story is not that simple. Michael Moore did not instantaneously pop up like a fatter, Boticellian blue-collar Venus rising from the sea. Nor did a Werner Herzog suddenly appear on the horizon, tilting at the form like a crazed Don Quixote.

Call it the zeitgeist or the hippie era, or don't call it anything. But it's certainly true that people were feeling and acting on a sea change years before the current craze. Consider the following declaration:

> Those of us who began applying an observational approach to ethnographic filmmaking found ourselves taking as our model not the documentary film as we had come to know it since Grierson, but the dramatic fiction film, in all its incarnations from Tokyo to Hollywood. This paradox resulted from the fact that of the two, the fiction film was the more observational in attitude. Documentaries of the previous thirty years had celebrated the sensibility of the filmmaker in confronting reality; they had rarely explored the flow of real events.[12]

Does this manifesto come from Moore, or Morgan Spurlock? The currently very quotable Herzog? Or his near peer in age and professional friend, Errol Morris? Actually, it's a statement from David MacDougall, generally recognized as the world's most famous ethnographic documentary filmmaker, a Canadian-American who currently lives in Australia. He was the winner of the Grand Prize at the Venice Film Festival in 1972 for his (and his wife's) film *To Live With Herds*, one of many acclaimed MacDougall films. The excerpt is from an essay he wrote in the mid-1970s.

He has correctly sensed that the paradigm has shifted. You can make a lot out of this—and this book hopes to—by saying that people are suspicious of the media as it presents reality these days, or distrustful of government versions of truth. You can get highbrow and say that everything is up for redefinition (or deconstruction) in a postmodern world which questions everything, even at times its own definition (and uses every available, not necessarily chronological, element to make its point; pastiche is the current critical term to describe this process). To put it in literary terms, it's reminiscent of the debate about realism and naturalism. Or in the analogy to journalism, the old "who, what, when, where, but not why" as taught by the AP and journalism schools of yore in contrast to the New Journalism which enlivened prose in the 1970s, forever altering even the Grey Lady of journalism, the *New York Times*, which currently tries for numerous witticisms and has first-person references even in its standard feature stories.

And if one might say that Albert Maysles is the Flaubert of documentary filmmaking in that he always has and still espouses the noninterventionist approach to movie making, calling it Direct Cinema, then the Zola Naturalism Award must go to Frederick Wiseman. Perhaps then Herzog is the Gauguin of documentarists, traveling to far-away spots to explain other cultures and, of course and more importantly, himself. Sometimes, it would seem, more like an obsessed van Gogh. And, if so, is Errol Morris the Matisse, looking again and again at the same subject to find and define its essence, and in doing so, reshaping a form?

Yet a number of documentary filmmakers reminded me that there were earlier films in the personal vein that inspired them and challenged their concepts of objective, newspaper-style documentary, and that some contained technical as well as creative breakthroughs. Some cited the work of Ed Pincus in the 1960s, particularly *Panola*, wherein some technical bits like a boom shot were left in the film, indicating immediacy and the filmmaker's presence. With reference to the then controversial issues of whether artificial or natural light was to be preferred, or even allowed, into the documentary format, a few documentarians poetically described the natural half-light in which Pincus filmed his subject, a poor African-American in the deep South, likening the filmmaker's work to that of Walker Evans and Dorothea Lange.

In the developing movement mixing fact and fiction techniques, it is important to note the precedent-setting work of Perry Miller Adato, a documentary filmmaker extremely active in the 1970s and 1980s with her series of films about women artists, including Louise Nevelson, Georgia O'Keeffe, and Gertrude Stein. Though Adato was working in establishment television where she had begun as a researcher, she challenged the form, and was aware she was doing so. In an interview with Herbert Mitgang in the *New York Times* about her film on Carl Sandburg, Adato said, "I'm taking a calculated risk by combining fiction and fact, drama and documentary. So far, I have a good feeling about the way it's going. But when I get into the cutting room over the next few months, I'll know more about which segments work, about what stays in and what gets cut."

Mitgang lays out some of the issues of the documentary:

> Almost since the beginning of this challenging art form, there has been a debate among documentary filmmakers about the roles of correspondents and actors. Should the correspondent be on or off camera? That is, should he be almost as important on screen as the subject of his interview? Or should he be, as in many British documentaries, simply an intelligent, detached interlocutor who is barely visible, so that the viewer concentrates fully on the subject? Then, too, the question of dramatizing facts has arisen—sometimes as an ethical matter. Should a name actor recreate the role of a historic figure—or should only film footage and stills be used to preserve the integrity of a subject?[13]

The year was 1981.

Today, documentary filmmakers seem to be putting a new and different spin on their own work or recasting the work of others to qualify for the current trend. Chris Hegedus, the partner of famed documentary filmmaker D.A. Pennebaker (*Don't Look Back, The War Room*), says that *Jane*, Pennebaker's 1962 film, is "almost like a fiction film because you had an actress in it."

Not that this kind of carbon-dating is the point, but this precedes both Wexler and Adato. It may be a case of the more you look, the more you find: who was doing what and when.

Yet still, the question remains. What kind of a name to give these films? Neo-docs? Sounds like sportswear. Meta-docs? Sounds too scientific. Nouveau docs? Too French. And, of course, too pretentious. How about hybrids? But that has a quasi-scientific connotation.

Also, should there be a special name for modern documentaries such as *Super Size Me* which some have called—disparagingly or not—a stunt doc? Or for films like *Fahrenheit 9/11* and *Bowling for Columbine*, with their extreme, even cartoonish characterizations and strong commercial and entertainment appeal? Their directors have, respectively, backgrounds in MTV and Internet editing, and muckraking journalism with a knack for publicity.

Where Women Fit In

A panel headed by Cara Mertes, currently head of the Documentary Program at the Sundance Institute and former head of the P.O.V. series on PBS, took place in June 2007 at the Brooklyn Academy of Music (BAM). The title of the panel was "Four Who Turned the Tide,"[14] and the four documentary filmmakers taking part were Barbara Kopple, Al Maysles, Raoul Peck, and Joan Churchill. Peck is an award-winning Haitian documentary filmmaker who now lives in New York. He directed the award-winning *Lumumba— Death of a Prophet* in 1992 and *Man by the Shore* in 1993, the first Caribbean film ever accepted for competition at the Cannes Film Festival.

Churchill, primarily a cinematographer and editor, had worked with her then husband, Nick Broomfield, on one of the films the panel was discussing: *Soldier Girls*. Apparently this was one of the films that had "turned the tide," in 1981, a movie about life in the barracks for women being trained to go fight in Afghanistan. In some sense, it was rehearsed: The women were playing themselves in scenes showing their daily lives in the Fort Gordon, Georgia, boot camp, and—as nonactors—they clearly know the camera is on them most of the time, and do act as if "acting themselves," occasionally mugging to the camera. And yet the need for the filmmaker to be spontaneous and flexible in order to capture an impromptu moment—about which so many documentary filmmakers have spoken eloquently—was emphasized by Churchill.

One such moment was the unexpected breakdown of the training sergeant, Sgt. Abing, possibly one of the most moving of all the film's sequences. The tough-as-nails fellow, seen in the film demonstrating how to bite the head off a live chicken when one is stranded in the jungle and needs protein, suddenly flips out and confesses how emotionally devastated he still is after his Vietnam tour of duty.

Given that flexibility was attributed to women in the workplace (historically for negative as well as good reasons), it would seem documentaries and the distaff sex are a perfect match. Add to this the fact that editing was one of the few sure entries for women filmmakers into the film business as editing—like docs of the recent past—is somewhat anonymous and behind-the-scenes. (Nevertheless it can be highly significant and sometimes thematically contributory, as we will see especially in the work of Charlotte Zwerin on the Maysles brothers films).

In fact, one of the first great newsreel compilers was Esfir Shub, and she became a documentary filmmaker, though she did not officially take the title. And according to noted historian Kevin Brownlow's *The War, the West, and the Wilderness*, Jessica Borthwick was the first woman filmmaker, having received some training in 1913 with a motion picture camera and spending a year in the Balkans making films in towns, prisons, and on the battlefield.[15]

The First Female Autobiographical Superstar?

There have been many terrific films made by female documentarians more recently: *Union Maids* by Julia Richert, which uses footage of labor struggles of the Depression years and focuses on three outspoken older women who see themselves in the footage and comment on it; *With Babies and Banners* by Lorraine Gray, Lynn Goldfarb, and Ann Bohlen, about an automobile strike in the 1930s; *The Wobblies* by Deborah Shaffer; *The Life and Times of Rosie the Riveter* by Connie Field; *Paris Is Burning* by Jeannie Livingston; and *The Kid Stays in the Picture* by Nanette Burstein.

Still, there has been no femme-superstar autobiographical documentarian to emerge yet in the sense of a Moore or a Spurlock; even in breakthrough films by two-time Oscar-winning Barbara Kopple you don't see a participatory narrator, though this is clearly her choice. In *Harlan County USA* for instance, you may catch an occasional question posed by the filmmaker to her subject. And of course there is the highly dramatic moment when she and her equipment are being attacked in the attempt to shut down shooting.

But you never hear her referred to as "Barbara," even in the offhand way that some of Michael Apted's subjects occasionally, if increasingly, say "Michael" in response to a question in some of the later installments of Apted's "Up" series. Certainly there is no neo-narrative paralleling her experience with those of her topics, such as making a comparison between herself and the Dixie Chicks, or comparing her struggles in balancing the demands of career and family to those of the Chicks (one of the topics of *Shut Up and Sing*). Think here of Michael Moore talking about his hometown of Flint, Michigan, in *Roger and Me*, giving us his family background about relatives who had worked on the assembly lines at the GM plant, or comparing his being fired to the experiences of the Flint inhabitants.

Speaking at BAM, this is what Kopple had to say about her approach:

I think there are many different ways to make a documentary—
there really are no rules. One obvious stylistic difference between
Michael's films and mine is that Michael appears in his films and I do

not. He is wonderful in that role, and his style is very effective and very powerful. I think we both come from the same place in that we both want to make films that challenge people. And we both believe, like many other filmmakers out there, that nonfiction films can and do play a role in the national conversation, in the movements for social change and in the ongoing fight for social justice.

Still, I really believe that every story is different. In *Harlan County* we lived with the mining families. We ate with them. We faced down violence together on the picket line. We wanted to tell a story about their community, about these brave women and men taking great risks to stand up for their rights and their families.

[And on the topic of the one-sidedness of the film,] we did not feel an obligation to speak for the company because the voices of the rich and the powerful are those most often heard. We wanted to help amplify the voices most often ignored. One of the reasons that the perspective did not seem forced is because we took the time to really get to know these people. They got used to our cameras and we got to understand them on a deep, very human level. We told their story honestly, in their own words, as it unfolded.

But there is one pioneer female precedent for the inserted, or interactive, female filmmaker: Leni Riefenstahl.

Here is what John Grierson had to say about her film *Olympia*: "It is a great film report of a public event, and no other film has ever been so splendid in its capture of the poetry of athletic motions. It is the greatest sports record I have ever seen in the cinema."[16]

And there is even a brief shot of Riefenstahl herself in the film, training. It's not a shot held very long, and not too much is made of it. Still, there she/it is, much more than a Hitchcock-like cameo, if not an on-the-spot Morganna Spurlock. It is deliberate self-insertion, and another example of Riefenstahl's being ahead of her time.

Riefenstahl had been an acclaimed actress, so it's natural that she is comfortable in front of as well as behind the camera, here including footage of herself training for an event. It's not highlighted in any grandiose way, as a Moore might have done, yet she fills the screen.

For my money, having recently taught both films, *Olympia*, Riefenstahl's film about the 1936 sports event, is a much more exciting, aesthetically pleasing, and innovative film than her more widely referred to *Triumph of the Will*. But if you don't believe me, biographer Judith Thurman gives an overview of the film's contributions in her review of Steven Bach's biography of Riefenstahl, even using this book's term for the new form, hybrid. According to Thurman, *Olympia* is:

…a hybrid, servile to Fascist ideals in some ways, defiant of them in others—especially in the radiant close-ups of Jesse Owens; America's black gold medalist. It was marketed as an independent production, though it was financed by a shell company and paid for entirely by the Reich. Rainer Rother, the author of an authoritative filmography, says that the closing sequence of Carl Junghan's documentary on the Winter Games—a slow-motion montage of ski jumpers—was shot by the same inventive cinematographer, Hans Ertl (one of Riefenstahl's former flames), who shot the slow-motion montage of divers that ends 'Olympia.' But even if Riefenstahl cavalierly appropriated imagery and techniques—and profited from the priceless gift that Hitler and history had given her—of a duel between the designated champions of good and evil—her use of multiple stationary and moving cameras, and her inspired placement of them (underwater, in trenches and dirigibles; on towers and saddles; or worn by the marathon runners themselves in their pre-race trials) brought a revolutionary, if not strictly documentary, sense of immediacy to the coverage of sports events.[17]

Riefenstahl's ideas were beyond breakthrough. To photograph a footrace, she laid flat in a wagon, holding a small camera, and was frenziedly pushed alongside the runners. To shoot pole-vaulters, she hid in a hole and shot them from below. Some of her ideas were impossible at that time—for example, her desire to be catapulted through the air with a camera in her hand. And when it was all over, Riefenstahl spent months editing *Olympia*, incorporating various strategies such as disguised reverse shots and forced perspectives.

Ingenious editing, yes. We knew some of that. But it teases us out of thought to think how much of herself—former actress that she was—she might have wished to use in her own brand of performance art on film.

And later in life she seems to have grasped which way the wind was blowing. The wily and willful Riefenstahl, who in many post-WWII interviews downplayed her Nazi connection by saying it was only the beauty of the cinematic images that interested her, was clever enough to leap onto the bandwagon of the neo-doc even in her nineties.

In an interview published in *Der Spiegel* on August 18, 1997, responding to the question, "When you photograph a Greek temple and at the side there is a pile of rubbish, would you leave the rubbish out?," Riefenstahl answered, "Definitely. I am not interested in reality."[18]

And as if to further emphasize her insistence on the ideal, as well as star power, the documentarian refused to give Jodie Foster the rights to her life because she wanted to retain control over the film. As a filmmaker, she knew the importance of final cut. She wanted Sharon Stone to play her, not Foster, or Madonna, who was also interested in the project. No doubt Stone must have looked more the Aryan goddess.

In the end, Jodie Foster did get the rights.

So now, add to Riefenstahl's roster of fame her work as a great propagandist, the inventor of sports film techniques which are still used today. And the first female on the block with the hybrid film, inserting herself, the director, in her movie. In this, she preempted even documentarians like Herzog, Morris, and Moore by many decades. She is discarding literal, or naturalistic, reality. In her documentaries, she is using a kind of expressionism.

Given our continual reevaluation of Riefenstahl, and the current zeitgeist, one might think there would be a plethora of women documentarians these days, even if they are not in the superstar mode.

There are some, though a cautionary comment comes from Mystelle Brabbee, the New York-based documentarian who made *Highway Courtesan* in 2006. When I asked her why there have been so few female documentary filmmakers historically, she responded that she had thought about the issue a lot and had decided some of it has to do with the male ego. "I went to a recent documentary film conference in Amsterdam," she told me in the fall of 2006. "All the big names were there. All men. I won't name them. You know who they are. And—not to take anything away from them or their work—they never seemed to doubt themselves. Whatever they were showing, whether it was something wonderful or a real piece of junk, they were just so proud of what they had done. Never questioned themselves or their work at all." Debbie Zimmerman, head of Women Make Movies, told me in the spring of 2007: "It is one of my pet peeves that so few documentary filmmakers get attention.... Please try to talk to Kim Longinotto [*Sisters in Law*] if you can." (See Kim's career modus operandi in the "Tips and Tricks" section of the book.)

One suggestion made by a male documentary filmmaker, who asked to remain anonymous, was that possibly women are not that terrific in the salesmanship aspect of documentary filmmaking, referring to the fact that to eke out a living as a doc filmmaker, one must constantly be on the hustle for grants or support from corporations or foundations.

But here is Kopple once more, with a counterview. And do keep in mind that she trained under a proponent of Direct Cinema with its touted quiet self-abnegation: "Women have a unique voice in film, and support for female filmmakers has never been stronger. In New York alone, there are several organizations dedicated to supporting women filmmakers and artists: Women Make Movies and New York Women in Film and Television." She goes on to say, "I think for me it's always been easier to make film *because* I'm a woman, because I can ask any question that I want. For example, in the film I did about Mike Tyson, I could ask heavyweight champs and big, tough sports critics any question I wanted, and I got the full answer because they assumed I didn't know anything about boxing. So sometimes it's easier being a woman."

Bearing this out, neither Kopple, nor the Emmy Award–nominated documentarian Lauren Greenfield (for the film *Thin*), which breaks a narrative into four parts and follows the story of four victims of anorexia, nor Rory Kennedy in her documentary *Ghosts of Abu Ghraib*, use any of the "imaginative" techniques of today's superstar documentarians. It follows, then, that these women filmmakers don't present themselves as representative of society in any way, nor apparently do they feel compelled to star in their own docs.

Revelations

Aviva Slesin, though, who won an Oscar in 1987 for her film *The Ten-Year Lunch*, a documentary about the famed writers and talkers who frequented the Algonquin Hotel dining room in the 1930s, made a film in 2002 which is in part personal and autobiographical. It is *Secret Lives: Hidden Children and Their Rescuers During WWII* and is about Jewish children hidden from the Nazis; Slesin was one, taken in as a baby by a gentile family. She narrates the film, some of which is about her own experiences. But the majority of the movie uses interviews and archival footage to talk to the now grown-up hidden children and the families who rescued them from certain death.

Still, "What I had thought of as my dream project for many years became my own personal nightmare," she told me in the summer of 2007, referring to the effort of finding, and talking to, the other lost children, and reliving her own memories.

And now comes Jennifer Fox with her highly personal (and very long, 5 1/2-hour) doc, *Flying*, about her own "issues," with similar stories from her friends and peers. She is both unabashed and brave in revelations about her personal struggles with romantic, financial, and reproductive matters, and she uses the doc mode to universalize her own experiences. Fox is working within the framework of the personal documentary, though using standard documentary elements of interviews with others (friends, family members), archival footage (her own family history), and travels to other lands in the tradition of the documentarian-explorer (South Africa and Germany).

The personal documentary is a format also cleverly used by any number of interesting male documentary filmmakers, such as Alan Berliner and Ross McElwee.

Look to Europe, though, for even earlier expressions of the neo-doc, or the autobiographical doc.

The World and My View

As we've seen, Herzog has always admitted to his movies being personal and subjective. His 2002 film *Grizzly Man* is one perfection of his approach to his subjects, a method he's been practicing since the early 1970s. Never holding back in declaring his thoughts about the adventures of the idealistic environmentalist Timothy Treadwell, who insisted on living in the wilderness with bears until he was finally killed by one, Herzog is only restrained when it comes to our listening to the tape of Treadwell's (and his girlfriend's) demise. The by-now familiar tones of Herzog narrate the film, setting his own attitude toward nature (and life) against that of Treadwell's. Certainly not as much as in a Michael Moore film but not entirely hidden either, we *do* see Herzog, or the back of his head, as Treadwell's former girlfriend listens to the tape of Treadwell being mauled to death by a bear. Herzog's hand is shaking as the details are heard.

With a few exceptions, Herzog has not made social intent documentaries with the purpose of changing the world—films such as *Roger and Me, Sicko,* or *Super Size Me.* As for the present-day popularity of films such as Moore's, or Sacha Baron Cohen's *Borat* (for short), Herzog said he considers Michael Moore "a great boar of an interviewer."

Yet the documentary filmmaker as an ironic presence or persona in his own film was actually seen as early as 1912, though it may not be the most estimable example.

> Mr. and Mrs. Martin Johnson, who had completed their first travelogue in 1912, were still successfully at it two decades later. Self-glorification was the keynote. Unabashed condescension and amusement marked their attitude toward natives. They started

Congorilla—about 'big apes and little people'—in 1929 as the transition to sound was under way, so they included brief sound sequences and narration to make it the first sound film from darkest Africa. Both Johnsons were constantly on camera in sequences demonstrating their courage or wit, or both. In a forest clearing we see them recruiting forty 'black boys' as carriers. When one gives his name, it sounds like 'coffee pot' to Mrs. Osa Johnson, so his name is written down as Coffee Pot. His idea of humor was to give a pygmy a cigar and wait for him to get sick; to give another a balloon to blow up and watch his reaction when it bursts; to give a monkey beer and watch the result.[19]

Perhaps this is one reason why the inserted or interactive narrator took almost fifty years to reemerge.

Underpinning all of this is how the presence of Flaherty affected *Nanook of the North*. Of course this has already been the topic of many articles and debates: How Nanook is hamming for the camera, how Flaherty's working a Victrola in Antarctica shapes the scene in an odd way.

Today, documentarian Errol Morris pithily says, "Flaherty's films were fables. They were heavily constructed, they were the antithesis of what we take to be documentary."

Fame, Infamy, and the Documentary

Not only has the documentary filmmaker made herself or, more often, himself a superstar—Flaherty certainly became one after *Nanook*—but sometimes the subjects of the films become stars as well. Nanook did, for a while. Going well beyond the new mix of fact and fiction in biopics, or movies about celebrities, such as Kopple documentaries about the Dixie Chicks, Woody Allen, and Mike Tyson (about whom Werner Herzog has also said he would like to do a film—what *is* the appeal there?) are films that confer fame on their subjects. In England, some of the subjects of Michael Apted's "Up" series have enjoyed (and others run away from) fame, and their moment (and longer) in the sun. Case in point is Tony, the owner of a fleet of cabs, who appeared with Apted at the 2006 Lincoln Center Film Festival panel about documentaries, and who in the latest installment, *49 Up*, has admitted on camera that he quite likes his celebrity status.

In one of the most famous instances of all, Errol Morris's *The Thin Blue Line*, Randall Adams, the film's subject, had his life altered inexorably—by the filmmaker's saving it. On its cinematic merits as well, the film is considered a classic of documentary filmmaking, with the chilling evidence piling up about the crime, all against the backdrop of the Philip Glass score. But in the category of curiouser and curiouser, after Adams's incarceration and death sentence were reexamined and he was released on the strength of the argument the film had constructed, the power of the doc form turned on itself, or anyway on the filmmaker Errol Morris.

Perhaps because of being so impressed with the ability of film to change lives, Adams ended up suing Morris for the rights back to his own life, to make, apparently, his own uses of his newfound fame.

Though Morris did not make his presence known in *Vernon, Florida* or *Gates of Heaven*, there is a clear sense of him in *The Thin Blue Line*. There are the audible questions in *The Fog of War*, such as, "Were you aware that this was going to happen?" (to Robert McNamara, about the "accidental" killing of 100,000 women and children during the firebombing of Hiroshima, Tokyo, and other cities). We hear Morris say, "The choice of incendiary bomb. Where did that come from?," just as we hear him comment, "At some point we have to approach Vietnam."

Some neo-docs use narrative voice-overs. In the recent *March of the Penguins* and in Ken Burns's documentaries—particularly *The Civil War*—recognizable tones of famous narrators both make the films irresistible and narratively tie events together. The neutrality of, say, the BBC style of earlier social documentaries has been replaced by attitude, tone, feeling—for instance, Morgan Freeman all throughout *March of the Penguins*, and again in *The Civil War*. And who can ever forget the voices of *The Civil War*'s Sam Waterston, Julie Harris, and many illustrious-sounding others? Of course, changing the form forever was the warning tone of Al Gore in *An Inconvenient Truth*. We didn't like hearing his voice on the campaign trail, but it seems to be an entirely different thing when he is a doc narrator/star.

Just as effective, if not as well known (which was probably not his intention anyway) is Sydney Pollack casting himself as a narrator/interviewer in his direction of *Sketches of Frank Gehry*. It is highly unlikely that a film such as this would pull in those who did not already know who Gehry is, but the director also relied heavily on his own recognizability as a familiar narrator/director/cameo-performer—who can forget Pollack playing Dustin Hoffman's outraged agent in *Tootsie* in the scene in the Russian Tea Room where Hoffman stays in drag and flirts with Pollack? Indeed, the DVD cover shows Pollack and Gehry in animated discussion, apparently arguing over the creative process and architecture, or one of the other topics of the film.

Possibly the ultimate compliment conferred on the doc mode is to have—in the ultimate role reversal—Hollywood be so impressed with a real-life documentary subject that superstar possibilities are glimpsed, and it decides to back a feature adapted from the doc. In Herzog's *Rescue Dawn*, the hero is Dieter Dengler, also the subject of Werner Herzog's documentary *Little Dieter Needs to Fly*. Art is imitating life, which was already art.

Credit Michael Moore. Or, if you're this writer, credit Werner Herzog and Haskell Wexler. Or, if you're Michael Moore, credit Peter Davis. Whoever assumes the mantle, it's undeniable that the form is now so popular, so hip, that it is being lampooned, a sure sign of success. A "Shouts & Murmurs" send-up in *The New Yorker* is tongue-in-cheekily titled "My Nature Documentary" (July 2, 2007). The Emmys started a Best Documentary Director award in 2002. Festivals devoted only to documentaries abound. There is a television channel, the Documentary Channel, which shows only documentaries, and of course HBO, the Sundance Channel, and the Discovery Channel, all of which showcase documentaries. Not to slight the original P.O.V. series on PBS. And there are now so many Web sites devoted to documentaries that there is a Web site to source them, *Survey of Documentary Web Sites*. Still, a couple might be mentioned: the popular *DocumentaryFilms.Net* and *The Documentary Site*, started in 2002, now prophetically posting the disclaimer "Formerly Reality Films." And finally the academy is joining up: There is now a refereed journal, *Studies in Documentary Film*, established in 2007 at Monash University in Australia.

Where Does Acting Fit In?

The phenomenon of the inserted director, as well as that of the superstar documentarian, has revived public interest in some of the issues which have been concerns of the documentary film movement from the very beginning. Yet even as recently as 2005, the Oscar-winning documentary *Mighty Times: The Children's March* was heavily criticized for its re-enactment scenes of thousands of children marching in civil rights protest marches in 1963. The directors, Bobby Houston and Robert Hudson, defended their film by calling it a faux doc. The Academy responded by forcing a redefinition of the eligibility rules for documentaries. Ultimately the critical consensus that seems to have come down the pike is that the filmmakers presented their footage "as if" it were real, and this was wrong.

Nearly every documentary director working in the cinéma vérité or Direct Cinema mode eschews re-enactment of events or historical facts.

Though for very different reasons, re-enactment may also not be an issue for a filmmaker such as Morgan Spurlock, since the entire structures of both *Super Size Me* and *Where in the World Is Osama Bin Laden?* stay in the present tense, making use of a kind of frame of "enactment" (you wouldn't really call it re-enactment) embroidered by some fantasy sequences. Director Michael Moore, while initially denying this, now admits that some narrative reconstructions have occurred, as well as some out-of-chronology editing. For Peter Davis, who Moore says inspired him, historical re-enactment is sometimes necessary, as in the *Hearts and Minds'* Revolutionary War "Minutemen" segment. Errol Morris has devoted much of his recent *New York Times* blog to discussing re-enactment, though he blurted out in a recent talk that "Re-enactment is a damn bad word and maybe we should find another."

That documentarians are making statements about their practices, about their positions on casting themselves as characters in their films, and even— now—if they should pay their performers, only speaks to the high interest in the genre.[20]

Highly significant arenas of people's lives are being affected. Not just food (Spurlock, Aaron Woolf) but health (Moore, most recently) and, of course, war (Morris, Kennedy, Bloomfield). But "lesser" areas of endeavor, such as the possible hoax of Abstract Expressionism in the art world, the surprise hit of relatively new filmmaker Amir Bar-Lev in his *My Kid Could Paint That*, a documentary which mixes both traditional and new documentary filmmaking techniques.

Consider how many times one has seen the title "Fill-in-the-Blank and Me." It's as if the name of Michael Moore's first major cinematic success has given credibility to individuals who are suddenly confident enough to reconsider all sorts of phenomena—the "and Me" part being the most significant.

As Al Maysles says about documentaries overall, "It's an idea whose time has come."

• • • • • • • • • •

Endnotes

1. Paul Rotha, *Documentary Film* (New York: Hasting House, 1952), 116–17, 106.

2. Rachael Low, *History of the British Film, 1906–1914* (British Film Institute and British Film Academy, 1948), 147.

3. David Hinton, "Triumph of the Will: Document or Artifice?" *Cinema Journal* (Autumn, 1975).

4. Michael Delahaye, "Leni and the Wolf: Interview with Leni Riefenstahl," *Cahiers du Cinéma in English* (June 1966).

5. Stella Bruzzi, *New Documentary: A Critical Introduction* (New York and London, Routledge, 1994), 5.

6. Richard Meran Barsam, *Non-Fiction Film: A Critical History* (New York: E.P. Dutton, 1973), 294.

7. Bill Nichols. See Nichols's 1991 book *Representing Reality*, with his breakdown of the new documentary into four categories: the didactic, observational, interactive, and reflexive modes, p. 32–75. He also adds the category performative in his book *Blurred Boundaries*, (1994), p. 95. Both books are published by Indiana University Press in Bloomington, Indiana. Nichols is honest enough to admit that many of these categories overlap, but still they are quite useful in getting a handle on some of the new documentaries, and the types they are exhibiting. It is not Nichols's observation but mine that the most obvious example of such a combination is *Super Size Me*, both didactic and performative.

8. Erik Barnouw, *Documentary: A History of the Non-Fiction Film* (New York: Oxford University Press, 1993), 21, 22.

9. Ibid., p. 63–65.

10. Janet Maslin, "When Bad Things Happen to Good Ideas," *New York Times* (March 2, 1990).

11. *www.nickbroomfield.com/bio.html*

12. David MacDougall, collected in *Movies and Methods*, ed. Bill Nichols, (Indiana University Press), p. 277. Reprinted from the essay "Beyond Observational Cinema" from *Principles of Visual Anthropology*, ed. Paul Hockys (The Hague: Mouton Publishers, 1975).

13. Herbert Mitgang, "Profile of Carl Sandburg: Do Fact and Fiction Mix?" *New York Times* (March 26, 1981).

14. The title "Four Who Turned the Tide" has apparently been used in the past at another BAM film series; it might not have been appropriately exemplified in 2007, as you have to wonder if Maysles and Kopple are really representing "the Tide" in this instance. Broomfield was originally listed for the panel—his inclusion might have made more sense—but as he couldn't attend, his ex-wife, Joan Churchill came in his stead.

15. Kevin Brownlow, *The War, the West, and the Wilderness* (New York: Knopf, 1979), 4–5. Original quotation from *The Bioscope*, May 7, 1914, in which the account of Jessica Borthwick's adventure appeared. In this context, consider filmmaker Jill Godmilow's comment in the Summer 1975 *Women & Film* interview by Patricia Erens, titled "Interview with Jill Godmilow." "I think more women are involved in editing than any other aspect of filmmaking because it's a non-physical job. It also

involves an enormous amount of what I call librarian work—classifying, coding, cataloging—and I think women are better able to slip in there than anywhere else. Editing takes a lot of patience, a supposed feminine virtue, but I'm not sure women make better editors than men. However, since those were the only jobs open, they've had lots of experience at it. Beyond that, I think women editors are less threatening to male directors. Without actually making a man feel challenged, women have found a way to give some creative in-put to a work. I think a male director is easier about taking suggestions from a woman." p. 38.

16. Grierson, quoted by quoted by Hollis Alpert, in *Saturday Review*, "The Lively Ghost of Leni," March 25, 1972. A film treating the work of Reifenstahl along with other women directors is *Women Who Made the Movies* (1992) by Wheeler Winston Dixon and Gwendolyn Audrey Foster, available through the ordering catalogue of Women Make Movies. Also of note is *The Wonderful Horrible Life of Leni Riefenstahl*, the 1994 documentary about her by Ray Muller, with footage of Riefenstahl at eighty-nine.

17. Judith Thurman, "Where There's a Will," *The New Yorker* (March 19, 2007). Reprinted with permission of the author.

18. Matthias Schreiber, Susanne Weingarten, "Realität interessiert mich nicht," Leni Riefenstahl über ihre Filme, thr Schönheitsideal, ihr NS-Verstrickung und. Hitlers Wirkung auf die Menschen, *Der Spiegel* (August 18, 1997).

Also see the interview with Riefenstahl in *Cahiers du Cinéma*, quoted by Stefan Steinberg, *World Socialist Web site*. September 15, 2003.

Also pertinent is her oft-quoted remark, "I can simply say that I feel spontaneously attracted by everything that is beautiful. It comes from the unconscious and not from my knowledge.... Whatever is purely realistic, slice of life, which is average, quotidian, doesn't interest me." Michael Delahaye, "Leni and the Wolf: Interview with Leni Riefenstahl," *Cahiers du Cinéma in English* (New York, June 1966).

19. Barnouw, 50–51.

20. A controversy erupted after the screening of *Standard Operating Procedure* at the 2008 Tribeca Film Festival, when Morris admitted that he had paid some of his interviewees, a practice most disavow except for a nominal payment, or if the person is indigent. However, according to Charlotte Zwerin as quoted by Liz Stubbs in *Documentary Filmmakers Speak*, this has been done before, though no one would go on record about it.

chapter two

THE PURIST AND THE PEEKABOO DOCUMENTARIAN: FREDERICK WISEMAN AND ALBERT MAYSLES

· · · · · · · · · ·

Though constantly being overturned, chipped away at, or mossed over, the rock on which the new documentary rests is the *oeuvre* of the two preeminent documentarians of our age: the reserved Frederick Wiseman and the ubiquitous Albert Maysles. Wiseman is a former law professor who left the law after three years, in 1967, after his highly successful (and highly controversial) documentary *Titicut Follies* created a small sensation. (He has said in numerous interviews he didn't really like the law, and spent much of his time in law school reading novels.) The film, which shows abuses in a Massachusetts insane asylum, is so influential, so legendary, that people who have never seen it know about it, and what effects it had.

Today, his work is considered the last holdout for purely observational cinema—no musical soundtrack, no obvious point of view, no manipulation of evidence or changing of time, to mention just a few of the signposts of a Wiseman film. However, and intriguingly, contemporary critics and historians may be revising their take on Wiseman. While most still see a Wiseman film (and those of Al Maysles to a certain extent) as a kind of last stand for the pure, non-interventionist style, a recasting of even *his* work is starting to take place, for instance in a book by Thomas W. Benson and Carolyn Anderson. Called *Reality Fictions: The Films of Frederick Wiseman*, it claims Wiseman himself uses fiction editing techniques and stresses one of his quotes describing his films as reality fictions.[1]

Titicut Follies created its own brand of observational tactics and proved indispensable in raising awareness of the abuses perpetrated on inmates, ultimately becoming a classic of a certain kind of documentary. It also proved, once again, that controversy can ultimately be good for one's reputation (and future sales). For our purposes, it shows observational cinema at its best, with a 1960s slant toward the social consciousness of vérité. After the furor of the film, however, Wiseman permanently shifted to less sensationalistic subject matter, and away from an attitudinally-based style of filmmaking.

To be sure, Wiseman focused on some of the more bizarre elements in *Titicut Follies*, the first in his series about life in America. And it is the most sensationalistic in subject and style, though the last Wiseman film using this approach. It is a detailed examination of life inside the Bridgewater State Hospital in the mid-1960s. One of the most harrowing documentaries ever made, *Titicut Follies* is the first of a continuing series of Wiseman films examining public housing, hospitals, the police, high schools, and social welfare in the United States.

The most recent Wiseman film, *State Legislature*, expands his particular brand of sociology in a three-hour doc about typical legislative goings-on in Idaho. It is one more in his series of films which examine institutions, and how individuals use and react to them. The picture of American life? It's there, but it's subtle, and you wouldn't get it from Wiseman as director—not ostensibly, anyway. (Most commenters seem to feel that the overall picture is that institutions demoralize individuals.)

Unwitting Sensationalism

Taking advantage of new lightweight cameras and tape recorders, Wiseman originally took viewers on a frightening journey into the Massachusetts facility. *Titicut Follies* begins and ends with a song and dance routine by prison officers and inmates, part of an annual vaudeville performance at the institution, and hence the name of the movie—theoretically good therapy for the patients.

But very quickly there follows an increasingly nightmarish series of scenes where it becomes clear the only decent exit for the patients will be death. Bridgewater is a place where seriously ill men, defined by authorities as criminally insane or sexually dangerous, are treated like wild animals and where boorish and sadistic guards physically and mentally abuse the inmates. Doctors give their so-called problem patients heavy doses of tranquilizers and let it go at that.

At times, *Titicut Follies* is so distressingly real that it is difficult to watch. As the film develops, distinctions between sanity and mental illness blur, the rehearsals and final performance of the song and dance routine underscoring this effect. One patient, Jim, a former teacher, is roughly washed and shaved each day and then returned naked to his cell, where he spends most of his time screaming and stamping his feet. Another inmate, an old man, has decided that life in Bridgewater is so horrible that he has resolved to starve himself to death. The authorities respond by taking him from his cell, stripping him naked, and force-feeding him. The doctor in charge casually smokes as he pushes a greased rubber hose down the inmate's nose. Numerous patients speak directly to the camera (as noted above, a format Wiseman eschewed in subsequent films), explaining their hopes and fears. One man urges authorities to send him to a prison facility so he can serve out a jail term and be released. A panel of doctors rejects this request and ignores his complaint that the tranquilizers are making him ill. Their recommendation? Prescribe a higher dosage.

Though Wiseman was given official permission to film inside the institution for twenty-nine days, state authorities launched legal action against the movie (even though it had been screened to much acclaim at the 1967 New York Film Festival). The Attorney General of Massachusetts barred public screenings, and the state's Supreme Court ruled that the movie constituted an invasion of privacy of the Bridgewater guards and patients. This ban remained in place until 1991, almost a quarter of a century after the movie was made. Later, Wiseman would call this a classic mistake on their part, obviously referring to the fact that this only called attention to the film.

Back to Basics

After *Titicut Follies*, as much as it put him on the map, Wiseman became more restrained in his filmmaking style, rejecting what he describes as a "naïve and pretentious view that there was some kind of one-to-one connection between a film and social change."[2]

Wiseman rejects the term "cinéma vérité" or even the less loaded label "Direct Cinema" for his films. He says that after *Titicut Follies*, he avoided outré subject matter, and never imposes a point of view or structure, though he is clear in stating that in selecting material, and editing it later, there is a built-in process of shaping. And that the final film may resemble fiction, though it is based on unstaged, nonmanipulated actions. He says he doesn't alter or shape the events, though he admits that editing, as well as shooting, can be highly manipulative. In 2000, he told Michael Atkinson of the *Village Voice*:

> Objectivity is not a word I would use. My films are biased, prejudiced, condensed, compressed, subjective—but fair. I say 'fair' not as a substitute, but as an alternative, to 'objective.' I mean, it's fair to my experience, of being in a place for a period of time, and then studying the material during the editing. But certainly not objective.... Everything I do represents a choice, of subject matter,

of how something's shot, the duration of a sequence. I never liked
narration, so I never used it. I don't like to do interviews. The idea
is, when this technique works, it works because it puts the viewers
in the middle of events and asks them to think through their own
relationship with what they're seeing and hearing. I would definitely
agree that my films represent my position on things—I'm an active
participant, just not a very obvious participant.[3]

Wiseman, based in Cambridge, Massachusetts, has made approximately
one documentary each year since 1967, mainly for WNET (public television)
in New York. There is no commentary or music, and no direct interviews
given to subjects in the journalistic one-on-one stance. His philosophy of
film, as told to Gerald Peary in the *Boston Phoenix* in 1998, is:

A lot of people think that the purpose of documentary films is to
expose injustice to those victimized, or that the films are made to
correct the filmmaker's idea of injustice. I think that's a strand of
documentary but it's certainly not the only use. My first films, *High
School* and *Titicut Follies*, were partly an example of that strand,
somewhat didactic. The Correctional Institution at Bridgewater was
a horrible place in *Titicut Follies*, but even within that horror, there were
people who worked hard and well. And since *Law and Order*, to the
extent that I'm trying to do anything, it's to show as wide a range of
human behavior as possible, its enormous complexity and diversity.

[*Law and Order* is Wiseman's 1969 documentary capturing the daily,
working lives of the police in an urban environment, including scenes of
how they deal with everyday problems with no pat answers. This includes
mundane tasks such as investigating the scene of an accident, disposing of
drunks, even handling family violence. In *The New Yorker*, Pauline Kael called
Law and Order, which won an Emmy as Best News Documentary, "The most
powerful hour and a half of television that I've seen all year."]

"*High School* is somewhat open-ended," Wiseman continues. "When it
was first shown in Boston in 1969, one of the people who saw it was Louise
Day Hicks, a very conservative member of the Boston School Committee.
I thought she'd hate the movie. But she came up and said, 'Mr. Wiseman, that
was a wonderful high school!' I thought she was kidding me until I realized
she was on the other side from me on all the value questions. Everything
I thought I was parodying she thought was great."

The way the interview reads, Wiseman seems pleased, for "I never thought
her reaction represented a failure of the film. Instead, we have an illustration that
reality is ambiguous, a complex mirror, that the 'real' film takes place where the
mind of the viewer meets the screen. It's how the viewer interprets the events."[4]

Scenes from *High School,* Frederick Wiseman's film about a typical day in an American high school. Photos courtesy of Zipporah Films.

A curious sidenote to this reaction is that not a few documentary filmmakers have also reported just this confusion in their initial audience screenings. One perhaps to-be-expected example is that Rob Reiner says that preview audiences thought *This Is Spinal Tap* was a real film about a real group, and complained they didn't understand why anyone would make a movie about a group so blatantly bad. The now deceased Michael Ritchie, the director of the film *Smile*, said that the audience thought his satire on a beauty pageant was real; he mixes it up even more by saying that he had been inspired by his time as a judge at a beauty pageant in Santa Rosa, California, and so insisted on using that as the location for his film. Perhaps contributing to the ambiguity was that he hired many not readily recognizable actors as documentary-like characters: pageant professionals, in this case. Ultimately those films became recognized as spoofs or send-ups (more of this to follow in chapter 7). Theoreticians have now decided that a spoof film should make itself clear, "foregrounding," in the currently popular critical phrase, its status by announcing its intent somehow. And even contemporary documentarians seem to agree with this ethical stance: When I interviewed director Davis Guggenheim (see chapter 5), he said he personally believes that as long as audiences know what is going on, a spoof in the doc mode is okay.

But point taken and made. Shaping reality makes it seem, at times, just that much more real.

Daily Life, According to Docs

In *High School* (1968), several months of school life are compressed into one day with some ludicrous results. Yet character portraits, or standard interviews with subjects, are not part of the film. There is, as in all Wiseman's films, a refusal to make a statement manifest through direct questioning, voice-overs and self-conscious attention-getting, or numerous cuts. Needless to say, there is no insertion of point of view such as we have become used to—not even archival footage or statistics—and his films thereby retain their purity. Wiseman says:

> To me, America has always been an undiscovered country from the point of view of documentary film. There are millions of good subjects, and the effort was to make movies about everyday experiences. The point is to always be on hand when these things take place. [And this is a sentiment echoed by Albert Maysles, Barbara Kopple, Joan Churchill, Spike Lee, and even those not working in the realistic tradition, such as Morgan Spurlock or Kevin Macdonald.] If you are lucky enough and hang around long enough, you can get some very funny things, sad things, benign things in ordinary experience that if they were scripted you'd think were part of an amazing imagination. Not that I thought it through very much at the time, nor gave it a label.

> I do always edit the films so that they will have a dramatic structure. That is why I object to some extent to the term observational cinema or cinéma vérité, because this implies just hanging around, with one thing being as valuable as another and that is simply not the case. At least that is not true for me. Cinéma vérité is just a pompous French term that has absolutely no meaning, as far as I am concerned.

> I was not the first one to make documentaries in America. There are Richard Leacock, D.A. Pennebaker, Tim Lipskin, Al Maysles, and Willard Van Dyke to name just a few.

> Where I *would* draw a distinction is that instead of making my subjects superstars, or picking superstars for subjects, I make a place for the star.

> If I focus on institutions, it's because they provide a boundary, serving the same function as the lines of a tennis court.[5]

To see how much the doc form has evolved, consider the following description from the book *Faking It*:

> Unlike the documentaries of Wiseman, for example, *Hospital* (1970), in which intimate portrayals of institutions are used for broader

33

ideological questions, [the genre] docu-soap merely makes a spectacle out of the ordinary.... [and] this particular spin-off combines aspects of documentary with those of soap opera, and to date appears to have developed most successfully in the United Kingdom.

These hybrid texts tend to take shape around an exposé or behind-the-scenes look at large institutions—especially those that have day-to-day contact with the public. Their documentariness lies in their claim to present real people, places, and events. Utilizing the observational mode, or fly-on-the-wall techniques, these programmes [sic] present a slice of naturally occurring everyday life. This visual mode of spontaneous reality is undercut slightly by an often-used authoritative voice-over which guides viewers through the narrative.

These programmes gain their credibility through their association with the documentary form, but their appeal lies in the way in which their narratives are constructed along the lines of soap opera.[6]

Backing Off from Sensationalism

But that is now. The way Wiseman managed *Titicut Follies* may be seen as typical of the way his mind works: infinitely subtle. *Titicut Follies* won the Best Documentary Award at the Manneheim Film Festival, and though its distribution was blocked in Massachusetts, Wiseman took the position that if an institution receives tax support, citizens have a right to know what happens in it, and reportorial access is also a constitutional right. If, at the time of filming, anyone objected to being photographed, Wiseman discarded the material, but this rarely occurred. More recently, he told an interviewer for the PBS Web site:

> Most inmates in *Titicut Follies* gave their consent. For those inmates not capable of giving consent, the superintendent of Bridgewater, as their legal guardian, approved the filming. This was one of the disputed points during the trial. My position was that Bridgewater was a public institution, i.e., supported by taxpayer's money. Public institutions in a democracy are meant to be transparent, open to public inspection. One aspect of public inspection is documentary filmmaking. In the year the film was made, there were also 10,000 visitors to Bridgewater who as part of their tour saw some of the same men naked in their cells. In a democracy the government is not supposed to hide information from the citizens except in cases involving national security.... The various scandals at Abu Ghraib are a current example of the public's need to know and receive information from photographs.[7]

Wiseman's films about teachers, doctors, social workers, and research biologists (among others and clearly an even fuller spectrum is to come) present individuals who are not categorized as either heroes or villains, leaving, it would seem, such conclusions up to the viewer. There is no dramatic focusing on one character, then another, and back and forth with the juxtaposition of shots making commentary, as even the early films of Errol Morris do in, say, *Gates of Heaven*. This model, based on the crosscutting of feature filmmaking, is not employed by Wiseman. Needless to say, there is never a sense of the filmmaker's presence. Nor is there even the taking heads television-type interview, which does imply another presence, seen or heard. And it follows that no character ever turns or says "Fred" or "Mr. Wiseman." He may be honest in giving an appraisal of his work as being not totally objective, yet he never, ever inserts himself in his films.

The documentary according to Wiseman definitely retains the documentary model of traveling to, showing, a new place or situation. Some of Wiseman's films starring a place are *Canal Zone* (1977), *Sinai Field Mission* (1978), *Racetrack* (about the Belmont Park Racetrack, 1985), *Central Park* (1989), *Aspen* (1991), *Zoo* (Miami Metro Zoo, 1992), and *Belfast, Maine* (1999).

He (and Albert Maysles) have not been shy about making explicit criticisms of Michael Moore and the kind of films he makes. "I haven't seen *Sicko*," Wiseman says, "but generally speaking I'm not a fan of Michael Moore's. I think he's an entertainer. I don't think he's interested in complexity. I'm not against the filmmaker appearing in a film. I think some of the greatest documentaries I've ever seen have been made by a filmmaker who's present in the film. I don't know if you've seen any movies by Marcel Ophuls—*The Sorrow and the Pity* or *Hotel Terminus*. Ophuls is a great filmmaker because he's a great interviewer and he has a very sharp and analytical mind. In the case of Michael Moore, I don't see any particular filmmaking skills, and I think his point of view is extremely simplistic and self-serving."

Yet it may be that Wiseman, unlike Al Maysles, is making some accommodation and broadening out his thoughts about the definition of documentary. In the same interview, he goes on to say, "One of my goals is always to deal with the ambiguity and complexity that I find in any subject. In *Titicut Follies*, for example, there are scenes where you see a guard or a doctor or a social worker being cruel to an inmate. But there are other situations where they're being kind. Some of them are both kind and cruel, if not simultaneously then serially."[9]

The Academy Wakes Up

For the very first time, in the fall of 2006, the Film Society of Lincoln Center gave a special tribute to Wiseman and the documentary, at the New York Film Festival. The program simply stated:

> At this point in film history, the documentary form has become more important and pervasive than ever. So we felt it was a good time to invite Frederick Wiseman, an important American documentary filmmaker, to come and share his thoughts on his work, and on the issues and implications arising from his films. No one is more eloquent on the subject of Frederick Wiseman's cinema than Mr. Wiseman himself, and this is a rare opportunity to see him discuss his films in person, illustrated by selected scenes.

This is, of course, exactly what took place. Wiseman, however, as deserving as he clearly is, may not be the current benchmark of documentary films, so he's a safe choice. Some might say, as Roger Ebert often has in his

Frederick Wiseman, documentary filmmaker. Photo courtesy Bowdoin College. Photo credit: Selby Frame.

complaints about the Academy of Motion Picture Arts and Sciences (the Oscars), that these official bodies are very much behind the times. As Ebert (and Siskel) pointed out in the extensive discussion of this non-phenomenon in the Criterion edition of *Hoop Dreams*, the stiffing of *Hoop Dreams* by the Oscars was a kind of backward thinking. Also setting the record straight is the Carl Plantinga journal article referred to in the last chapter of this book about the Academy's behind-the-curve stance on major documentary filmmakers.

New England Origins

That Wiseman received such a high—if long overdue—accolade from the New York Film Festival might have galled a less generous spirit than Albert Maysles, a near peer of Wiseman (Maysles was born in 1926, Wiseman in 1930) and longtime contributor to the New York City film economy. Also originally from Massachusetts (Brookline for Maysles and Brighton for Wiseman), Maysles has lived in New York for nearly all his working life as a documentary filmmaker.

In his self-assessment, Wiseman is perhaps more frank or possibly more self-aware than Maysles, who insists that he does not interfere in any way with the picture that emerges from his documentaries, that he doesn't select his subject matter with any more intent than just being there. Maysles further clarifies that he does not interfere with the order of events as they took place in his documentaries, and that he wants to put the viewer as close to his subjects as he was in filming them.

In this regard, the movie *Salesman*, which Maysles made with his brother David, is perhaps the most frequently cited example of Direct Cinema. The Maysles brothers, who themselves had worked as salesmen, follow four Bible salesmen through their door-to-door attempts to sell the Bible, driving through New England snowstorms and even at one point in an odd-seeming (to them) Spanish outskirt of Miami. We go behind the scenes into their hotel rooms and listen to the banter of the four as they play cards, watch television, and generally discuss business. We end up focusing on Paul (the Badger) more than the others, yet the documentary feel and intent is retained. (And perhaps it is the latter-day aesthetic that makes a contemporary viewer start to see the emphasis on one character over the others as feature-film derived.) Only occasionally do we think about the fact that the scenes are being filmed at all.

Even in the car-driving sequences, it appears that the Badger is just talking to an anonymous observer about his life on the road, and certainly in the interior shots of people in their homes as they are being pitched to, the neutrality is evident. It is as if a completely omniscient or anonymous entity (God, or reality, as Al Maysles would have it) is controlling the scene and there is little, if any, self-consciousness at all among the characters.

Still, we do feel tremendous empathy for the salesmen, especially for Paul, who feels he is losing it and unable to sell anymore. The comparisons with Mamet's play *Glengarry Glen Ross* cannot help but come to (my) mind, although the four salesmen with their narrow, black, early 1960s ties reminded one of my students of the characters in *Reservoir Dogs*.

Albert Maysles says *Salesman* is most likely his favorite film, and to him the best example of his Direct Cinema, although he sometimes makes a case for *Grey Gardens (1976)* or *LaLee's Kin: The Legacy of Cotton*, his 2001 documentary.

Impact on the Subjects

To put and get things in perspective, when *Salesman* came out it was attacked for not being purely journalistic enough (remembering here that the Drew Associates approach to objective reporting had been in operation and in vogue for a while). Defending his film, Maysles has always said there was no manipulation of reality or subjective involvement with his subjects, citing the fact that the (then new) portable equipment became invisible to the subjects after a while, and that people were therefore not self-conscious in the camera's presence, and so act as they would under normal circumstances.

Yet he told me that much more important than a concern with equipment is to "gain access and maintain rapport through eye contact and empathy." Still, even in a film with a sensationalistic subject matter, such as *Gimme Shelter*—the Maysles' film of the rock concert in Altamont with the Rolling Stones and other groups which turned out to signal the demise of the sixties love era with its captured murder of a concert-goer by an over-assiduous Hell's Angel guarding Mick Jagger—Maysles disavows, in his words, "any shaping of the film inconsistent with the essential character of the footage." Charlotte Zwerin, who ultimately received co-director credit on the film along with Al and David Maysles, served as editor with David Maysles supervising. Some revisionists, particularly feminist film historians, say the Maysles allowed editor Zwerin (and other women editors in other films) to emphasize certain aspects of the unfolding of the events. And that, in doing so, the Maysles in effect passed the buck, or the decision making, onto Zwerin while still maintaining their "purist" stance.

Today, Al Maysles seems both honest and generous in kudos to Zwein for her editing work. Yet another point of view on the film, showing how current some of the controversies surrounding it still are, is "The Stage of Death" from the *Sunday Times* (London) by David James Smith, March 27, 2005. This article, available online, details the Stones settling out of court with the murder victim's parents. It also has some fascinating updates on the Hell's Angels, the Stones' bodyguards and those responsible—or not—for the murder.

Wiseman here is in counterpoint, saying that he has always admitted a film is the product of deliberate choices. Speaking about his latest film, *State Legislature*, Wiseman said, "My opinion is always expressed indirectly through structure. I hate didactic movies, or didactic novels."[10]

Of course he is definite about his disapproval of re-enactments: "I guess that I have a sense that most people know when they are being conned and they can tell the difference between staged and unstaged events. It's not that some really good filmmakers can't do things that appear to be unstaged but are staged, yet ultimately they will give the game away because they want to take credit for it. I don't think people are that stupid."[11] He has often gone on record stating that if he thinks somebody is putting on for the camera, he stops shooting, or doesn't use it in the editing room.

He has also said that he doesn't think people have the capacity to change their behavior and become suddenly different just because a camera is present. Wiseman called the discussion about whether a filmmaker's presence colors the events being filmed a basic discussion of documentary filmmaking. It is usually referred to as the Heisenberg principle, a theory of physics about the mutability of particles which documentary theorists adapted in wondering if people behave differently when a camera is present. Al Maysles says he agrees, and he's sure his brother and Zwerin, would agree with this. (This concept is the basis for criticisms that Michael Moore received, particularly for *Bowling for Columbine*. This is discussed at length in chapter 3.)

Wiseman on the "Heisenberg Principle"

Says Wiseman:

> When you are making a movie, most of the time you are hanging around. You're not shooting. But the camera is

always there because you have to be ready to shoot. Part of the technique is to be able to go at least at a second's notice, and the mic is always prominent. It's quite funny to watch, and it's amazing.

People's behavior is not different, whether the camera is on or off. I think it's because all I ask permission for is to be present when they are going ahead doing what they ordinarily would be doing when I'm not there. Also, I don't think that the camera really changes the way that people behave. I have asked people who have been in my films about this. For example, I made a film about a welfare center and, while the workers in the center knew that there was a movie being made, it didn't seem to affect the clients at all. They just walked through the door, did not seem bothered at all, and it did not interfere with what they said or did.[12]

Upon hearing about Wiseman's above comment, Maysles says that he would agree, but that he still thinks it's wrong for the filmmaker to pretend not to be there.

Old/New Controversies

Yet in a reflection of the changing times, even the stalwart advocates of Direct Cinema, the Maysles brothers seemed to a certain extent to be lightening and loosening up the form. They took some heat for this in the early 1960s, from even the generally liberal Vincent Canby. In an article in the *New York Times*, Canby draws analogies between the social movements of the times and the New Journalism. "Salesmen," Canby quotes Maysles as saying, "is the record of almost a hundred such confrontations [between two strangers]," and is described by Canby in a kind of "gotcha" mode as "a sort of secret cinema in which, it was suggested by the young hero of Norman Mailer's *Why Are We in Vietnam?*, everyone thinks he may be starring. In their next film, which they've already started to shoot, the Maysles are becoming even more personal. They are making a movie starring themselves and their family, headed by their widowed 72-year-old mother."[13] This critical finger-wagging from Canby sounds funny today, when such subjective filmmaking is in vogue; at the time it seemed as if Canby were holding back the tides; today it is Maysles.

David Maysles had an intriguing response to Canby's criticism—ironic when you think of Albert's present position—observing that a particular blend of journalism and fiction-influenced narrative was something Truman Capote was also taken to task for in Capote's nonfiction novel *In Cold*

Blood. He said, "What we [me and my brother Albert Maysles] are doing is in direct parallel in motion picture form to what Capote is doing in the literary form....He, for instance, is very conscious of intruding upon his subject, of making any kind of intrusion. That's why he doesn't take notes. The same way that we try to build our equipment. We try to gain a certain kind of rapport, some relationship with the subject, as Capote does. To establish this relationship, we have perfected a camera that doesn't make any noise."[14] This comment is revealing, in fact, when considering some recent re-interpretations of David Maysles, particularly what Celia Mayles, his daughter, has to say in chapter 9.

The Lovable Dean

Al Maysles, a ubiquitous and charming eighty-something, is less acerbic but perhaps ultimately more propagandistic than Wiseman. "I prefer the term 'Direct Cinema,'" says the popular fellow, who has trained filmmakers ranging from Charlotte Zwerin to Ellen Hovde, Barbara Kopple, Muffie Myer, Joan Churchill, and numerous others along the way and, apparently, to come. Some of these women began in the business as interns in Maysles' shop in Manhattan's West Fifties. And it's more common than not to see, when skimming biographies of numerous documentary filmmakers, that they, too, worked for a time at the Maysles'. Many revere him, and a few—even the highly successful Morgan Spurlock—worry about what he thinks of them and their work.

Albert Maysles. Photo credit: Kendall Messick.

It's interesting to note that not everyone is a Maysles disciple, however. One who is not is Henry Corra, the director of a number of personal documentaries, who once trained with Maysles Films. He calls Maysles' stance "the Dogma." Maysles counters that Corra once worked for him, and "attempted to contradict the Maysles' method when he was supervising the editing of the Maysles' *Christo and Jeanne Claude Umbrellas* film and exaggerated the drama with music and sped up the editing with short takes." Maysles says that he dismissed Corra at that point.

Nor is the twenty-seven-year-old estranged niece of Albert Maysles, Celia (daughter of David), who works with and for Corra. Her philosophy of filmmaking is very different from that of her uncle. A full discussion of her film *Wild Blue Yonder*, which concerns a family rift—a split which, in part, mirrors the history of the documentary form in the last fifty years or so—is in chapter 9.

Most of today's doc-appreciating audiences, however, applaud and adore Albert Maysles. A wildly enthusiastic crowd came to see him at the Brooklyn Academy of Music, at an event called "Four [Documentary Films] that Turned the Tide," in June of 2007, choosing to hear Maysles speak after showing his clips rather than attend the movies of the other filmmaker/documentarians, which were being screened at the same time. And when the panel convened after the screenings, with filmmakers Kopple, Churchill, and Raoul Peck on hand, there was a funny moment when Kopple described her own observational film technique—not imposing a point of view—and being on hand to capture whatever serendipitously comes the filmmaker's way. Maysles was apparently so pleased with this description that Kopple mockingly patted herself on her head: Yes, she had learned her lessons at his knee quite well.

This writer met with Maysles twice in New York, first in the fall of 2006 at the suite of rooms on the top floor of the building in the West 50s so well known in the business that it was referred to as the Maysles Building. The brothers Maysles produced not only documentaries but also commercials there, with the editing and all else done on the premises. In doing so, they adopted one of what seems to be three standard career models for documentary filmmakers. They either make commercials (Morris, Corra, Maysles come to mind), teach at a university (like Ross McElwee or Peter Davis), or get by on grants (Wiseman and Alan Berliner, for instance).

One would have to say that only in the past decade, with the advent of the superstar documentary filmmaker, has it been possible for a documentarian to be successful enough to make a living at only that. Clearly,

Morgan Spurlock and Michael Moore have made this breakthrough possible. Even so, the road ahead may be dicey, as Amir Bar-Lev attests to in chapter 9.

The second time I met with Al Maysles was at his then new offices on Lenox Avenue in Harlem. In the spring of 2007, Maysles (without his brother, who died in 1987) moved to Harlem; bought two buildings for his four children, wife, and himself; and owns a building nearby that houses his office, editing rooms, and a movie theater that shows, in his words, "documentaries of interest and value to the community."

Maysles still wears his trademark heavy black glasses, has white hair, and is spry-seeming. A favorite activity of film reporters, especially online, is Maysles-spotting at numerous festivals around the country: an active sport, as he seems to never miss such an event. Gentle-seeming and beneficent— "the trick is to love people," he says more than once in explaining how he managed to produce so many great films on a variety of topics—he still manages a moment of irritation when at one point referring to Frederick Wiseman: "I know Wiseman doesn't like the term 'direct cinema,'" he says. Maysles says that he does not believe in shaping his material even as much as Wiseman admits to. One of Maysles' favorite quotes comes from Alfred Hitchcock: "In a fiction film, the director is God. In a documentary, God is the director." The documentarian should simply be there, says Maysles, an attentive observer on hand when something memorable takes place and relying on serendipitous happenings.

Film historian Brian Winston, himself a widely respected documentary filmmaker, says that Maysles is casting his work in a new, more benevolent light these days because, he believes, Maysles is in his eighties, senses his own mortality and may want to appear more mellow. Winston asserts that if one takes a truly objective look at, for instance, *Grey Gardens*, the movie is actually filled with shots which are both critical or negative of both Big Edie and Little Edie.[15] Curiously, a similar criticism was leveled at Michael Moore for the "Pets or Meat" sequence in *Roger and Me*, in which it was felt he was condescending to the woman who must raise and sell rabbits, for one purpose or another. Both objections are clearly a matter of interpretation.

That "critical attitude" is discussed at all may emanate from the fact that the camera does linger on its subjects as if they were characters, making statements using angles and editing, employing a kind of narrative (fiction) technique.

It's an issue that would never come up in questions about the films of Frederick Wiseman, at least those subsequent to *Titicut Follies*.

"As for how I got to be a documentary filmmaker, and develop this style," says Maysles, "I may have attention deficit disorder. And one thing with people like that—they are very silent. And always, into my twenties, I was a very silent person. I learned to look at people and listen. That's how you draw them out."

Upon close questioning, Maysles acknowledges that there are scenes in many of his films where his presence is not to be denied. For instance, in *Salesman*, one of the traveling Bible salesmen will, on occasion, refer to Maysles by name—Al—as if in a kind of dialogue. It's rare, but it does happen. But, for the most part, even while the salesmen are driving their cars or knocking on doors of potential buyers—and though the viewer *must* know that someone is there capturing all this on camera—the film gives the illusion that the footage came about magically.

Peekaboo, in Spite of Himself

However in *Grey Gardens*, it is impossible to watch the now-famous documentary without being aware of the Maysles brothers' filming. The more jiggly camerawork, for instance, is one thing. But even more significantly, there is an active interchange between Big Edie and Little Edie, indicating their awareness of the Maysles. The mother and daughter often pick at each other verbally and by way of little digs against each other wonder "what Al will think." There are moments of direct address to Al, especially by Little Edie. And of course she dances and performs for his camera, trying on various poses and outfits, performing, as it were, for the filmmakers. According to Celia Maysles, "It's so obvious that [Little] Edie is in love with my dad."

For his part, Al Maysles denies any intervention: "Almost anybody else making *Grey Gardens* would have placed the blame on either the mother or the daughter. We saw that each got something they both did and didn't want out of their relationship. But we preferred to not take sides. To me, it's an example of Direct Cinema, the term which is highly preferable to cinéma vérité."

However, there are shots in the film where the Maysles point the camera at themselves. For example, the highly artistic—even self-consciously quaint—shot of the two brothers in the oval-shaped mirror in the house of the two Edies, a shot held for quite some time.

While you might see this as a kind of signature moment, in the way that Rembrandt put himself in a portrait, Maysles gives a technician's reasons.

Big and Little Edie regard the filmmakers, Albert and David Maysles, and the audience, in the film *Grey Gardens*. Courtesy Maysles Films.

"Otherwise the viewer would be asking: 'What are we doing here? Is there a hidden camera?'"

Bottom line? "It wasn't posed, but I didn't edit it out either."

This interviewer thought she had trapped the director into some contradiction with his Direct Cinema stance, but he was ready. "Actually there are two shots where we are in the film," Maysles says. In one, Al Maysles even has a camera slung over his shoulder.

Still, Maysles emphasizes, "The Maysles' never regarded their presence as a violation of their methods. They are, after all, not 'flies on the wall,' immobilized and without mind or emotions."

In fact, there is a shot of Maysles in *Gimme Shelter* as well. And in this film there is a scene just too stylized to be described as anything other than a set piece. Jagger is at the Moviola, watching himself sing "Sympathy for the Devil," and looks dismayed, but he stays put. David Maysles is seen in the footage and so is the editing equipment. Maysles has said Jagger had asked to see the footage and "we took advantage of that request to film their reaction to the events filmed." Charlotte Zwerin had come back from Paris to edit the film, and according to an article by Michael Sragow on *Salon.com*, "Gimme Shelter: the True Story" (August 10, 2000), it was cinematographer Stephen Lighthill's footage of Mick Jagger that was compressed by Zwerin in her idea to give a narrative hook (and look) to *Gimme Shelter*. This adds a special irony as the movie shows Jagger at the moviola, essentially watching himself, then the knifing.

The web-accessible Sragow piece is worth looking into not just for a technical history of the film, but also for putting the concert in context. Now we think of it as the demise of the '60s love era. True enough. But he also makes come alive the fact that the concert brought together superstar cinematographers, rockers, and even celebrity critics.

Again, Maysles maintains his stance of uninvolved, Direct Cinema: "Some have criticized me for not showing enough of the murder. For not giving enough shape to the film. Maybe I could be criticized for not having a point of view. That is, was it an accidental killing or a murder? The movie doesn't make it clear. What was the guy doing with the gun?" Still, the Maysles footage was considered so important it was subpoenaed for the trial of the gang member who had knifed Meredith Hunter, the eighteen-year-old black man who the Hell's Angel thought was threatening Jagger. (In the action footage of the film's narrative we see and hear the footage in which someone calls out, "He's got a gun!")

A letter to the *New York Times*, signed by Albert, David, and Charlotte Zwerin, says, in response to the piece by Vince Canby:

> He [Canby] calls us humanists but says he is depressed by the 'exuberant opportunism with which it (the movie) exploits the events'—referring to Altamont and the killing there. 'It probably would have been a kind of mini-Woodstock,' he says, describing what the film would have been without the killing, which he later calls a 'murder.'

> Altamont and the killing in front of the stage *happened*. It was not Woodstock!... We hope these same readers will see our film and not take his other charges as the truth, but draw their own conclusions.

> The space we have been given, although appreciated, precludes our answering all his charges in detail. In *Salesman*, we did not put the Bible salesmen into artificial situations nor send them to Miami, any more than we wrote the Stones' songs and sent them to Altamont. The Stones say they did not hire the Angels. The Angels say they were not hired.[16]

Maysles says both at the time and now that he did not actually film the footage of the knifing—he saw it but was too disturbed to capture it—and that he couldn't see the event from where he was standing on the stage. It was his brother David with cameraman Baird Bryant who happened to be able to see the knifing, he says, and filmed it. [Other sources have also credited cinematographer Eric Saarinen with capturing this footage.] Congruent with his "happenstance" theory of filmmaking, Maysles adds that he had been filming the Stones while they were touring when Altamont just came along, the "next stop" on the tour.

Everything Old is New Again: Event Manipulation

What is more shocking, possibly, is that *The New Yorker*'s critic Pauline Kael, in her review of the film (sarcastically titled "Beyond Pirandello") actually accused the Maysles—via an associate of theirs—of setting up the event by encouraging the use of that particular venue for the concert.[17] In doing this, she not only made accusations about truth altering and careerism, but even assigns some blame for the murder. Of course, implied here is her belief—probably a vérité-influenced one—that documentary filmmakers do have a societal function. When a new print of *Gimme Shelter* was released a few years ago, some critics characterized Kael's take on the film as a kind of snuff film. (A subsequent collection of Kael criticism slightly toned down the accusations in this review as it was initially printed.)

Maybe this is why the generally gentle-seeming Maysles still gets livid at the mention of Kael: "I called Mr. Shawn (the then editor of the *New Yorker*) to complain, but got nowhere with it. This was in the days before fact-checkers, but still. They should have made it right. Everyone always said how brilliant she was. Should have been 'Pauline Kael, a goddamn liar.'"

Delinquent Disciples

So, then, how does he feel about the current uptick in the documentary mode? Or the popularity of documentaries, whether purely fact-based or fiction-influenced? Maysles just smiles: "Well, what's the phrase? It's an idea whose time has come." And what is his opinion of the new participatory documentary? Here he minces no words, especially when it comes to filmmaker Michael Moore: "He takes something you and I might agree with, but he pushes so hard that he hurts his own case. I think sometimes point of view works against the filmmaker. For instance, I think the son pushes too hard in *Tell Them Who You Are*. But of course, Haskell Wexler is a friend of mine.

"What I regret," Maysles says, "is that the movement has not taken on the character of Direct Cinema. So much of what is out there now is propaganda. A filmmaker's point of view rather than an open-ended investigation. Even some of the better ones won't accept the responsibility for telling the full truth. They blame the photographer, the editing. But if it's truly a documentary, then it should be a work of nonfiction. For example, [look at] the memoir that Oprah Winfrey got in trouble with [Note: Maysles refers to James Frey's *A Million Little Pieces*]. But there isn't a ruckus over inaccuracies in documentary films such as Michael Moore's."

In Maysles' film-formative years, he worked for a time for Robert Drew, of Drew Associates. Drew had been an editor at *Life* magazine, then started to work for television, forming a company of what would turn out to be future documentary geniuses: Maysles, Richard Leacock, and D.A. Pennebaker. Their preference for the purity of the image, and their insistence on noninterference, stuck. For Maysles, the term he took away from this association was Direct Cinema. It was generally referred to at the time as the American School of documentary (as opposed to the European brand of agitprop or more socially motivated cinema vérité), and Maysles still holds firmly to the credo.[18]

When I interviewed Morgan Spurlock (see chapter 6), he asked me a bit trepidatiously if "Al" had anything bad to say about him. No, was the answer, and then Spurlock laughingly recalled a panel where he and Maysles appeared together, where the older filmmaker attacked him for not being a real documentary filmmaker. "'Well, then, what is it I've made?' I asked Al. 'It's reality as I experienced it.'"

Still, Spurlock spoke of Al Maysles with the highest regard and respect. Even, in fact, a bit of terror.

One More Lucky Accident

Increasingly in the past few years, Maysles has been regarded as the true doyen of documentary filmmaking, so some are surprised to learn that he started out accidentally as a filmmaker. "I went to Syracuse University, where I studied psychology. One course in hypnosis especially inspired me, and I went on to get a graduate degree in psychology at Boston University. I was teaching there when, at age 28, I went to Russia to film patients in mental hospitals. I had borrowed a camera from CBS in New York, and after that I never looked back."

Maysles says his father was a very bright guy who "should have been a musician" but made his living as a postal worker. His mother, whom he eulogized in what he says was never-before-seen footage shown at BAM, was a staunch civil libertarian. Maysles is married to a family therapist and his four children, some of whom work at Maysles Films, are all in their twenties. He still takes on interns, whom he pays some small amount, and is actively involved in giving back by reaching out to the community and teaching budding young filmmakers who might not otherwise have a chance at such a training. A particular focus is on children who have a family member who is incarcerated, and when the films made by those kids are finished, copies are sent to the family member in prison.

"You know, of course, the theory that people who are violent tend to have a history of lack of self-respect with no creative outlet to counter their shame," he queries rhetorically. And though it sounds corny (unless you are there in his presence), Maysles says that compassion is an essential element in the character of a great documentary filmmaker, adding, "I can't imagine if we had really gone to Iraq [before] and filmed those people with compassion, we'd be in this mess now."

Working very much within the tradition of documentarian as world traveler, Maysles' current project is to take long distance trains to various places out of which will emerge a number of dramatic stories. As an example, at BAM, he showed a clip of this doc in the making about the reuniting of a family when the passenger got off the train.

Without his brother, who did much of the sound work on their films, Maysles carries on with various other partners. Charlotte Zwerin was one, though she too has passed away, from lung cancer ("smoking," Maysles gestures, puffing on an imaginary cigarette, and in a "too bad" way). David Maysles' interest in filmmaking started when, serving in the Korean War, he met a fellow soldier who later introduced him to the photographer, Milton Greene, who most famously photographed Marilyn Monroe. David Maysles became his assistant when Greene got into making Marilyn Monroe films. Many I interviewed characterize David Maysles, the business decision-maker, as the more high-strung of the duo and definitely the more flamboyant, becoming increasingly personally and professionally expressive before his sudden death (by aneurysm). Nearly all agree that it was a very successful partnership, both personally and professionally.

Happy-Go-Lucky Hustler

There is a kind of radical innocence to Maysles which seems to coexist with a shrewd business sense. He is extraordinarily generous in giving of his time for interviews; still, Maysles always seems to have his ear cocked—and why not?—for the business at hand. The second time I met with him he was waiting to hear back from HBO about the screening of *The Gates*, the most recent of his films about Christo and Jean-Claude. Never inattentive or impolite, he would nevertheless stop talking when the phone rang to find out if, indeed, this might be a call worth taking. Maysles is a humanist who takes care of business. One of his favorite phrases to answer a proposition from someone is, "If it is mutually beneficial." From anyone else, this would sound cold, but for some reason, from Al Maysles, it just seems honest.

He is ever on the hustle. At this moment, Maysles is a bit frustrated, because he doesn't understand why he can't get funding for a certain pet project—the totally false accusation that Jews kill Christian children to take their blood and mix it with Matzos to celebrate Passover, a belief Maysles says is still held internationally. (Fueling Maysles's anger is that recently the Hezbollah has made a propaganda film broadcast on satellite TV asserting this.)

It seems from this vantage point that the Maysles brothers made many shrewd guesses in picking subjects for their films. Case in point, of course, is their interviewing Little and Big Edie for *Grey Gardens*, especially considering the ultimate success of the film, its eventual classic status, and that it was made into both a musical on Broadway with Chrstine Ebersole and Mary Louise Wilson, and a feature film with Jessica Lange and Drew Barrymore. Maysles says he is not working on the feature, but was sent the script as a courtesy, and liked it. Yet for many years, the film *Grey Gardens* was a commercial flop. Today, it is ironic to see the clip which Maysles is now showing around, a bit when Albert and David are being interviewed on a contemporaneous talk show. The interviewer remarks that the doc has been a commercial failure. Al just nods, in a whatcha-gonna-do way, and then David says bravely, "Well, it may make some money yet."

He also did a movie on Brando, the revelatory *Meet Marlon Brando* (1965), in which the young actor promotes his (then) latest movie, *Morituri*, by hitting on female journalists and interrogating the interrogators. And *The Gates* was selected to close the Tribeca Film Festival in the spring of 2006. Currently listed in the many films of the company is *What's Happening! The Beatles in America* (1964), the only film about the Beatles' first visit to the United States which has footage of the Fab Four cavorting inside the Plaza Hotel just after they arrived in the States. As the explanatory notes for the June 2007 BAM event state, "Produced by Granada Television, this film documents The Beatles' historic first arrival in the United States. Many versions of this film exist, and this scene is often excised." For other films, the Maysles snagged footage of Muhammad Ali, John F. Kennedy, Paul Newman, Sophia Loren, and Truman Capote, to name just a few. And he owns footage of Roman Polanski and Sharon Tate, a sure shot for high interest if it does ever get used for a film.

The Maysles brothers seemed to have a knack for publicity, too, whether good or bad. For instance, though Martin Scorsese's *The Last Waltz* was a highly regarded documentary about the last appearance of the group The Band (and though Scorsese himself, intriguingly, did appear in the film), it never received the attention of *Gimme Shelter*. Similarly Taylor Hackford's acclaimed documentary *Chuck Berry Hail! Hail! Rock 'n' Roll* was high on every critic's "best" list, but it isn't as well known as the Maysles' Stones doc; nor are Leon Gast's documentaries—*Salsa*, which featured Rubén Blades, and *Our Latin Thing*, which explored the music scene. Gast even made a documentary about the Hell's Angels, but, needless to say, it did not receive the same recognition as did *Gimme Shelter*. Given the huge output of Maysles Films, some might say that being in the right place at the right time was a happy inevitability due to statistical probability. As Maysles says, "I just believe in luck, don't you?" Well, yeah, but you've still got to get access.

· · · · · · · · · ·

Endnotes

1. Carbondale: Southern Illinois University Press, 1989.

2. Nick Poppy, "Frederick Wiseman," *Salon.com* (January 30, 2002).

3. Atkinson, "Frederick Wiseman's Fair Game," *Village Voice* (February 8, 2000).

4. Gerald Peary, "Too Good to Win an Oscar," *The Boston Phoenix* (March 23, 1998).

5. Kaleem Aftab and Alexandra Weltz, "Fred Wiseman," *www/iol.ie/-gaalfilm/ filmwest/40wiseman.htm.*

6. Craig Hight and Jan Roscoe, *Faking It: Mock-Documentary and the Subversion of Factuality* (Manchester and New York: Manchester University Press, 2001), 37.

7. Interview with Frederick Wiseman, PBS Web site, "Ask Fred," *Independentlens* (2008).

8. Jesse Walker, "Interview with Frederick Wiseman," *www.reason.com* (December 2007).

9. Walker, ibid.

10. Bilge Ebiri, "Documentarian Frederick Wiseman on How the Idaho Legislature Can Help You Understand Barack Obama," *New York* magazine (February 20, 2008).

11. Aftab and Weltz, "Fred Wiseman."

12. Ibid.

13. Vincent Canby, "And Now, the 'Spontaneous' Film,'" *New York Times* (December 23, 1970).

14. Quoted by Jonas Mekas in "Mekas's Movie Journal," *Village Voice* (March 3, 1966).

15. Brian Winston, "North American Documentary in the 1960s," *Contemporary American Cinema*, ed. Linda Ruth Williams and Michael Hammond (New York: McGraw-Hill, 2006), 78.

16. *New York Times*, "Movie Mailbag," signed letter, December 27, 1970.

17. Pauline Kael, "Beyond Pirandello," *The New Yorker* (December 19, 1970). In a subsequent collection of her reviews, Kael slightly modified some of her assertions.

18. Following is a statement about the difference between Direct Cinema and cinema vérité, important to keep in mind here, for even subsequent documentarians seem to use the terms incorrectly at moments. Direct Cinema hopes to unveil truth through detailed outward observation of events and/or subjects; cinéma vérité seeks any means to explore ideas of truth and in some cases is connected with the revolutionary guerilla filmmaking of the 1960s. In the words of one critic, "in Direct Cinema, truth is what steps in front of the camera and what the filmmaker chooses to highlight. But in cinéma vérité, the role of the filmmaker can either assist in the process of discovering/revealing truth or detract from it." Many, many use the phrases interchangeably, but historically—in the original definition of the words—this is incorrect. Eric Barnouw's exceptionally well-written *Documentary: A History of the Non-fiction Film* (Oxford University Press) gives a thorough historical background of the terms.

chapter three

THE PROFESSOR AND THE RABBLE-ROUSER: PETER DAVIS AND MICHAEL MOORE

· · · · · · · · · ·

Nothing makes a point better than a little historical perspective. While we may be very well used to the neo-doc by now, and even in most cases expect to be entertained as well as edified when we go to a documentary these days, consider the following beginning paragraphs from the review of the film *Hearts and Minds* in *The Nation*:

> Peter Davis's *Hearts and Minds* is an admirably paced, continuously passionate, frequently moving, sometimes shocking, once or twice savagely funny propaganda film and I would be as well pleased if it were not being shown. Since it is edited from pre-existing footage, it is being called a documentary, but that is an absurd designation, for the picture makes no pretense of being an even-handed report. But because its bias is overt and one that I have held about Vietnam for, it sometimes seems, most of my adult life, I do not object on that score.
>
> The fact is that it operates to arouse hatred against hatred, to induce a gut reaction against gut reaction, and by doing so serves to sustain a morbid emotionalism of the very sort it claims to abominate...it manipulates its viewers, as for example when it juxtaposes Westmoreland's notorious statement about the low value Orientals place on human life against scenes of Vietnamese families mourning at the open graves of their beloved dead. That sort of editing teaches nothing except that we should despise Westmoreland, which is a waste of nervous energy.[1]

Propaganda is the real put-down word in this review, and yet it is a word that is rarely mentioned these days when documentaries are discussed. Perhaps we currently see ourselves as sophisticated enough to see through such tactics, or possibly there is such a loss of faith in institutions and government that the word has lost its meaning. As Cara Mertes, head of the Documentary Fund at the Sundance Institute and former head of *P.O.V.*, the documentary series on PBS, suggested to me, in explaining the new popularity of the documentary, "The political climate is such that people are ready to hear the truth on film."

Hearts and Minds really irritated *The Nation* reviewer, R. Hatch, and just think: Davis himself doesn't even appear in the film. (Most know by now that the title of the film came from a speech by LBJ about winning the "hearts and minds" of the Vietnamese people, and was also used by Robert McNamara in his defense of the Vietnam war.)

Hatch does admit, however, that *Hearts and Minds* "aspired to be an American version of *The Sorrow and the Pity*, a compassionate look at the commonplaces of everyday life that inspired the people of a large industrial nation to follow their leaders in a war against a remote peasant society far from its shores."

Hearts and Minds: Relevance for Today

But why should we order up *Hearts and Minds* on Netflix now or buy it on Amazon? There is a general consensus now that Vietnam was a dreadful mistake; most seem to agree that the point of view Davis took was correct.

Nevertheless, some of the cinematic devices employed—the use of music for emotional editorializing, the sensationalistic if brilliantly connective cross-cuts—have been capitalized on and made into a recognizable mini-genre by Michael Moore and other contemporary documentarians. *Hearts and Minds* alternates between eminent talking heads interviews, stock footage, testimony from veterans, and clips from Hollywood films. Still, there is no official narrator, humorous or otherwise, as in a Moore film.

Yet Michael Moore, born in 1954 and so not exactly a spring chicken himself, credits what he calls an "old film"—*Hearts and Minds*—as having been his inspiration. The generally immodest Moore is giving some credit where credit is due.

It is also, he says, the best documentary ever made.

There can be little doubt that Moore took *Hearts and Minds* as a template. And the outstanding structural likeness between the two films points up that before the 1975 film, there was no documentary which satirically placed mainstream cinema clips side by side with serious subject matter. (For his part, Davis says he appreciates the compliment, has only met Moore on one occasion, and does have a few "problems" with some of Moore's tactics.)

For instance, in *Hearts and Minds*, a character in a feature film clip asks, "Will we ever understand the Eastern race?" followed immediately by a cut to Bob Hope in an "on the road" movie, lolling about with courtesans on some pillows. The next clip is from a 1940s film where a woman declaims against "you hideous yellow monsters." And shortly thereafter is a scene of General Westmoreland giving his view that Orientals don't value life as much as we do.

The last listed sequence is first comically intercut with feature film footage, then goes into a cinéma vérité type statement. After the Westmoreland quote, there is a scene of a little Vietnamese boy grieving at his father's funeral.

In the spring of 2007, after a talk about *Hearts and Minds* at the New School for Social Research, Davis said, "I was criticized for using that quote in that spot, and of course Westmoreland himself said I took it out of context. But the truth is that there is no place where there wouldn't have been some kind of shock value to the quote."

Did I Intervene?

When you look at this sequence today, it out-Moores Michael Moore himself. It is funny, it is cutting, and of course it is editorializing like mad.

From today's vantage point, you have to ask yourself how in the world the relatively straight-laced acting and looking (well-bred, beautifully mannered) Davis came up with this idea. True, he had worked as a documentary filmmaker for CBS News. But his movie's structure clearly uses the kind of juxtaposition that no major television channel would have allowed at the time. Another possible source for his inspiration is that, as he says, "I grew up in a screenwriting household, but with screenwriters who were thoroughly disillusioned with the studio system. So while, yes, I was very familiar with movies, in some ways I was inoculated against the movie business and wanted to make documentaries as a kind of counter to all that."

There is also his clever use of the patriotic spirit–inducing World War I song "Over There." "I especially wanted to use 'Over There,'" Davis says. "I realized as far back as World War I, we were seeing ourselves as the world's saviors. I wanted to evoke that and, in doing so, question whether we should still be applying that principle to Vietnam at the time of the movie, and of course today as well."

He laughingly admits, "I spent an awful lot of time getting rights to film music and permissions for film clips."

So it seems that sequences in Michael Moore's films, such as his use of the song "Fire Water Burn" when soldiers embark on bombing raids in Afghanistan in *Fahrenheit 9/11*, are not exactly novel, though they may appear that way to a new generation of documentary film watchers.

Brand New Methods

Music to comment editorially on film action (as opposed to just setting a mood) may not have been entirely novel, but certainly it was popularized successfully by Davis. Yet nostalgic film clips used for commentary seem to be the cinematic conceptual breakthrough of Peter Davis.

Moore, like Davis, has been accused of manipulating audience reactions and of being too heavy-handed. In *Bowling for Columbine*, for instance, Moore goes from President Bill Clinton announcing the bombing of Kosovo to a shot an hour later of Clinton announcing the fact that there had been a school shooting in Columbine. Davis shows two GIs with some prostitutes, then cuts to a scene of the burning of Vietnamese villages. He sets up the viewer to watch a few Vietnam veterans talking to the camera before pulling back to show that they are amputees and/or in a wheelchair. We have listened to Robert Muller talk for quite a bit in the film before the camera shockingly pulls back to reveal his wheelchair; similarly we don't know for a while that William Marshall has lost his arm. Is this manipulative, or just incredibly effective?

Davis comments on the criticisms that his movie is too subjective: "It is not to say the film doesn't have a voice and that the voice is not mine. But I tried to leave spaces in the film so the viewer will come to his or her own conclusion, not pound it into the viewer. I was accused of being one-sided in that I did not show any of the atrocities committed by the South Vietnamese. Surely they did do terrible as well as, I'm sure, inspiring things. They believed they were defending their own country against a foreign invader. But that wasn't the film I was making. My movie was about why Americans were in Vietnam, what we did there, and what it did to us in the process."

To this viewer, some of the most clever edits are in a section in which Davis uses a shot of marching soldiers from *This Is the Army*, in a section of the film about patriotism, followed by a montage of scenes which satirically comment on America's fear of Communism. After some footage of the McCarthy hearings—which now seem prophetic of Michael Moore's cinema tactics—there is a scene from the 1952 film *My Son John* in which a mother

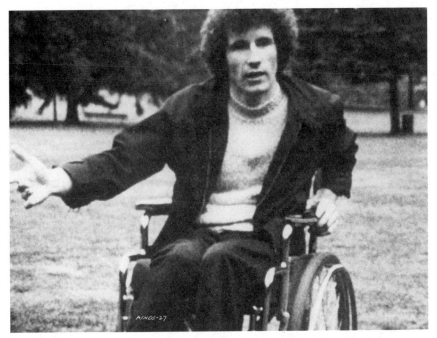

First criticized for being manipulative, then lauded for its surprise effect, the viewer doesn't know Muller is in a wheelchair until the camera pulls back in *Hearts and Minds*. Photo courtesy of Warner Brothers.

asks her son to take an oath that he is not a Communist. When he does, she gratefully clasps his hands to her face.

These edits are used satirically and are worthy of the best of the tongue-in-cheek editing style of Moore, to make a critical anachronism.

To Narrate or Not

One way in which Davis's film is different from Moore movies is that Davis did not use any voice-over narration, autobiographical or otherwise (though there are moments in the film when we see a mike or hear a very occasional question). This is Davis's rationale: "I had been working in television and I noticed that with a lot of TV footage of people suffering there is always a reporter, but the more eloquent the narrator, the less you identify with victims. So I wanted to remove that curtain." And *Hearts and Minds* does begin with a fairly straightforward chronological history of our involvement in Vietnam, tracing through American presidents, from Truman on.

He also disavows any set-up scenes, such as Michael Moore has been accused of. Davis said that the scene, for instance, in which the deserter living in Canada comes home to tell his mother in Detroit that he wishes to return to the US, even if it means he will have to do jail time, was completely spontaneous. Crediting his cinematographer, Richard Pearce, with the companionable and unself-conscious relationship Pearce set up between the camera and his subjects, Davis says that the mother and son were at that point ignoring the camera—an affirmation of the fact that after a while their subjects forgot they were being filmed.

Still, the intensity of this scene in the way the cutting is handled—back and forth medium close-up shots—makes the characters seem as if they are in a feature film; we become that intimately connected with them, and their reactions and interactions.

Davis also says that, while he is not sure if the Vietnamese ever accepted his and his small crew's presence in some of their villages, they did at least "get used to us. I wouldn't say they accepted us, of course. I have no idea what they thought. But it did seem that after a while they got used to us, ignored us."

He also observes, like a lot of filmmakers who have come after him, that in making a documentary, some of the most significant footage occurred accidentally. The example Davis cites is the Emerson family, who lost their son in the war: The filmmaker met the family while the crew was in Concord for another mission. And that filming these scenes of the grieving family—descended from the distinguished New England family of Ralph Waldo Emerson—was so painful for Pearce that the cinematographer decided to leave the world of doc filmmaking and go into features. Which he did—he directed *Country*, the 1984 film about the farm foreclosures produced by and starring Jessica Lange. Curiously, or maybe not, it has a doc-like, historical sensibility.

The Trouble-Making Gentleman

There was enough controversy over *Hearts and Minds* when it came out to warm the cockles of even Moore's heart. When Peter Davis and Burt Schneider, the film's producer, won the Oscar for their documentary in 1975, Schneider read a statement from the Viet Cong expressing friendship. This was followed by Frank Sinatra reading aloud a disclaimer (a disclaimer he subsequently disavowed by saying Bob Hope thrust the paper before him, forcing him to read it) from the Academy absolving its members from any guilt by association from anyone making a political remark during the telecast. Somehow, it makes Michael Moore's booed acceptance speech at the 2002 Oscars when he won for *Bowling for Columbine* a bit tame by comparison.

Peter Davis, who currently holds a post teaching documentary film at the New School for Social Research in New York City, and has taught broadcast journalism at Yale University, was, during the making of *Hearts and Minds*, a newsman who wrote and directed such acclaimed pieces as *Hunger in America* and *The Selling of the Pentagon* for CBS News. He says:

> I had thought about the [Vietnam] war a great deal without coming to many conclusions about the reasons for it, or even what the war served—or failed to serve—in our society. I never thought that being for or against the war was the whole story.
>
> I shot 85 percent of the footage with my own crew, in Vietnam and the United States. The rest came from outside sources, ranging from old movies to other newsmen. I was not content with interviews. And when we shot interviews, I didn't just shoot some guy at his desk. . . . I always stayed with people much longer than I did in television—until they were starting to get tired of their own public masks.
>
> I was also interested, as much as possible, in getting close to people's experiences. It seems to me that's one thing the movie form can do. Television can try, but it does much less well with such a small screen. I've always been interested in the nonfiction film, and particularly how you can get people to be as interested in that as they are in fantasy.

With these comments, he acknowledges the complexity of the relationship of subject and director. Joan Didion may have said it best, if cryptically, in her famous comment, "Never trust a writer." In cinema, perhaps because it is a newer form, the occasionally voracious and vicarious nature of such symbiotic relationships hasn't yet been fully acknowledged and analyzed. This may be particularly true in the development of the "new doc" with its implied relationship between director and subject.

You can hear Davis in the Criterion DVD extended interview: "I ended *Hearts and Minds* with the accusation from the veteran who says, 'You guys were over there too, with your cameras.' He was right. We were implicated in the war too."

Benevolent Royalty

Davis was born in Santa Monica, California, in 1937 to screenwriter parents. (He was later married to Joanna Mankiewicz, the daughter of Herman Mankiewicz, the Hollywood screenwriter.) After graduating from Harvard, Davis traveled to India, where he was struck by the extreme disparity of wealth and poverty, and his social consciousness was stirred.

Davis worked briefly at the *New York Times* and was then chosen to research Franklin Delano Roosevelt for a television series on this president. This provided a segue into the documentary film world, and at CBS News in the late 1960s and 1970s, Davis made films on student rebellion, poverty, racism, mental illness, and war. His investigation into Defense Department propaganda began a conflict between the Nixon Administration and broadcast journalists that led to reforms in the Pentagon's structure. When he left CBS in 1972, Davis made *Hearts and Minds*.

Davis spent a year shooting the film, picking up two journalistic nuggets of information along the way: showing former French Foreign Minister Georges Bidault revealing an offer by John Foster Dulles, previous to the 1954 Geneva Convention, to provide a pair of A-bombs to French forces in Indochina; and Gen. Nguyen Kanh playing a taped telephone call from Gen. Maxwell Taylor confirming Washington's decision to force him out as president of South Vietnam. In Washington, Davis had been unsuccessful in getting interviews with American policy makers from President Nixon and Henry Kissinger to McGeorge Bundy, Robert McNamara, and Dean Rusk.

"None of the Americans believed themselves accountable for their actions," said Davis.

Reversal of Fortune: the Upside

Where once the film was trashed for being one-sided and emotionally out of whack, now it is praised. Consider the review, for instance, of the re-released *Hearts and Minds*, shown in 2004 at New York's Film Forum, and the words of *Village Voice* reviewer Michael Atkinson:

> Davis's trump moments are strictly Eisensteinian: cutting from a Vietnamese capitalist hopefully outlining his future plunder to a busy factory rapping out prosthetic limbs or a heartbreaking funeral scene, complete with loved ones assailing the coffin, followed by beefeater General Westmoreland asserting that 'Orientals' don't put the 'same high price on life as does the Westerner.' Even if you think Davis went too far in scoring images of village razing and torture with a bouncy rendition of 'Over There,' the all-important equation of official jingoism and murderous destruction is tough to dicker over.[2]

It seems that editorial comments are now acceptable, and—depending on how you feel about Eisenstein—the mix of fact and fiction or narrative fiction-like techniques is now not only acceptable but brilliant. The techniques of fictional feature films are now considered praiseworthy inclusions in documentary cinema.

Music, for instance, is used effectively by Davis, and is similarly employed by Michael Moore. Extremely effective are Moore's use of the lyrics, "We don't need no water, let the motherfucker burn/Burn, motherfucker, burn" (from the song "Fire Water Burn" by Bloodhound Gang) set to bombing scenes in *Fahrenheit 9/11*. This music and destruction sequence follows a talking heads type interview where a soldier is describing getting pumped up for flying and bombing. And for a long time after seeing the film, one can't get the lead tune to *Bowling for Columbine*, "take them bowling," out of one's mind (or anyway, this writer couldn't). Moore's using music this way was hardly pioneering, though: It's just as incendiary to hear "Over There" in *Hearts and Minds* as Vietnamese villages are being razed.

Don't Blame Just Michael Moore

Moore has taken some heat for not making logical connections in *Bowling for Columbine* about America's predilection for violence, guns, and the scenes from its historical past. Critics suggest that parts of the movie are nothing more than deliberately propagandistic; for instance particularly the segment titled "White Man's Fear of Black Men," which juxtaposes footage from the Willie Horton rape references and accusations about a mythical black man by murderer Susan Smith during her trial for killing her kids.

But in the cross-cuts, the use of music, and the placement of certain interviews, it turns out that Davis could be accused of not quite connecting the dots as well. Davis makes connections between a violent high school football game, a re-enactment of a Revolutionary War setting of 1776, and then cuts to a scene showing Ho Chi Minh expressing his hope that America will be empathetic to the similarly righteous Vietnamese war against the French. He goes from a rampaging football game "back home" in the States to the Tet Offensive. Moore, in a not dissimilar structure, cuts from bowling alleys to random violence to the shooting death of the Colorado students to the NRA and Charlton Heston.

One significant difference between the two documentaries, however: *Hearts and Minds* has no scenes which were set up in advance such as Michael Moore has subsequently admitted to, nor are there any chronologically out-of-sync contemporary events presented. (And, of course, there is no narrator, or narrator/star.)

So, here's Stuart Klawans in *The Nation*, in a complete reversal from the original *Nation* critique: "[*Hearts and Minds* is] one of the great feats of filmmaking: a coolly comprehensive assessment of America's war against Vietnam, completed while the shots were still being fired." He also writes:

> Davis got all sides into the movie: American Presidents, generals, and planners; Vietnamese leaders, prostitutes, and peasants; French colonial officials; US veterans, from the heartbroken to the vehemently pro-war; mourners; flag-wavers; coffin-makers; amputees; even a high school football team, whose coach helps set the tone for the movie by instructing his players to kill. By creating a counterpoint among these many voices, Davis composed a work that is simultaneously an expose of the history of the war, an exploration of American martial culture, and a deeply humane portrait of the victims.[3]

Same Methods, Different Sources

One way in which the two filmmakers are personally dissimilar: Peter Davis is ever the gentleman, restrained and elegant, from an elite background. And Michael Moore is, well, Michael Moore—slapdash, sloppy, and all that we have come to know, accept, and (some of us) love about his baseball-capped mask/persona. And there is a huge economic difference: *Roger and Me* was the first film to break the million-dollar ceiling for the gross for a documentary film. And since then, of course, more, much more. Two unarguable facts jump out, and even a Moore detractor could not counter them. *Bowling for Columbine* was the first documentary which was a box-office success to win an Oscar for a documentary since *Woodstock*, and *Fahrenheit 9/11* was the first documentary to land in the weekend top five, in addition to making it to number one.

Born outside of Flint, Michigan,[4] Moore is from an Irish Catholic family, which he refers to frequently in his films, a family of relatives who worked for the town's main business, General Motors. Though Michael Moore had signed up to start work there, he didn't actually turn up on the job for his first day at the GM plant. He felt he was bound for other things, as indeed he was: He started a newspaper in Flint, then had his own radio show, followed by a six-month gig in California at *Mother Jones* magazine before being fired (and ultimately suing and settling for wrongful termination, a settlement used in part to finance *Roger and Me*).

Undoubtedly, Michael Moore's heritage will be the high visibility he brought to the documentary form. *Roger and Me* was a financial watershed.

And as David Lynch said, speaking for the unanimous decision of the committee at the Cannes Film Festival when Moore won a Palme d'Or for *Bowling for Columbine* (becoming the first documentary to be so recognized at Cannes in nearly fifty years), movies should be about something. There is "so little of that, especially in America."

Still, though Moore is prominent in both *Roger and Me* and *Bowling for Columbine*, he says, "I didn't set out to be a celebrity. I've never really been comfortable being on screen for obvious reasons. When in doubt, cut me out," he told Larissa MacFarquhar in *The New Yorker*.[5] Perhaps. Still, it's nearly impossible to watch a Michael Moore documentary without either hearing or seeing him; and, of course, his first big success, *Roger and Me*, starts out as a kind of autobiographical, personal film.

And though he certainly did not invent the subjective documentary, or the neo-doc, he most definitely has capitalized on it, popularized the form, and driven it deep into our collective consciousness. As critic Adam Hart concludes in *Senses of Cinema*, "Michael Moore has made it okay for directors to state an explicit point of view—not that either he or Errol Morris were the first, of course."[6]

Motivations from the Home Front

Here is the story of the genesis of *Roger and Me*. No, I did not go to Flint or trail after Moore on his many publicity stunts following the release of *Sicko*; Moore lives in zip code 10024 in Manhattan, at least quite a bit of the time, a fact which he doesn't exactly hide, but he does sort of keep on the Q.T. Indeed, all home references in Moore's films are to Flint and only Flint. He always goes back or home to Michigan in his movies—not just in *Roger and Me*, but in all his movies.

"After I got back to Flint from California and the *Mother Jones* debacle, I was in a pretty big depression. It got even worse when I found out that GM intended to close eleven assembly and production facilities locally. Of course, it was all because GM wanted to take advantage of the lower wages in foreign countries, and in the span of a decade, Flint—my Flint, my family's Flint, and a town of 150,000—lost 30,000 jobs. Unemployment and crime rose, and according to *Money* magazine, Flint became the least desirable place to live in the country. I was incensed."

His identification with his hometown may be one reason for the highly personal quality of his film. Still, it's quite startling, if a bit disingenuous, that he starts *Roger and Me* with the voice-over, "I was kind of a strange child," in his now familiar, unabashed way. We are treated to pictures of his childhood birthday parties, and home movies of him in Flint as a kid.

Then, a bit into the film, "I wrote, I phoned, I faxed—no Roger. I wanted to get him to meet those losing their jobs." Next is a cinematic juxtaposition typical of (some would say typically illogical of) Moore. There are scenes of the rat population, much larger because, according to Moore's narration, now that everyone is leaving Flint the town can't afford more than a twice-weekly garbage pickup. You might call it a Michael Moore type analogy. It works on film, maybe because of the cartoonlike grotesque exaggeration, but not if you think about it too much.

Naturally humorous—he was his high school's class clown, after all— Moore even allows himself to be color-analyzed. Janice, a friend of Moore's and a former feminist radio talk show host, is trying new career possibilities in light of Flint's decline: She is working as an Amway salesperson, color analyzing women in their homes to determine their season, and what colors they should wear. She has a mini-crisis when she realizes that she herself has been mis-analyzed. To help her feel better, Moore allows her to analyze him in one of the marvelously burlesqued images of the film. He dons a cone-shaped white paper hat to cover his hair in order to not throw off color schemes.

When contemporary audiences saw *Roger and Me* in 1989, it was a bit of a stunner to have the individual filmmaker making such a strong connection between himself and a city, himself and a whole socio-economic stratum. In retrospect, it was probably a great thing that it was in a humor vein; spoonfuls of sugar always making things a bit easier to go down.

Though the parallels are not precise, in Ed Pincus's 1981 documentary *The Diaries*, there are connections made between his marriage, career, friends, and family and his era—the early days of the women's liberation movement. *Le Monde* called *The Diaries* "an epic work that redefines an art, forcing us to rethink what we thought we knew about the Cinema."[7]

Trouble in the Making

Even so, Michael Moore had trouble financing *Roger and Me*, though he sold his home and used his settlement money from the *Mother Jones* lawsuit. So he started a weekly game of Bingo, which was somewhat profitable (PBS was refusing to advance more funds). Finally, Moore took the movie around to festivals such as the Telluride, Toronto, and New York Film Festivals. "I shanghaied Roger Ebert away from a Peter Greenaway Gala essentially accosting him on the street, and talked him into going to *Roger and Me* instead," Moore remembers proudly. Ebert got behind the film, it created a small sensation, and Moore sold the distribution rights to Warner Brothers for $3 million. When it was released in 1989, *Roger and Me* pulled in more than $25 million at the box office, which made it the highest-grossing documentary at that time, subsequently surpassed by *Fahrenheit 9/11* and *March of the Penguins*.

And as for his methods and the shape of his film, which seems to have popularized and solidified this type of filmmaking, Moore says, "Basically, I made a virtue of a necessity. I had worked as a journalist. I know how to interview people. I know how to research.

"When I couldn't nail down Roger Smith, I just decided to go with it and use that fact for the film."

But after this first great success with *Roger and Me*, there came backlashes and criticisms of his editing style, factual tie-ins, and the chronology of the film's timeline. In late 1989, Harlan Jacobson, at the time the editor of *Film Comment* magazine, the official publication of the prestigious Film Society at Lincoln Center, correctly accused Moore of fudging the chronology of the movie, to make it seem that events that took place before GM's layoffs—like the city of Flint's attempts to revive, such as creating a theme park called AutoWorld—were a consequence of the layoffs, though this was not what actually occurred chronologically.

Covering, Moore told Jacobson that he considered the story to have started in his childhood, not when he returned to Flint. Influential critic Pauline Kael further publicized the controversy by mentioning the fracas in her review in *The New Yorker*.

But later, Moore stopped being apologetic: "If Jacobson wanted exact chronology, he should have watched C-SPAN."

Will the Real Chronology Please Stand Up?

This is reminiscent of some of the comments that a filmmaker such as Werner Herzog has made about not wanting to "merely" portray an accountant's truth in his films. Yet in Moore's case, it seems that the presentation might have been intended to deceive, or in a better light, were just a bit careless. And of course, most of what Herzog creates would not be considered muckraking, with its implied obligation to fact.

For instance, in *Bowling for Columbine*, the audience is led to believe that the two teenage killers at Columbine High School may have become inured to violence by the proximity of a local weapons factory. Yet it later came

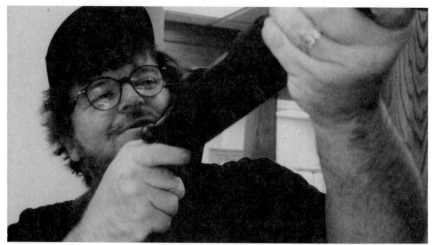

Easy access to ammo in the film *Bowling for Columbine*. Courtesy Metro-Goldwyn-Mayer.

out that the factory produced nothing more lethal than rockets to launch TV satellites. This is a little more than sloppy editing—perhaps even a bit duplicitous?

Documentary's progenitor Al Maysles has declared: "Sometimes Moore hurts his own cause [by overstating it]." Other critics of Moore have noted this as well: For instance, Moore's calling Bush a deserter (it would have been just as effective to tell the truth: that Bush went AWOL from his National Guard duties). Shooting himself in the foot by such overstatement might be a subconscious way of creating more controversy, and calling more attention to himself, but that's a guess to which Moore won't respond.

The chief complaint against him as a documentary filmmaker—that he has changed chronology in some of his films—in some cases, oddly enough, unnecessarily—was also made about Davis for *Hearts and Minds*. But the cause and effect charge about timeline presentation did not apply to Davis's film. There is little doubt that the cavalier attitude of some of the soldiers Davis shoots has to do with being in Vietnam or that the generals interviewed had an impact on the decision to go to war.

Here is what Moore has to say in his defense about the offending, often referenced scene from *Bowling for Columbine*: "In the spring of 2001 I saw a *real* ad in a *real* newspaper in Michigan announcing a promotion that a *real* bank would give you a gun as your up-front interest for opening up a certificate of deposit account: 'More bang for your buck!' Even the Chicago *Sun-Times* wrote about it. When you see me going in to the bank and walking out with my new gun in *Bowling for Columbine*—that is exactly as it happened. Nothing was done out of the ordinary other than to phone ahead and ask permission to let me bring a camera in to film me opening up my account. I walked into that bank in northern Michigan for the first time ever on that day in June 2001, and, with cameras rolling, gave the bank teller $1,000—and opened up a twenty-year CD account. After you see me filling out the required federal forms, plus saying 'How do you spell Caucasian?,' which I am filling out here for the first time, the bank manager faxed it to the bank's main office for them to do the background check. The bank is a licensed federal arms dealer and thus can have guns on the premises and do the instant background checks." (*www.MichaelMoore.com*)

In *Bowling for Columbine*, the Michael Moore style is established, especially in the cartoon sequences. "A Brief History of the United States of America" is a witty and, of course, highly exaggerated cartoon sequence written by Moore and animated by Harold Moss and FlickerLab (animator Moss provided a similar service in *Fahrenheit 9/11*), followed soon after by the sequence, "White Man's Fear of Black Men."

The cartoon is a witty run-down of American history with a slant toward demonstrating Moore's points about slave labor, and "Fear of Black Men" focuses on the American tendency to always assume it was a black man who committed a crime.

It is followed by footage about rapist Willie Horton and also the famous scene from *Birth of a Nation* when Mae Marsh is pursued by a leering and

From the "Don't Kill Me Big Black Man" segment of the animation in *Bowling for Columbine*, "A Brief History of America." Animation cels courtesy of Harold Moss and FlickerLab.

threatening black man, jumping to her demise to escape a fate worse than death.

Both these sequences point up what will probably turn out to be some of Moore's longest-lasting impact on the documentary form: cartoon-like animation, sometimes intercut with film clips, scored by ironically used music. If some have compared his dramatic editing style to that of Eisenstein, it is not unexpected (though some reviewers like Anthony Lane in *The New Yorker* call Moore a "blunderbuss" in his broad and clumsy editing). The cross-cuts of Eisenstein were once considered outlandish too, and yet, like Moore's, they were in the service of a social cause: At the time, Soviet documentaries were the first to develop the format for social intent and were also accused of being propagandistic.

On the downside, some filmmakers, such as Aaron Woolf, the director of 2007's *King Corn*, say Moore's slanting, maybe even twisting, of interviews has made it more difficult for other working documentary filmmakers to get people to agree to be on camera.

Wild and Wooly Innovation

Those who reference *Hearts and Minds* say Michael Moore is perhaps the most ideological and emotive editor since Davis. Others do go back to Eisenstein for a comparison citing his montage of shock and statement. Juxtaposing heroes and villains, Moore moves with ease between political comedy and tragic reality. And in most of his films he intercuts with exemplifying newsreels, or film clips used for ironic counterpoint. In *Roger and Me*, for instance, his return to Flint after having been fired from *Mother Jones* is commented on using "nostalgia" clips from decades-old films of soldiers returning home from the war.

A Michael Moore documentary has a recognizable, even frequently imitated, pattern. For instance, the 2004 film *Michael Moore Hates America* by Michael Wilson is very much in Moore's trademark—shall we say *auteur*-ish?—style. Mimicking *Roger and Me*, Wilson begins with his own blue-collar Midwestern background, relating how his father was laid off from work but kept his family together and sent Wilson to college. Much of the developing storyline traces Wilson's semicomic attempts to get the elusive Moore to sit down for an interview, in effect turning Moore into his own version of Roger Smith. The Canadian filmmakers Rick Caine and Debbie Melnyk took a similar tack in their 2004 film *Manufacturing Dissent*, a movie that asserts that all of *Roger and Me* is based on a lie, since Michael Moore has omitted the fact that indeed he had once met and interviewed Roger Smith, a couple years before the making of *Roger and Me*. (See especially "Michael and Me," a clever commentary plus interview with Moore in Cannes by Andrew Anthony in the May 23, 2004 *Observer*, which both skewers and appreciates the filmmaker. It also has a notorious interchange with Moore about enrolling his daughter in an exclusive Manhattan private school.)

And while adapting it to their own style of quicker cuts of MTV-style editing and the visual superimpositions of Internet-style editing—use of animation as images piled on top of other images which do not disappear—many other filmmakers, including Morgan Spurlock, have given Moore the compliment of following suit. Spurlock's film *Super Size Me* begins with his own family pictures of his mother cooking dinner in their family kitchen—photos arranged like snapshots in an album. While a purely personal documentarian like Alan Berliner (*The Sweetest Sound, Nobody's Business*) was occasionally taken to task by critics for having too much of himself in a film, we no longer blink an eye at this convention, even if the movie is ostensibly about a "cause." Save those family photographs, in case you ever do decide to make a documentary!

Moore does still use standard documentary conventions, such as maps detailing his journey: Flint to New York, highlighted on a US map, New York being where Moore has to go to try to track down Roger Smith, at the Waldorf Astoria. He also identifies certain interviewees on film with titles for dramatic purpose. For example, GM's official spokesperson Tom Kay, whom Moore interviewed throughout *Roger and Me*, always took the laissez-faire position about business and its employees (emphasizing that General Motors did not owe the town anything), but in the end he lost his own job. At the end of the film there is a shot of Kay, with the subtitle: "Laid off. Office closed." Also in the doc tradition/heritage, Moore uses actual, sometimes archival footage in *Roger and Me*, for instance, of Ronald Reagan, Dan Rather, and Ted Koppel.

A Form Too Far

By Moore's standards, *Sicko* was restrained, as he himself and others have noted. His typical hallmarks are present, however: Moore and a small band against the forces of imperialism. Filmmaker Roy Frumkes (profiled in chapter 7) declared taking a boat to Cuba the stunt doc aspect of *Sicko*.

But the style of interviewing is more straightforward and seems less staged. "The material speaks for itself," Moore said. "I hardly had to do a thing to it. I made this film in hopes of reaching across the great divide in this country, so I made it in a nonpartisan way. I started with the premise that illness knows no political stripe.

"And, of course, ultimately *Sicko* may end up being a more dangerous film because it's less controversial, because it does reach out and will appeal to all kinds of people and not just the Democrats. And because of that, if it reaches more people, it has a better chance of having some impact."

Sicko had the second-highest grossing opening weekend of a documentary, after *Fahrenheit 9/11*. As usual, Moore has been brilliant at marketing the film, beginning with his showing of clips of the at-the-time uncompleted doc at the 2006 fall Toronto International Film Festival. All heard of the subpoenas Moore received to testify about his trip to a Communist country, or of legal papers to suppress the film.

For our purposes, it's interesting that in this film Moore reverts—if in his usual exaggerated style—to interviews with people, for the most part presented straightforwardly, and without some of the satirical apparatus of his other films. Except for the few-years-old sequence about Hillary Clinton, if that even qualifies, there is no quasi-historical archival footage in the movie. And only a couple cartoons.

Sicko does not abandon the standard documentary form. Moore, the *benshi* of our time, travels to England, to France, to Cuba to make his points. Is it ethnographic? Yes, it is. There are locals photographed and talked to. Some may be Americans living abroad, in Paris, but they speak for themselves. And as for the footage of Cuba, it can't really be questioned. Are there testimonials from experts? Yes, the comments of the various Cuban doctors who look after the American victims that Moore is traveling with: emergency workers from 9/11, veterans, and others who cannot afford American health care. And, of course, the victims themselves, giving their own live guinea-pig-like statistics about the cost of health care in America for their very own specific cases.

It may be a concept documentary, and a Michael Moore concept at that. But it is still a documentary.

And on a Personal Note...

Multimillionaire Moore lives quite comfortably in his apartment on Manhattan's affluent Upper West Side, as of this writing, though he does go back regularly to his properties in Michigan, which he prefers to emphasize as his official residence. Another thing he doesn't spread around is that his moviemaking operation is also based in New York City. Unlike the offices of an Errol Morris, or an Al Maysles, when you call Michael Moore's place of work, the telephone answerer gives an anonymous, "Studio." Some of this is passed off to a need for secrecy in project creation and making, and this is surely understandable, given some of the pressures and even harassment Moore has received in government attempts to suppress *Sicko*. Still, it is not exactly in the proletariat vein to have your living situation and working headquarters in some of the priciest real estate in the country. The last time this interviewer spoke with Moore's publicity company, a junior publicist insisted that Moore was going to sell his New York condo and move permanently back to Michigan.

To point up some of the murkiness around his place of residence, check out some of Moore's own e-responses to online complaints that such a populist would live in an elite city area. Then, take a look at an article in the *New York Times* in December 2007, devoted to praising Michael Moore and photographer John Robert Williams for restoring an historic theater in downtown Traverse City, dark since 1978.[9] Though the article asserts that Moore and his family had relocated to the town in 2002, doormen still receive packages for Moore at his condo on the Upper West Side, there are sightings in the area, and many Internet sites snipe at him for living in high bourgeois splendor in the West 80s. As Maysles says in another context, it might be just as easy to not muddy the waters.

Moore is married to his long-time partner Kathleen Glynn, whom he met in the office of the Flint *Voice*, which Moore founded. She works as a producer on his movies. Alternately defensive about and proud of the fact that his movies have made so much money, Moore never hesitates to bring up the foundation he has set up, the Center for Alternative Media, for other less well-heeled filmmakers, or to mention the Traverse City Film Festival, now in its third year, which he started, conveniently near his lakefront summer home in Michigan.

Experts Put It in Perspective

One thing he is not at all apologetic about: the form of his films, and their mix of fact and fiction. "I make movies," says Moore. "I write books. I don't write nonfiction books or fiction books. Same thing for movies." A similarly quotable parallel is his famous Oscar acceptance speech for *Bowling for Columbine*, in which he dismisses any cavils about his film, and about it not being a doc film in general, by saying, "We have a fictitious president." (In other places, the ever-quotable Moore has said, "We like nonfiction because we live in fictitious times.")

Syracuse University's Robert Thompson, a media expert and professor who likens the current surge in documentaries to the effect *The Simpsons* had on animation, predicts: "There are twenty thousand people out there who want to be the next Michael Moore, on both sides of the fence. Many are called. A few will be chosen." No doubt.

Both Peter Davis and Michael Moore, though from very different worlds and parts of the country, are working within—still—the didactic mode of filmmaking. The social intent of documentaries is their chief motivating force, and they even employ many of the same techniques, though of course one has inspired and of course preceded the other. [10]

The expressionistic stretch or reach that Moore has made to include himself in all his films—in fact, taking himself as an emblem of sorts—sets his movies apart from those of Davis, who is perhaps too reserved for such an effort. Or, perhaps the idea just did not seem appropriate to the type of film he was making, although the personal film was already a convention in the 1970s.

As to which films are the most incendiary, or effective, that's a judgment call.

That their similar styles of filmmaking have indelibly altered both the serious, political, or cause-y doc, and the doc as entertainment, is not arguable.

And overwhelmingly, supporters and detractors agree: The current fascination with documentaries, and much of their success, simply would not have occurred without Michael Moore.

• • • • • • • • •

Endnotes

1. R. Hatch, "Review of *Hearts and Minds*," *The Nation* (April 12, 1975).

2. Michael Atkinson, *Village Voice* (October 20, 2004).

3. Stuart Klawan, *The Nation* (November 15, 2004).

4. Jason Clarke and David T. Hardy, *Michael Moore Is a Big Fat Stupid White Man* (New York: Harper Paperbacks, 2005).

   "Throughout his career, Moore has portrayed himself as a Flint native whose consciousness is shaped by the city's industrial experiences. 'Ben [Hamper] and I both grew up in Flint, Michigan, the sons of factory workers,' he writes in the introduction of Hamper's book *Rivethead*. *Roger and Me* constantly hearkens back to Moore's life in Flint. His speaker's bureau describes him as 'born in Flint,' his Web site calls him a 'Flint native,' and his production company's Web site informs us that 'Michael Moore was born in Flint, Michigan, where his father and most of his relatives worked in the automobile factories.' Asked to describe the source of his empathy for the worker, Moore told *People's Weekly World* that 'I think it's just the function of growing up in Flint, Michigan.' These claims are reflected in almost every biography: Moore is described as 'a Flint native,' 'the man from Flint,' or as hailing from his 'hometown of Flint.' But in fact, Moore was born and raised in Davison, Michigan and attended Davison High School. While Davison is near Flint, proximity doesn't translate to similarity between the two towns. Davison is the wealthy white bedroom town of the area, largely inhabited by management, not labor. Davison's median household income is one and a half times that of Flint."

6. *www.sensesofcinema.com*, December 2004.

7. *www.wikipedia.org*, quoting *Le Monde*.

8. For comments critical of Michael Moore, see *www.moorewatch.com*, edited by Jim Kenefiche. In yet one more example of Moore's brilliant ability to handle publicity, he anonymously paid for Kenefiche's wife's much-needed medical treatment when Kenefiche couldn't, a gesture which pointed up the difficulties of paying for medical care in the US. The word did get out, however, and Moore has said that he supports "the guy's right to say nasty things about me," as well as to have medical care.

9. Keith Schneider, "Curtains Rise Again," *New York Times* (December 5, 2007).

10. His influence is so widespread that the [missed] potential for more effect has upset other filmmakers. According to Virginia Heffernan in the *New York Times*, Ken Burns the documentarian "condemned Mr. Moore [for not arranging] for *Fahrenheit 9/11's* broadcast on television before the election. A political documentary, he said, ought to be seen by as many people as possible." "America's Arty History Teacher," September 11, 2004.

chapter four

THE PRACTITIONER AND THE VISIONARY: WERNER HERZOG AND ERROL MORRIS

• • • • • • • • • •

O ne of the new doc movement's most constant practitioners—
perhaps even one of the definers—is Werner Herzog. Ironically,
though, he happens to echo some of the statements of his philosophical
opponent, Direct Cinema advocate Maysles, in defining documentary.
"Sometimes things fall into your lap you couldn't even dream of.... It's the
inexplicable magic of cinema," Herzog says in his voiced-over narration
to *Grizzly Man*.

And he says it in person, too. Over and over. If one had to put a pat
psychological label on Herzog (therapy being one of the things he says he
despises), it might be obsessive-compulsive. Tall, casually if conservatively
dressed, the now iron-gray-haired Herzog was ever ready to talk about his
movies and their drive toward his even more favored phrase, the "ecstasy
of truth," at a retrospective/homage to his work in May of 2007 at New
York City's Film Forum; at Goethe House, a center for German culture in
Manhattan on Fifth Avenue; at festivals worldwide; and even on YouTube
with the Dalai Lama—and in an interview with me.

In his public appearances, he is sometimes accompanied by his
fresh-faced wife Lena Piesetski (his third marriage). With her sheaf of
wheat-blond hair tied in a clever but not overly cute bun arrangement, a
sticklike sprig or two of blond hair poking up at just the right angle, Lena
is adoring but not clingy. And Herzog is adroit these days at handling
questions from audiences and the press, and with some nicely thought-
through answers. (God knows he's had enough practice: He's been making
films since his teen years and has had international successes since
the 1970s.)[1]

Huckster for the Cause

Until he gets tired. Which always seems to take place around 10 P.M., on schedule, like a good German, even a transplanted one. Though there was some grousing by some of the Film Forum staff that Herzog had—in their words—"crapped out" on some of the Q&As after a few of the evening screenings, it seemed to this attendee that he was dutifully on hand and for the most part enthusiastic.

And to this interviewer, very polite, and disarmingly charming. A profile in *The New Yorker* by Daniel Zalewski portrayed Herzog as looking old ("rheumy-eyed" was one of Zalewski's phrases to describe Herzog) and even malevolent at times, perhaps owing to the stresses he puts himself—and others—under during the making of his films.[2] But this did not seem to be the case in the spring of 2007, in Manhattan. Belying some recent photographs (perhaps they play to the popular belief that he stresses out himself and his crew when he is making a movie—the more difficult and obscure the terrain, the better), Herzog looked every inch a middle-aged man enjoying the accolades for his *oeuvre* now apparently properly termed documentaries, and he reveled in the attentive company of the thirty-some-year-old Piesetski, a Russian-born photographer. She is a US citizen, and the couple live near Los Angeles. But Herzog has elected not to become an American citizen, because he says he doesn't wish to belong to a government that supports capital punishment.

Herzog is very much a gentleman, always, with excellent manners, and also very much an intellectual, or smart (sometimes a smart-ass) guy. He's fast on his feet in answering questions, and he is not even making retorts in his native tongue (though of course he did go to college in Pennsylania as a young man, for a very short time).

Basking, and How I Got To

A polished performer by now, Herzog takes his films on a kind of traveling show to various film festivals and academic centers across the US and the world. Some reports are that he complains in talks to American academic audiences that he is under-appreciated in Germany. (Still, the center of Herzog's business is in Munich; if one wishes to get in touch with him, or to obtain an official update on his work, this is where one must start.) He has said that his films may get negatively reviewed at first, then in about 10 years or so the German critics come around.

When I spoke with Herzog, he was really pushing his feature film *Rescue Dawn*, the real-life story of Dieter Dengler, also the subject of one of Herzog's best known documentaries, *Little Dieter Needs to Fly*. With Christian Bale as Dengler, *Rescue Dawn* opened to generally good reviews on July 4, 2007, though some of the more discerning critics—in *The New Yorker* and in the *New York Review of Books*, for instance—thought the feature lacked the energy, even the narrative drive, of the documentary. Herzog says he had always envisioned *Little Dieter* as a feature film, but it took him almost a decade to secure the funding, location, and stars. Instead, he went first to Dengler, who was by then living in Northern California.

Dieter Dengler has since died, but here is an excerpt from his interview in *Indiewire*, an important source for news about documentaries and independent films:

Interviewer: How did you and Werner Herzog meet?

Dieter Dengler: He called me at home in San Francisco, and explained to me very briefly his idea to do a movie about my life. I had never heard of him before, so I was like "Who the heck is he?" I said to him, "You want to talk to me, come on over." So a couple of weeks later he's standing in front of my door with a movie crew, about eight or ten people, with cameras and boxes and all this stuff, and I said, "What's this all about?" And he said, "Well, you said to come on over...." We started to make the film in German, and Werner said, "Why don't we make it in English as well?" But this was difficult, because Werner is hard to work with sometimes.

Interviewer: Why's that?

Dengler: There's no script. He would stand behind the camera and do like this [Dengler hooks his finger into his mouth and bugs his eyes out crazily]. He'd make all these hand signals, and I'm trying to figure out what I'm supposed to say, and I said "Werner, I have no clue what you're trying to tell me! Why don't you just put up a sign that tells me what you want me to say?" And Werner said, "I don't work like that. I want you to just say what comes to your mind."[3]

In the long run, the ten-year delay between making the documentary and the feature (he tried to do the feature first) will probably work to the advantage of Herzog's reputation as a filmmaker. As Ian Buruma says in his *New York Review of Books* review of *Rescue Dawn* and of Herzog's recent appearances in the New York area, "Somehow his story, re-enacted in the feature film, fails to catch fire in the way it does in the documentary. It looks oddly conventional, even flat."[4] Perhaps there's something to be said for not planning ahead, at least where Herzog is concerned.

In this context, it's amusing to read early press releases about Herzog. Initially publicists had some difficulty labeling him. Promoting someone who was a documentary filmmaker was not easy in those days. For instance, the Twentieth Century Fox press notes to the 1984 film *Where the Green Ants Dream*, his documentary about a land feud between a mining company and the aborigines of the Australian desert, lists Herzog as having done fourteen "shorts" and thirteen features. Obviously struggling with a way to cast his work and with the doc concept in general, nowhere does the press release mention the word documentary.[5]

If you are a Herzog fan, it seems the documentary label has finally come around to him, to what he's been doing all along.

To the filmgoing community, he was a pioneer of the expressionistic, subjective documentary as early as 1973 in his *The Great Ecstasy of the Woodcarver Steiner*, which included footage of the almost preternaturally gifted ski-flyer Walter Steiner. For just an obvious few, up through *Wings of Hope*, his recent documentary success *Grizzly Man* and his latest film, *Encounters at the End of the World*, Herzog's narrative presence cannot be ignored. Often it is his narrative voice giving shape to the documentary, but sometimes he appears in the films as well, in some sort of combination of journalistic commentator, explorer/participant, and—yes—at times a star or self-inserted narrator/director. (One fascinating exception is that it is critic Lotte Eisner's voice reciting the Mayan creation myth in *Fata Morgana*, his metaphoric documentary capturing mirages in the Sahara desert.)

Do You Have to Go to the Edge?

There's Herzog in the jungle reminiscing with Juliane about the flight she took (and Herzog almost did, too) which crashed. There he is on top of a mountain chatting about mortality with the climber Reinhold Messner in *The Dark Glow of the Mountains*. There he is talking like mad in *Grizzly Man* in his narrative voice-over; there he is re-arranging a nonindigenous frozen fish in Antarctica. If he were Michael Moore, we would be duly sick of these antics by now. But Herzog seems to have no particular axe to grind, and he's not been as successful as Moore in self-promotion, so it's not really an issue. And of course he hasn't exactly been in every multiplex in the last decade.

Herzog is still and always has been very much within the primary documentary tradition of travel. He goes to faraway places (*La Soufriere*, the Caribbean volcano about to erupt which didn't; the Sahara in *Fata Morgana*, for just some of his many documentaries set in exotically remote spots).

He films the indigenous people. The more difficult the terrain (of course, being Herzog) the better. And to practice a bit of pop psychobiography, Herzog very much admired his grandfather, an archaeologist who conducted excavations on the Greek island of Kos.

Even one of his most critically and commercially successful films, *Grizzly Man*, is set in the wilderness of Alaska. The subject is the American Timothy Treadwell, who was killed by some of the bears he lived with in the wilderness and felt he was protecting. And was filming. As Herzog puts it in his own narration, "It was as if he had become a star by virtue of his own invention. As a filmmaker he captured such glorious moments, the likes of which the studios would never dream of." Herzog gets his own slams in at the feature film studio system, but the thrust of the movie is to show that Treadwell's philosophy of "seeing bears as humans in bear costumes," as one critic put it, had a disastrous end.

And it is Herzog's view of the universe which prevails, by narrative voice-over as well as the real-life events of the film. He says, "I believe the commonality of the universe is chaos, murder," a comment which accompanies a short sequence of a look into the (apparently) vacant eyes of a bear, more than suggesting that a bear's inclination is undoubtedly about food and survival—if anything—not the Disneyesque feelings Treadwell has assigned to his friends. Herzog's voice declares, "To me, there is no such thing as a secret world of the bears, and this blank stare speaks only of a half-bored interest in food."

Herzog has been making films since he was fifteen, when he first started submitting scripts to German producers. Later, he worked nights as a welder for two years to make money to finance the making of a prize-winning original script for a short film. More acclaim came his way when he won a prize for *Last Words* in 1967 at the Oberhausen Film Festival, and in 1968 his first feature, *Signs of Life*, was shown at the Cannes, Berlin, and New York festivals. Herzog's life, art, and personal mythology often mix and meld, and there are many wonderful stories which have come out of this: how he stole a camera in order to work on his first film; how the plaster falling during his childhood inevitably altered his view of life; how he never dreams (though sometimes he says he rarely dreams) and maybe this is why his films emerge by intuition nearly fully formed.

At this point in his career, he no longer defends his subjective techniques, but rather is extremely proud of the fact that he was one of the first of today's generation of well-known documentarians to use them.

Few question this. For instance, in his very first short film, *Herakles*, which he made in 1962, Herzog was introducing a kind of feature film-like structure, juxtaposing footage of bodybuilders with a famous racing accident at le Mans. It ain't Eisenstein, or even Peter Davis or Michael Moore, but it is definitely a "statement" in a documentary film.

"Those scenes with Dieter were rehearsed," declares Herzog cheerfully, about *Little Dieter Needs to Fly*, an admittance that would be anathema to a filmmaker such as Wiseman or Maysles (or perhaps even Michael Moore, for that matter) referring to the scenes where the older Dengler, now an American citizen, goes through his house in California opening doors for the camera, explaining that he can't stand to be confined after having spent time in a POW camp. For the bit where the director wanted a perfect image of a jellyfish (a metaphor in any case, so already once removed from literal documentary reality) in a fish tank, supposedly in Dengler's house in Northern California, the two actually went to the San Diego aquarium to film the scene. "Yes, let's go there," Herzog says Dengler had agreed enthusiastically.

Almost to assuage his guilt (though he still can't resist a little last-minute twist), he says, "The turkey [which Dengler eats in the documentary] was real. Thirty-six pounds. But we had it roasted for him."

He has even admitted to paying local people to be in his other documentaries to appear as natives carrying cargo, or rowing boats. One of the most often referenced examples of his toying with some tenets of the documentary form is that he hired local winos to play Pilgrims in his film *Bells From the Deep*.

And though it may have been because he was promoting *Rescue Dawn*, Herzog seems in the summer of 2007 to favor *Little Dieter Needs to Fly* over some of this other films. He implies that this may be because he has a background similar to Dengler, who also spent his childhood under dire circumstances during World War II.

Still, he makes it clear that he is partly in the subgenre of the autobiographical documentary. "I grew up in a mountain village," says Herzog. "I had no idea of the outside world until I was eleven." (Indeed, Herzog's mother took her sons to live in a remote village in the Bavarian Alps at the end of World War II.) Apparently like his attraction to many of his subjects, he picked Dieter Dengler to make a movie about because, "I too was growing up without a father, starving, in a remote place." He first heard about Dengler in an article in *Der Sturm*, a sensationalistic newspaper, he calls it. Still, he says what he most admires about Dengler (who recently passed away) is that he embodied the "American attributes of self-reliance, courage, loyalty, and optimism."

How Documentarians Find Their Doppelgangers

True enough, Dengler does seem to have a courageous, untouched innocence on screen and of course an incredible will to survive, and struggle, against truly insurmountable odds. And he did end up in America, as has Herzog.

Christian Bale, who plays Dieter in *Rescue Dawn*, lost thirty pounds to look like the captured flier during his imprisonment. But where his star opts for realism, and Herzog inserts fiction techniques into his documentary form, Herzog went for a more spontaneous look in the feature *Rescue Dawn*. For instance, the director deliberately kept some scenes mismatched at times, à la the more cheaply made, less expensive doc mode, and much to the dismay of his studio-trained crew. As he might say, perhaps subconsciously he knew that his "deeper truth" was in the doc format.

Yet despite the use of some archival footage, mainly at the beginning of the movie, there seem to be few innovative techniques in *Rescue Dawn*, certainly nothing as imaginative as Herzog has come up with in his documentaries. Perhaps the only unexpected element, which he proudly showed in a clip at the Film Forum, is when Dieter as done by Christian Bale explains his childhood to his buddy, played by Steve Zahn.

Recounting his childhood memory of being attacked by an Allied bomber—so close he even made eye contact with the plane's captain—Dieter-by-Bale then concludes the monologue with the almost humorously uttered, "Little Dieter needed to fly." There's nearly a wink at the camera, certainly an acknowledged hesitation, as he emphasizes the "-ed" of "needed." It sounds funny, especially as the circumstances of the prison camp are by contrast so grim.

Let's just call it one of the few ironic moments in a film in which Herzog and his hero are otherwise straightforward and heartfelt. The not-occasional irony of the self-reflexive, and therefore self-aware, doc form rears its head here.

Such "in jokes" may tend to disrupt the narrative flow in an action film such as *Rescue Dawn*. Though if excerpted as it was at the Film Forum, it brought down the house, if one can say such a thing about such an earnest venue.

Here is Ian Buruma's reflection on the reverse adaptation. "The difference, I think, has everything to do with Herzog's use of fantasy. In the documentary, his method is actually closer to that of a fiction writer than in the feature film. *Rescue Dawn* sticks to the facts of Dengler's story, without adding much background, let alone any hint of an inner life. It looks like a well-made docudrama. In the documentary, however, it is precisely the collage of family history, dream images, personal eccentricities, and factual information that brings Dieter Dengler alive as a fully rounded figure. This doesn't mean that the same effect cannot be achieved in a feature film. But it does show how far Werner Herzog has taken a genre that is commonly known as documentary film but that he calls 'just films.'[6]

Perhaps another element to be considered is that the doc was made a decade before the feature: There is something to be said for spontaneity, for freshness, as so many doc makers say in these pages.

I Got It From My Life

Herzog was born in Munich, in 1942. In the short documentary *Portrait Werner Herzog* (1986), wherein Herzog profiles himself, is one of the rare sequences in which he actually seems to be enjoying himself on film, laughing and drinking beer in a typical Munich beer hall, making remarks on the Bavarian temperament. Born Werner Stipetic, he renamed himself Herzog—which means "duke" in German—after his father came back from WWII with that nickname. He, his brothers, and their mother moved to the tiny town of Sachrang in the Alps after the house next to theirs was destroyed during WWII. And the family returned to Munich when Herzog was twelve, sharing an apartment with Klaus Kinski.

No matter how many times he has told the story, Herzog always seems to take particular delight in telling the tale of Kinski's berating him throughout the making of *Aguirre: The Wrath of God*, calling him a dwarf director—Herzog had done a feature on dwarfs, and was also a novice director, according to Kinski (with whom Herzog would eventually make five films). *Even Dwarfs Started Small* is a nihilistic black comedy set in Africa about inmates who rebel and take over their asylum; they are short-statured people, and the film is filled with surrealistic images.

In the mountains, the family lived, barely surviving, for the rest of the war, set apart in a remote landscape which the filmmaker believes deepened his sense of isolation and perhaps formed his predilection for finding and surviving difficult conditions. Part of the director's personal mythology is that their house was hit by a bomb during the war when he was a baby, and he still remembers a piece of plaster falling on him. He has said he believes this incident has affected his subsequent view of life.

In his 1975 film *Heart of Glass*, Herzog (in a translation by Alan Greenberg) says that as a child, "I was quite silent, and wouldn't speak for days. My parents thought I was insane or retarded. I was very dangerous; my character was peculiar." Herzog's father was mostly not around when Herzog was growing up, having had a series of wives, and children with each. Today, Herzog laughingly calls the different families of half-siblings his father's "litters." Herzog himself has three adult children from earlier marriages and one arrangement.

Herzog's mother, whom he adored for her incredibly hard work in raising her boys by herself, has said, "He was a difficult child, always in a rage and spending a lot of time alone, in silence." She too is interviewed in *Heart of Glass*, and says, "When he was in school, Werner never learned anything there. He never read the books he was supposed to read, he never studied, he never knew what he was supposed to know, it seemed. But in reality, Werner always knew everything. His senses were remarkable. If he heard the slightest sound, ten years later he would remember it precisely, he would talk about it, and maybe use it some way."

"Many of my films have been about flying," Herzog observes of his work, and indeed this is so, from *The Flying Doctors of East Africa* in 1969 to *The Great Ecstasy of the Woodcarver Steiner* in 1973 to *Wings of Hope*, the 1999 film about Juliane Koepcke, who survived a plane crash in the jungle, to *Little Dieter Needs to Fly*. "*Steiner the Woodcarver* is particularly close to my heart," says Herzog, about a film set in a remote spot in the Bavarian mountains, one of the first movies to look at the phenomenon of ski jumping. "It is almost like an ancient Greek drama," he says, "like Icarus flying close to the sun, and then being punished.

"*Steiner the Woodcarver* is the first nonfiction film in which I appear on camera," Herzog observes, and yet "I had already started to make films with a clear handwriting." And he told me, "*Steiner* is about redemption, too. My best friend was a ski jumper, like Steiner, and almost died. He did recover, but I went into deep shock. I never went up again, ever. And now I never look when someone crashes. It can never be like before.

"But the ski-jumpers are not like that. Otherwise they would never fly. If they do ever cancel, it's out of 'respect for conditions.'

"Steiner flew like a Frisbee, with a true sense of flight. He was a real Daddy Long Legs, though of course a bit awkward. Somehow he became a real person, like an inner brother to me. And, let's face it," he laughed, "I do look a little odd, shivering away there in my thin jacket, especially compared to the heavy parkas of the ABC team." And true enough, even in his sports interviewer mode in this early film, Herzog is quite focused on Steiner's personality as well as abilities, inserts his own opinions, and has long, lingering, and quite breathtaking shots of the skier at work. In this 1973 film, he is more, much more, than a normal interviewer.

Indeed, the camera does stay on Herzog for quite a while, as he makes some analytical statements about Steiner throughout the film, likening him to one who, like Icarus, tried to fly too high. And in some of those shots you see the high poetic sensibility of the Herzog to come, though those sequences are also mixed in with some more prosaic ones capturing a sports event.

In talking about the film at Film Forum, one of several personal favorites of his he culled for the retrospective of his work in May 2007 in New York City, Herzog points out that some of his commentary was part of the journalistic assignment at the time—almost as if he wishes to place on record his reasons for even the few standard television news techniques seen. "But still," he insists, "I believe I started something. Let's face it, in this film I'm a bit different than the basic newscaster. Maybe because I was freezing, I felt I had to get more personal."

Getting Me in the Credits

You get the feeling these days that Herzog wants to get credit for being in on the aesthetic ground floor, inventing the new form. It certainly is true that he has been speaking out against Direct Cinema (he usually calls it cinéma vérité) for decades now. And of course there is the work.

One film in which he seems to be intensely working out some personal issues is *Wings of Hope*, the documentary in which Herzog's voiced-over narrative continually comes back to the fact that he (and his crew) nearly took the same flight as did Juliane Koepcke. In 1971, Koepcke, a Dutch teenager, was the sole survivor of a jetliner crash in Peru and somehow made it out of the jungle. The now middle-aged Juliane, as seen in the 1999 film, traces her memories of the crash and steps through and out of the jungle. Like Dieter Dengler, she was rescued against all odds, and like Dengler, she survived against every statistical probability.

But despite Herzog's proddings throughout the film, Juliane is a much more reluctant remember-er and has some memory blocks or emotional places she can't or won't go to. Not particularly proud—or guilty either— about the fact that she survived, she is much more contained, though rueful about the death of all the other travelers on the plane, including her mother. Herzog reminds her (and us) he almost took the same flight. What is the significance of this, the filmmaker asks over and over in the film. Yet his somewhat resistant doppelganger, while obediently walking again those jungles where she almost died, is too self-contained to delve into her own issues to help Herzog parse his own escape from death.

In his most effective films, it's obvious Herzog is attracted to subjects for his own reasons. And though one may find exception to some of this (Timothy Treadwell comes immediately to mind), he says, "I never make interviews with people I don't like." Yet even in Treadwell's case, there is Herzog's own obsessive need to go to the wilderness, to test or try nature.

In *Wings of Hope* there was no need for Herzog to rearrange the landscape by inserting props, or to alter the timeline. For one thing, the contrast between the earlier taken/not-taken flight, and the jungle as it is now, is a built-in structure of the film. So when Juliane goes back to the airplane crashed in the ground, the rusted-out parts and growth of the jungle plants having overtaken the airplane wings are striking enough even for the eye of director Herzog. Yet perhaps the most shocking image is the angle of the seats of the plane—jutted forward, driven into the earth by the force of the crash. The torque survived time, so even Herzog didn't have to alter it.

Herzog's proclivities for ironic juxtaposition have been taken care of for him by nature and time.

Time Means Nothing to Me Or My Films

In other films, such as *Encounters at the End of the World*, Herzog seems to take particular delight in challenging or changing chronology. The film is referred to as the "first poetic feature film" about Antarctica on the National Science Foundation Web site, which in part funded the film. Like a mischievous school kid, Herzog fantasizes about how old a fish might actually be, if it is even indigenous to Antarctica, or if it was brought by some Russian sailors who were there before he was. For a while he pretends it may be from New Zealanders who left it. (This is what the locals believe.) He wonders what people might think in the future when they find it, after having moved or placed the fish in a certain spot.

But long before *Encounters at the End of the World* the filmmaker was moving in the direction of what he describes as showing a deeper truth in his documentaries.

Herzog's particular brand or blend of documentary and fiction is something he has been practicing since his late teenage years. He is credited with fifty-five documentaries, and he has done feature films as well, though there have been so many documentaries made about *Aguirre: The Wrath of God* that the feature seems almost a part of the canon of Herzog documentaries. He has said teasingly that his feature film *Fitzcarraldo* about a late nineteenth century robber baron played by Klaus Kinski is the best documentary he has made (the journey up the Amazon alone should qualify it, one would think). However, the Zalewski feature in the *New Yorker*, as have many critics have said about his work, characterizes Herzog as being well known for the difficulties of the circumstances in which his films are made, placing his crew as well as himself in danger. "No one has ever been hurt on my set!" he declared, a tiny bit defensively, at the Film Form series of Q&A's.

But if indeed there is a leitmotif to be found in Herzog's documentaries, it is the parallels between his own life and those of his subjects. In *Wings of Hope*, Herzog's narrative voice-over, and sometimes his literal presence, quizzes Juliane Koepcke about her flight. But it is never very far from his (and consequently the viewer's) mind that he might have met the same fate except for a quirk.

"This film lay dormant in me," Herzog's narrative voice declares, and he comes back to this theme again and again in the film. "We were in the same airport twenty-seven years ago. There was an announcement. My flight was canceled. In the end, only Juliane's flight took off." And when they go back together to visit the jungle in which she crashed, "This time we flew the same flight and sat in the same seats.... This time Juliane landed safely." (Apparently the airline company on which both were scheduled had deliberately overloaded its flights, and this caused Juliane's to crash.) As much as Herzog tries to get her to talk about her experiences, he admits that she has "a protective shell [around her] to lead an ordinary life." He sounds a bit disappointed.

Though Juliane is too silent for him, Herzog still manages to elicit what he can, mainly during the only scene she seems to want to return to: that of the three airplane seats still jammed headfirst in the ground. She wonders about the sheer force of the crash that could have forced the seats to go in at such an angle (and, of course, stay there until the making of the movie).

Herzog is pleased to discuss his attempt to control reality, formerly known as documentary reality, in his films. About *The White Diamond*, Herzog told me, "I recorded the music before the film was shot," a fact which pretty much states his intentions about the emotional color of the film to come. *The White Diamond* is the story of an aeronautical engineer who is trying to go back to the scene of an accident in Guyana and figure out why an earlier doomed balloon flight failed—to fix the past, in a way, something which seems to be in tune with Herzog's temperament.

Naturally, he goes up in the air with the balloonist/engineer.

He also laughs about the way he handles some of his film subjects: "One said to me, 'I'll show you a diamond, but only if you don't show my face.' But, of course, I did show his face."

How outrageous is this behavior in a documentary filmmaker? Where do issues of trust—with those appearing in his movies and with the audience too—figure in? It's essentially hard to accuse someone of something when they admit it outright first, but these are still interesting questions. One pithy response to such questions is when Herzog defends himself by saying he is after ecstatic truth, as opposed to a filmmaker like Michael Moore who, Herzog jokes, is "after corporeal truth."

He has perfected his official patter, a stance he made very real at the Telluride Film Festival in 2002, on a panel with D A Pennebaker, Chris Hegedus, Michael Moore, Ken Burns, and Steven Cantor. Moore was talking when Herzog interrupted him: "I'm interested in an ecstatic truth in my documentaries, in my films. Ken, here, is interested in an emotional truth. And you, with your big belly, are interested in a physical truth." To Pennebaker, he said, "And you, I think we are enemies. Cinéma vérité is the cinema of accountants."

Always forthright about his methods, Herzog seems more than ever to want to go on record with such statements, staking out his claim to being an early practitioner of the new form. He's everywhere these days with much the same message, and some of the same anecdotes, progressively more outrageous in his proclamations given at retrospectives of his films across the country and around the world. In 2002, he told Paul Cronin, in the book *Herzog on Herzog*: "Even though they are usually labeled as such, I would say that it is misleading to call films like *Bells from the Deep* and *Death for Five Voices* 'documentaries.' They merely come under the guise of documentaries,"[7] meaning probably that those films are not strictly fact-based.

Perhaps Karen Cooper, Film Forum's director, put it most pithily: "I think he's created a genre that's all his own."

Where We Diverge

Until recently, Herzog's methods, his genre-blending, and even the numbers of films he has made seem not to have occasioned the kind of attention, outrage, and high accolades as have the films of his friend and near peer in age, the American filmmaker Errol Morris, born in 1948. Morris has made films—not as many, and there have been longer intervals between them—in the new format as well. While Herzog seems to opt for the tactic of voice-over narrative as well as personal appearance on film in most of his work, Morris's patterns are not that easy to spot, though his impact on the film form, and film history, to date anyway, has been more profound. [2007 was a good year for Herzog, the artistic tortoise of their tortoise-and-hare-like contrasting work methods, and for Morris his latest film, *Standard Operating Procedure*, seems a fall-off from some of his earlier films.]

Through an increasingly obvious involvement with his subjects, Morris starts to question facts, fiction, and the point of view of his various subjects. It's a kind of postmodern and subtle view of reality. Of course, to present and further examine ambiguity is not totally unexpected, as Morris is a trained philosopher.

Possibly the true significance of Morris's achievement—and the coming importance of the documentary mode—can be seen in the ripples (or is it tidal waves?) around *The Thin Blue Line* in 1988. The movie was on every major critic's "best" list, and though it won the documentary of the year award from both the New York Film Critics Circle and the National Society of Film Critics, it was too difficult to categorize, and too controversial, to be nominated for an Oscar. The documentary category should be "nonfiction" and *The Thin Blue Line* was not therefore a documentary, said the Academy. Most damning was the fact that it had used re-enactment footage. From today's vantage point, with films brazenly tampering with chronology and re-enacting at will, this seems tame indeed.

But here, and for the record, the film begins with some eerily beautiful shots of Dallas, where the crime the film dissects took place. The tones are noir-ish blue, and Morris has managed to find some buildings in Dallas which are lit electrically, gothically, with a look that might remind the viewer of some of the impressionistic and beautifully lit city documentaries of the early twentieth century.

Point of View and the Doc

But the structure of the film has some straightforward elements (and initially is almost old-fashioned, in a talking heads kind of way). The two protagonists, if you will, on whose point of view and different versions the film hinges, are given equal time in the standard journalistic doc way in the beginning of the movie. In the interview with them, Randall Adams explains how he found himself in Texas, how he found himself at the scene of the crime. Then David Harris gives a bit of his own background. He is in orange prison uniform.

So far, compelling. But not necessarily anything "new."

Then into the continued blue tones of the reconstructed murder scene—intercut with close-ups of the red, swirly lights of the top of a police car, the jarring image of a spilled Burger King milkshake (an image often referred to as iconic by cineastes), an illustrated image of a gun (obviously artifice, in case we don't get the point about the whole scene), and some shots of the slamming of car doors.

This is not reality, but an imagined view of what events must have occurred to thrust a cop killer—allegedly Randall Adams at that point—into jail.

All is interspersed with archival footage—newspaper clippings of the time, and of course interviews with the police, the investigators, those who testified against Adams. Bit by bit the full picture emerges. Witnesses change their testimonies in order to have the defendant, Adams, convicted, and forensic psychiatrists give purposeful statements on his mental health. This chain of events resembles a classic police drama: a high-profile case requires that a guilty man must be found, and quickly.

About the film, Morris has said wittily that he created the first *film noir* documentary.

Unlike *The Children's March*, a documentary which got into perhaps more legitimate difficulty with the Oscar voting committee since it tried to pass off new footage as authentic, Morris instead calls attention to his re-creations and re-enactments of past events.

Demonstrating the Truth

Morris said he still feels that *The Thin Blue* line is "a triumph over vérité." He also said that he acted on his intuition (honed after an earlier three-year career of working as a private investigator) that the police had the wrong man. Increasingly he came to see that the stricter style of observational cinema did not accommodate the different possibilities for truth that he wished to present.

Still, it's done gradually and quietly. The most condemning part of all—when you hear a bit of the interview which shows that the actual person who committed the murder is not the person in jail—is not sensationalized in the least. In this sequence, it is simply a tape recorder that we see, and hear; watching a close-up of the swirling Sony tape with what David Harris is saying printed on the screen as well. (In fact, this seems to have turned into a visual signpost for Morris: The filmmaker focuses on a tape recorder accompanied by the words of Lyndon Johnson talking, with McNamara responding, in *The Fog of War*. By then—and perhaps due to the outcry—the Academy of Motion Picture Arts and Sciences seemed to have gotten used to such tactics, as it *did* award the subsequent *The Fog of War* an Oscar fifteen years later, whereas it ignored *The Thin Blue Line*.)

About this, Morris says that while David Harris does assent to his guilt in the film, there is an even more conclusive admittance off-screen. "David nodded 'yes' when I asked him directly," said Morris, and though you don't see this in the film, Morris says it was a nod accompanying the tape we do get to hear. In New York City in the spring of 2008, promoting his film *Standard Operating Procedure*, Morris laughingly admitted that what occasioned what critics refer to as another "iconic" image of just the tape recorder, which Morris uses for a scene in the film, was accidentally occasioned by what Morris calls "a filmmaker's worst nightmare. I was on the outskirts of Dallas late on a Friday night, and the camera broke. I had no choice except to just get whatever I could on the little tape recorder and go with that."

Morris, who has just turned sixty, is in graphic designer dweeb garb: khaki pants, white button-down shirt hanging out over his slight paunch, sneakers, and (here his iconoclasm shows) socks too short, which he periodically yanks up. Hair more white than iron gray, in a close, very good cut. Gone are the curls which made him seem impish in earlier decades, but he is still a provocateur, if an affable and very funny one.

To a questioner who says he can't access Morris's blog because he can't afford the Internet, Morris readily quips, "Clearly this calls for some arrangement." He takes some questions from people who have come to hear him talk about *Standard Operating Procedure*, but most of the queries are still about his most well-known films, *The Thin Blue Line* and *The Fog of War*.

"David Harris hurt a lot of people," Morris says. "As far as he was concerned, Randall Adams could've been executed for a crime he didn't commit. And David Harris did not care a whit about it. And yet in Dallas, he did the right thing. He made it absolutely clear to everyone concerned that Randall was not the shooter, and that he was. And he has this very odd way of speaking. It didn't amount to an all-out confession of murder, but everything he said made it absolutely clear that he was guilty and that Adams was innocent. And when I interviewed him that one time on audiotape—this is the very end of *The Thin Blue Line*—I asked Harris whether he was in fact the killer and he smiled and nodded his head. You can't hear it on audiotape, but it's something quite unforgettable for me."

Breakthrough, but Condemned

The Thin Blue Line can be seen as a watershed. If it took some knocks from the Academy Award voting committee, it had a positive social effect of righting a wrong, and brought the issue of the definition of a documentary front and center. It created a sensation especially in the major urban centers, perhaps already believing—in the spirit of the times—that the thin blue line of police solidarity also protected police corruption. It achieved an incredibly difficult thing: proving the wrong person was in jail, finding the actual killer, and forcing the release of the wrongfully accused.

With all this, you might say the American Morris, at the time, eclipsed his colleague and sometime mentor, Werner Herzog.

And while *The Thin Blue Line* may have legitimized the new creative metamix for documentaries, it also achieved the old-fashioned, Grierson-esque purpose of social intent. It won the release of Randall Adams from prison. Two of the important strains of doc filmmaking were met, and met brilliantly. Yet like many innovations—one might even say especially those which are successful—the innovator was punished for his achievements.

No Good Deed Goes Unpunished

But in a postmodern touch, Morris reminds me that Randall Adams eventually "sued me for the rights to his life story. And he felt as though I had stolen something from him. Maybe I had, maybe I just don't understand what it's like to be in prison for that long, for a crime you hadn't committed. In a certain sense, the whole crazy deal with the release was fueled by my relationship with his attorney. And it's a long, complicated story, but I guess when people are involved, there's always a mess somewhere [laughs]."

Even more ironic is the fact that Morris apparently had an ongoing correspondence with David Harris the entire time Harris was on death row, and up until the time of his execution. (Morris says he had always suspected that Harris was the killer and had this belief throughout the making of the film.) "I'm interested in liars," he adds. "David Harris, [Robert] McNamara, Fred Leuchter" [the subject of Morris's film *Dr. Death*].

So, there is an ambiguity that Morris either is attracted to or elicits. The actual murderer keeps up a correspondence with the fellow who blew his cover, while the person whose life he saved sues him. It's what you might term a Morris-like complexity, in which people are both liked and vilified at once. And unlike the possibly simpler worldview of good/evil, them against us (read: me and Herzog).

And just what does this contribute to the development of the new doc?

"One thing that's very odd about my filmmaking is that I'm never in an adversarial position with the people that I film. I don't want to be. I often think that if I don't like the person that I'm talking to, I can't do it, I can't do what I do. It's essential for me to have some kind of emotional connection," said Morris. (He also said that his interviews are getting longer and longer; he spent seventeen hours over the space of two days interviewing General Janice Karpinski, who was in charge of Abu Ghraib.)

Softening of the Form

Example in point: McNamara saying to Morris in the beginning of *The Fog of War*, in the conversational tone we all use for intimates: "You won't believe this," prefacing one of his comments. And of course we hear Morris's voice respond and question McNamara throughout the movie, again, signaled by the impatient-sounding Morris voice saying, "Go ahead." The instructions are given almost as one would to a child, urging McNamara on to complete a thought he had been mulling over.

Errol Morris interacting with his "subject," Robert McNamara, in *Fog of War*.
Photo courtesy of Fourth Floor Productions.

All this implies the relationship that both the director and his subjects have said developed throughout and even continued after the making of the movie. How different this is from the quasi-scientific attitude of the standard documentary! And how unabashed in contributing, whether purposefully or not, to the new form/format of the neo-doc. It goes without saying that Morris is more involved, and more open about being involved, than the gentle and approachable Maysles of the objective school, who admits that he might never see his subjects again after the shooting is over. Even the self-proclaimed inventor of the new form, Werner Herzog, says that there are very few of his subjects he maintains any contact with once a film is completed, the chief exception being of course the late Dieter Dengler, and his friend and legendary soccer coach, Rudi Gutendorf, who is the subject of *The Ball is a Scumbag*. A more sophisticated analysis of the new doc's sometimes complicated relationship between filmmaker and subjects is offered by director Amir Bar-Lev in chapter 9, as he tries to unravel the truth about a family he becomes fond of in *My Kid Could Paint That*.

Connecting with My Subjects

The possibilities for such complex, potentially continuing, relationships, is admitted by Morris: "Take a movie like *The Fog of War*," he says offhandedly. "It creates an entirely subjective account, but it's McNamara's subjective account of his experiences. To that end, I interview him at length and he tells me stories. Like any first-person account, it may be filled with factual errors, it can be self-serving. On the other hand, it can be incredibly revealing and can reveal things that very, very few people know about.

"There's a model for how we're supposed to make these kinds of films, and what I do violates that model," he says. "But I would argue that the model that is supposedly a guarantor of truth is no such thing. The model is, of course, an adversarial model, it's the Mike Wallace school of interviewing. You take the subject, you interview him, you back him against the wall, and if you hear something you believe to be untrue you confront him with that fact and force him to address it. I suppose it's the idea of a courtroom drama, and you are supposed to arrive at the truth.

"One of the funniest questions I got about *Standard Operating Procedure* was from a government contractor who was curious about my interview techniques," says Morris. "He asked me how I broke someone. I don't break people. It's not confession. I'm not a priest. I guess I would have to say I'm a participant."

Morris has another, perhaps a more clever, method of condemnation. Sometimes kindly and sometimes not, we hear his voice asking McNamara about the killing of 100,000 women and children—"Were you aware this was going to happen?"—as well as Morris posing the question, "The choice of incendiary bombs. Where did that come from?" We also hear him declaring to McNamara, in a somewhat harsher way, "At some point we have to approach Vietnam."

These voice-overs, his use of music, even the magnifying-type glass zeroing in on certain map sections, were simply not used in public affairs documentaries of twenty or thirty years ago, unless the other side was also presented, in the standard balanced approach. Morris even pointedly asks the question, "To what extent do you feel you were the author [of the Vietnam situation] or were you the instrument of things outside of your control?" And finally, "After you left the Johnson administration, why didn't you speak out against the war? Do you feel you were in any way responsible for it? Do you feel guilty?"

And at this date, rather than being defensive about these techniques, the director has a bit of braggadocio about using them. A questioner after Morris's New York City talk observed in a somewhat accusatory manner that he counted at least two times when his (Morris's) voice is heard in the film, asking questions. "Actually," he rejoined rather proudly, "There are eight times."

'Nuff said.

He gives a typically witty Morris explanation: "I've always had a fear of hearing my own voice. But after the first time I heard it on film, I thought, well, maybe it isn't so bad."

One issue *du jour* that Morris seems taken up with is the pros and cons of re-enactment. "Re-enactment is a damn bad word," he finally spat out after his semi-complicated explanation of why it is often necessary to go back and reconstruct (or re-enact, a topic he took up in his *New York Times* blog in 2007 and 2008.) "I'm just trying to put audiences in the same spot I've been in." With particular reference to *Standard Operating Procedure*, he says he wanted the re-enactments to look unmistakably different from everything else in the film. And he puts it right out there: "No, I did not go to Iraq to make this movie. I made it on a sound stage in Hollywood. Later I found out it was where *I Love Lucy* was filmed."

My New Methods

Morris gives credit to the Interrotron, a new method he devised first for *Fast, Cheap, and Out of Control*, followed by its more famous use in *The Fog of War*.

You can read his explanation of the Interrotron on his Web site. He lists some of its features: two cameras, but one is hidden. And in ironic Morris-like humor, the function of the Interrotron is the "facilitation of interspecies communication, homo sapiens to homo sapiens, successfully tested with orangutan (Bam-Bam; see Quaker Oats commercials)."

In person, and more literally, he says, "The Interrotron adds to the difference between faux first person and the true first person. There's an added intensity. The Interrotron inaugurates the birth of true first person cinema."

The interviewee is on the monitor while looking directly at the camera, which lets Morris and his audience achieve eye contact with his subjects. As this reporter understands it, there is a modified teleprompter, and the Interrotron allows Morris to project his own image on a monitor placed directly over the camera's lens. Interviewees address Morris, or his image anyway, not just the camera as in the standard documentary.

The new format seems to work. And the neo-doc is on display, in that we, the audience, are also more aware of the interviewer—Morris himself, though we do not ever see him physically. We do hear him. It becomes obvious that McNamara is responding to someone he knows, the interviewer. An intimate, intricate portrait gradually emerges. It is simply not the kind of good-versus-bad standard analysis that we sometimes see in a Michael Moore film, nor of course the detached observation of a Frederick Wiseman.

Keats-like Negative Capability

Morris says, "I have this style of letting people talk, of not having a specific agenda, not knowing what you're going to hear." If you look again at *Vernon, Florida*, and *Gates of Heaven*, he's been up to this sort of thing for years. And any working journalist has to ask himself, "How did he get those people to say all that?" But it's so bit by bit, if you listen objectively to the responses, that it's clear that the effect is cumulative. Subtle.

The director says he changed his mind about some of the issues brought up in the film: "I ended up liking Robert McNamara. Before, I had the clichéd idea about him that he was responsible for all the evil of the Vietnam War. But as we went on, it seemed that he thought he could do more good by staying on. And I realized the historical problems of our involvement in Vietnam, going back through the Johnson and Kennedy administrations to the Eisenhower years."

Originally there was to have been only an hour of interview time for a television show. But in the end, McNamara talked to Morris for twenty hours. Morris says he had been attracted to the project because McNamara had published a book about his public service, neither an apologia nor a disclaimer.

And though I did not talk with him, McNamara has said on multiple occasions that for the most part he accepts the film and what it shows of him, his motivations and decisions in explaining his thinking about the United States' continuing involvement in Indochina. According to a *New York Times* piece by Nancy Ramsey from December 23, 2003, McNamara said, "I don't think he had a particular story line. We just talked. Errol's such an extraordinary, interesting conversationalist."[8]

I Ended Up Liking My Director

Some of the mutual respect is evident in the shots of the two of them, used to publicize the film. They appeared together on *The Charlie Rose Show*. This is difficult to imagine in a standard adversarial or even purposefully revealing doc. And of course McNamara is featured on the cover of the DVD.

Backing up all of this are Morris's work methods: He pored through reams of declassified documents and listened to countless hours of audiotapes of Oval Office conversations that had only recently been released by the JFK and Lyndon Johnson Libraries. Morris acknowledges, "I started out believing the same old stuff. The hawk McNamara pushes a reluctant president into war. But [according to the tape recordings] it's the opposite—a bellicose president pushing a reluctant McNamara into war.

"My theory—and I believe this is not just some lame excuse—is that he knew the Joint Chiefs wanted to seriously escalate the war and he felt he could mitigate and control. I don't think I've made an apology film, and I do think it's fair to McNamara. He may quibble with elements of the film, but I believe McNamara thinks it's fair as well."

And one can't top Frank Rich's analysis in the *New York Times*:

Errol Morris is not a historian or an ideologue but a profound student of the quirks of human nature. As he dramatizes Mr. McNamara's efforts to make sense of his own history, we see that it is the man's vanity, his narcissistic overestimation of his own 'skill set' (to use current CEO lingo), that leads him into a mental fog and his government into a quagmire. Such a classic tragic law is personal, not political, which is why *The Fog of War* is moving in the end. We see its protagonist inexorably heading toward disaster, in his case taking a country with him, and we are powerless to stop it.[9]

Yet possibly the true import of *The Fog of War* comes not from a film critic, scholar, or historian, but from Peter Hall, who teaches political science at the Center for European Studies at Harvard (and is a friend of Morris's): "I think *The Fog of War* is a film about moral confusion. It's a rumination on the human condition. McNamara is the original whiz kid from the American automobile industry, a statistician in World War II. But he discovers that in the midst of war it's not clear what is a fact and what is not a fact. And that facts provide no clear guide to moral action."[10]

Morris himself says, "One of the things I find deeply fascinating about McNamara's account, his life in public service, is the element of caprice. On the one hand, people believe everything is directed, everything is controlled. My own two cents worth of opinion is that most things are deeply out of control." It is a world view that he seems to press for even in *The Thin Blue Line*, asking Harris—in jail at that time but for another crime—repeatedly how much chance or luck, had to do with the law incarcerating the wrong man. Wrong place, wrong time and all that. But Morris just doesn't let it drop. He keeps hammering away, even at this inmate, about the way the universe is constructed.

His method is audible questions, not the Herzog device of conclusive narrative voice-over, such as: "I believe the universe…" (and then his view of it) in *Grizzly Man*. These are both, of course, forms of editorializing voice from working filmmakers.

Where I Got My Ideas

The Fog of War may be seen as one more step in Morris's involvement with the merge of fact and fiction, the inquiry into what really is the truth, and his use of certain cinematic devices to get there. "In my films," he says, "people are talking directly to the camera or to me, without any kind of question-and-answer formula. And, yes, they do take on the character of monologues. The Interrotron was a way of doing a lot of different things at once. It removes me from the area around the camera. Instead, there's just a half-silvered mirror, an image of me floating in front of the lens. It allows for direct eye contact with me, and out at the audience at the same time. Which I don't think has ever existed before. I don't think anyone else has ever done that. You may see it, of course, when people are reading text on a TelePrompter—a newscaster or a politician—but it's different for someone who's talking to me extemporaneously and looking right at the audience at the same time. I think it has an arresting effect." Morris credits his wife, art historian Julia Sheehan, with coming up with the term "Interrotron" to signify a combination of interview and terror. "I've been obsessed with eye contact; it's wired into our brains. I think it's important for the subject to be looking at me instead of a camera."

Morris says, "I like to work in the gray area between fiction and film." For precedent, he cites the early and pioneer documentary *Nanook of the North*. According to Morris (and others), "Flaherty's films were fables, they were heavily constructed, they were the antithesis of what we take to be documentary." He says he was also inspired by *Lessons of Darkness*, the 1992 film by Werner Herzog: "I've often thought of documentary starting as expressionistic filmmaking partially because of that film." *Lessons of Darkness* examines the toll that the first Gulf War took on Kuwait by setting shots of bomb craters and burning oil fields to the music of Mahler and Wagner, providing a kind of editorial commentary, much more typical of a feature film use of music.

Morris also mentions the more restrained *Sinai Field Mission*, the Frederick Wiseman film which lets the onscreen images speak for themselves. The 1978 film tells the story of a U.N. peacekeeping mission to monitor Egyptian and Israeli activities in the Sinai after the 1973 war. Morris says, "There's this one great scene where a guy is using a broom to sweep sand off the road and the wind keeps blowing it right back on. It's really sick but really funny."

Overall, Morris sees himself in the tradition of Vertov, who pioneered the use of a variety of innovative camera techniques—including split screens, slow motion, and freeze frames—to depict the lives of ordinary people in the Soviet Union. *The Man With the Movie Camera* (Vertov's film), according to Morris, is "visually stunning. Watching this 1929 movie taught me that documentary film wasn't about creating images, it was about capturing them. *The Man With the Movie Camera* or Vigo's *A Propos de Nice* to me are expressionistic films, although in some sense, some very real sense, they're composed of what we would today take as documentary images. I like to think that my films in part are a return to part of that kind of idea: that documentary really isn't journalism at all, but can be a kind of pure filmmaking."

Blurring the Boundaries: Fact and Fiction

Morris's movies so consciously and consistently blur the lines between fact and fiction, reality and fantasy, objectivity and subjectivity, that the use of real-life subjects and lack of a prewritten script sometimes seem to be their only common thread, except for certain thematic constants such as the difference between reality and people's perception of reality. For instance, another of Morris's films, *Dr. Death*, deals with a real-life individual: Fred Leuchter, a self-styled technologist who was hired by Holocaust revisionist Ernst Zundel to find evidence that the Holocaust never took place. It's a topic perfectly suited for Morris, it would seem, in that he is concerned with, maybe obsessed by, the shifting relationships among reality, myth, and memory.

It is fascinating to read this former philosophy student's comments about these topics on his blog for the *New York Times*, particularly the July 2007 entry where he analyzes the impact and importance of images with and without captions, with and without a context. He starts with his own family photographs, then takes off into a clever disquisition about a photograph of a ship, querying the reader how differently he or she would feel to know this was a photograph of the Lusitania, the sinking of which precipitated US involvement in World War I.

When he made this blog entry Morris was still working on his film about Abu Ghraib, *Standard Operating Procedure*. After showing some preliminary clips of the work-in-progress, he told a group at Brandeis University: "I can't say for certain what will happen fifty years from years from now, but I have the feeling that [the notorious] photographs from Abu Ghraib will be the iconic photographs of the Iraq War. Not even because of the torture or cruelty. But some of them were so nuts. Nuts in a senseless kind of empty way that is even more disturbing." And in New York City to promote *Standard Operating Procedure*, he said, "When I first saw Sabrina's photographs [the one he particularly refers to is where the soldier, Sabrina, is leaning over a dead body, giving a thumbs-up] I thought, 'What a monster!' Then I learned she was not responsible. That's where pictures can both conceal and reveal. She just wanted to make a record of some of what was going on. Is the crime to have taken a picture? Or is the crime the murder? In another culture, she would have won a Pulitzer Prize, but instead she's the one in jail. I think it's wrong to have the little guy always be the one to get the blame."

Acerbically, he answers a question from someone in the crowd about why he was interested in Abu Ghraib. "The photographs," he says. "I was interested in the photographs. But nobody talked to the people who took them. I thought, 'I'll remedy that in short order.'" Then Morris laughs, shaking his head at himself. "Short order. Ha. Three years later."

He also says, quite wittily, that no government official tried to stop him from making the film. "No. It was a little disappointing, actually. The only one who got in my way was myself" (referring to his well-known habit of procrastination during the making of a movie).

Making a Living and Making Docs: Not Always the Same

Like Wiseman and Maysles, Morris supplements his income from filmmaking by doing commercials. In fact, according to Morris, this is his main income; he says he never "made a dime" on *The Thin Blue Line* nor on the Oscar-winning *The Fog of War*. Morris has been, however, the recipient of numerous grants and honors, including a MacArthur Fellowship, a kind of genius grant, which carried an award of $250,000 when he received it in 1989. Along with award-winning ads for Hewlett-Packard and Quaker Oats, Morris has created clever commercials for Apple Computers, using his interview technique to talk to people who have had bad experiences with Windows, and so decided to switch to the easier-to-use Macs. One of the interviews, with a friend of Morris's teenaged son, became so popular it has achieved cult status on the Web.

Morris's breakout film was probably *Gates of Heaven*, a 1978 movie constructed around two narratives (a well-known and much-used fiction film technique originally taken from literature) juxtaposing and revealing two different approaches to owning a pet cemetery. One is based on a desire for a successful corporate setup, the other on humane—or rather animal—concerns. But where the first, run by a family but based on a business model, is successful, the other is not. The latter is owned by a fellow who sincerely cares about the decent disposing of the animals. Bit by bit, we find that his business is failing. (And the film is dotted with one-on-one interviews with people talking about the peace of mind they have when they know their little Fifi or whomever is in a safe place, and what he or she meant to them.)

In the way he shows the two contrasting stories, it becomes clear which business, and which owners, are the more decent, the more humane. Yet it is hard to tell exactly how and when this judgment comes about. Here, you might say, is Morris's genius. In fact, we don't even dislike the brothers who are inheriting and running the successful, if venal, business, as Morris gets them to tell their tales and as we spend a bit of time with them. Learning about the two sons who will inherit the business from their dad, and who are basically in it for the money, once again a complicated picture emerges. The brothers are not that much alike, and we see that they have come home to work in the business for complex personal reasons. They're not so bad, after all. Or are they?

Morris says that *Gates of Heaven* got scant attention when it first came out, and might have died on the festival circuit, but that Roger Ebert saw the film, loved it, and—in the words of Morris—kept "reviewing it over and over, almost obsessively so. Up until then I figured it was an unmitigated disaster." He also says that Diane Keaton saw *Gates of Heaven*, liked the interviewing technique Morris was using, and talked Warren Beatty into doing something similar in *Reds*, which was also being made around that time.

Early Examples

We also see a bit of the kind of subjective documentary or neo-doc that is to come in Morris's work: a satirical use of archival footage used to show the reverent way Egyptian animals were preserved, compared to current practices like factories extracting glue from animal hooves. In *Gates of Heaven*, Morris cuts to some footage of Egypt: pyramids—an ironic establishing shot—which he follows with the imagined preservations of animals, a very far cry from the brutal descriptions of the contemporary disposal of animals and their parts (and the odors from same in the factories that do this kind of work, described by even one of their owners—how did Morris ever get him to say all that?).

Vernon, Florida, Morris's next film, which garnered him wide attention, was a modified version of the movie he really wanted to make, to be called *Nub City*. It was to be about a Florida town known for the deliberate self-amputations of its residents for insurance money. The most admired in the town were the amputees who had "cashed in" for both an arm and a leg, a fact which carries the fascination of the grotesque. "I was starting to receive death threats," Morris says, explaining the modified slant the film eventually took. *Vernon, Florida* focuses on seemingly straightforward interviews with the idiosyncratic townsfolk: an unsavory turkey hunter paddling his boat around a swamp, wishing there were as many turkeys flapping around as buzzards. A more gentle but just as bizarre fellow keeps certain odd animals for pets; and we also get to meet a couple who take their vacation in White Sands, New Mexico, where the atom bomb was tested. They bring home different jars of sand, believing and showing (to the unseen filmmaker) how the sand in one of the jars is glowing due to radiation.

The movie *Vernon, Florida* was in part funded by his friend and fellow documentarian Herzog, who forced him to take $2,000 to finish the movie. The story, now legendary in film circles, comes from Herzog. "We were in a motel room in Minnesota. I gave Errol an envelope with $2,000 in it, and he went to the window and threw it out. I went to the parking lot, carefully picked up the bills, and said to him, 'Please don't do that again.' The next time he took the money."

(Another insider story is that Herzog bet Morris, then a graduate student in philosophy at Berkeley, that Morris would never finish *Gates of Heaven*, but "If you do I'll eat my shoe." Morris and Les Blank documented the eating of said shoe in the short film *Werner Herzog Eats His Shoe*, which premiered at the first public screening of Morris's film. The recipe was from Alice Waters: duck fat, herbs, hot sauce and garlic.)[11]

When I mentioned to Morris I would have much preferred to see the original *Nub City*, with its amputees, Morris just laughed and said he might not be alive if that film had been made. Morris, born in 1948, is originally from Long Island, and as a youth went to the Putney School in Vermont. He is a graduate of the University of Wisconsin in Madison and was a graduate student at Princeton and at UC Berkeley. While at Berkeley, Morris always sneaked into to the Pacific Film Archive, according to Tom Luddy, its director, who also says that Morris always denied this. Another tale is that Morris got into both Princeton and Berkeley not by a formal admissions process, but by showing up and barreling his way in through an impromptu, forced interview. Morris is the winner of three NEA Fellowships and a Guggenheim grant, as well as the aforementioned prestigious MacArthur Fellowship. He lives in Cambridge, Massachusetts, where his production company is based, and is a member of the Cambridge-based American Academy of Arts and Sciences.

His wife says that when she met Morris in Wisconsin he said to her, "I've been talking to a lot of mass murderers lately, but I just couldn't get you out of my mind." Though he says he immediately regretted the remark, Sheehan says it was "one of the nicest things anybody ever said to me."

Method to Their Madness

So from these two filmmakers, Morris and Herzog, descend the chief strains of our era's neo-doc. In Herzog's work, there is the obvious use of fiction filmmaking techniques such as voice-over narrative with its editorializing comments, the inclusion of his own person on film, and, occasionally, the use of faked evidence or props. We also see some deliberate ignoring of timelines. Pitting his protagonists (and himself) against nature and going to remote places are also tied into his cinematic themes, and at times seem an obsession.

These are all extreme devices and practices, yet possibly because of Herzog's grave and sometimes lugubrious manner, his methods never seem as sensationalistic as those of Michael Moore. And his films are so remote in setting, and also so poetic, that they never achieved "hot topic" status. Obviously, too, he is German and working in a different tradition. Some call it romantic; to other critics it is expressionist. (Though to dissociate himself from the nature and "Mountain" films of the Nazi era, Herzog avoids a connection with this romantic idea. Film historians say his allegiance to Lotte Eisner comes from her "teaching" him about earlier German filmmakers not associated with the Third Reich.)

Morris also used highly imaginative or even surrealistic sequences in *The Fog of War* to comment on the proclamations of its subject. When McNamara, for instance, as an executive at Ford, seeks out data on casualties from auto wrecks, he is told that if people were packaged like eggs, the rate of survival would improve. Whereupon the film shows us a carton of eggs splattering on the kitchen floor, and skulls in white cloth falling in slow motion down a stairwell, cracking against the floor below.

(The skull image came to Morris, he says, while listening to McNamara talk about research, but the image expanded to things falling from above, such as the bombs dropping from the sky onto the fields of Vietnam, and by extension McNamara's direction of that war. Even a conventional re-enactment—lines of dominoes tumbling onto a map of southeast Asia and later reversing literal numbers—an ironic comment on the numbers of dead that McNamara's voice-over admits to—tumbling surrealistically on the map of a battle scene, are hypnotic. And his use of war footage has an eerily beautiful—almost mystical—quality, not unlike that of *Hearts and Minds*; particularly, in this viewer's opinion, in the strangely compelling lights of bombs and battlefields.)

Perhaps most uniquely, the filmmaker has created a subtle and subjective style of interviewing, which I have come to believe will be Morris's most lasting contribution, as well as an ability to create an imagined timeline, and images that seem susceptible to infinite interpretations.

But whereas Herzog has clearly tried for lasting fame for some of his subjects—Walter Steiner or Juliane Koepcke, for instance, and especially Dieter Dengler—it doesn't look as if they will go down in the canon of remembered personalities.

Perhaps Herzog is just a bit removed in his approach, in the end, and Morris's more complicated involvement with his subjects will have a longer-lasting impact.

As Frank Rich put it: "There has been no more unlikely movie star this season than Robert McNamara, the only living character in Errol Morris's documentary."[12] Unless, of course, you count Errol.

Another area where Herzog's and Morris's creative and temperamental differences emerge is in their use of music, an extremely important part of their filmmaking. "Music is one thing I've always been good at selecting," says Herzog, a bit immodestly if correctly. And each of his films does seem to have a highly appropriate score, specific to the film, almost like a feature filmmaker seeking out just the right mood-making and -altering music for the topic at hand. There is no particular composer with whom he is associated, though, or seems to favor.

Morris, though not using any music in *Vernon, Florida* or *Gates of Heaven*, starts to use music in his later films, in order to make an editorial and emotional point. The composer he has most frequently and effectively employed is Philip Glass, particularly in *The Fog of War* and *The Thin Blue Line*. It's as if he has found the music which most perfectly expresses what Morris clearly sees as a tension between perception and reality: Glass's scores are tension- and goosebump-causing, unexpected, and keep the viewer on the edge. (A possible influence is that Morris's widowed mother supported her family by giving music lessons; Morris studied the cello in Paris with an instructor who had taught Glass.) In *Standard Operating Procedure*, a movie which has not fared that well with critics, not that this is the reason why, the original score is by Danny Elfman, a well-known, and award-winning, Hollywood composer. (And when speaking about Elfman's industry reputation, Morris was perhaps a bit defensive about using such well-known feature film talent.)

If Herzog is a romantic, or anyway a post-romantic (read modern) in that he sees himself in nature, or inserts his own persona as a reflection of the lives of others, or even more frequently the reverse, Errol Morris is postmodern. It's not about him, though he may get pulled in. All time is present all the time. Plus, the lines of demarcation between fact and fancy are so muddied—if ever so interesting. In his worldview, people can never be either good or bad, or perhaps are both at once. But in the fuzziness is the fascination.

• • • • • • • • • •

Endnotes

1. For an excellent and thorough summary of the career of Werner Herzog, see "Profile of Werner Herzog" by David Church in *sensesofcinema.com*, June 2006.

2. Daniel Zalewski, "The Ecstatic Truth," *The New Yorker* (April 24, 2006). According to a 1985 article by Roger Ebert, one of the first American critics to champion Herzog,

"He makes films that exist outside the usual categories. He takes enormous risks to make them. In a widely discussed *New Republic* article last autumn, Stanley Kauffmann wondered if it is an item of Herzog's faith that he must risk his life with every movie he makes." (*Chicago Sun-Times*, January 16, 1983).

3. "Learning to Fly: Dieter Dengler Speaks about Werner Herzog's Latest Doc," by Doug Stone, *www.indiewire.com/people/int_Dengler_Dieter_980414.html*. By permission of *indiewire.com*.

4. Ian Buruma, "Herzog and His Heroes," *New York Review of Books* (July 19, 2007).

5. Press notes, Billy Rose Theatre Collection, Lincoln Center for the Performing Arts.

6. Buruma, "Herzog and His Heroes."

7. Cronin, Paul, *Herzog on Herzog* (London: Faber and Faber, 2002).

8. Nancy Ramsey, "Strangely Hopeful in a World of War and Caprice," *New York Times* (December 23, 2003).

9. Frank Rich, "Oldest Living Whiz Kid Tells All," *New York Times* (January 25, 2004).

10. Peter Hall, quoted by Nancy Ramsey in "Strangely Hopeful in a World of War and Caprice."

11. Les Blank's name is frequently linked with these two, yet of course he is a major documentary filmmaker in his own right. His current film is *Tea*, a fairly traditionally presented film about finding the perfect unadulterated, organically grown tea. Often he works in the interactive mode, though, as in his 1990 film *Yum, Yum, Yum! A Taste of Cajun and Creole Cooking*. Although Blank is only seen briefly on camera, those interviewed turn to address him and the crew directly, and we hear the questions: Chef Marc Savoy: "Les, know what's better than a bowl of gumbo?" Les: "What?" Marc Savoy: "Two bowls."

12. Rich, "Oldest Living Whiz Kid Tells All."

chapter five

THE CHARISMATIC COMMENTER: AL GORE, LEON GAST, DAVIS GUGGENHEIM, CHRISTIAN SLATER, SPIKE LEE (AS NARRATOR)

· · · · · · · · · ·

The idea to have a familiar, famous voice narrate a documentary is not new. A form that was once considered earnest, even dull in some people's eyes, might need some "glamming up" or some creative credibility. Plus, only too obviously, sometimes things have to be explained or tied together. For instance, in 1977 the Canadian director Harry Rasky picked a highly distinct, distinguished voice—that of James Mason—to narrate his *Homage to Chagall*, a film which was an Academy Award nominee for Best Documentary Film in its year, and which won an Emmy in that category. There are plenty of elegant voices around, yet Mason's is truly tony. Perhaps more importantly, it is a recognizable voice, giving a kind of aura to the film. In 2007, Paul Newman's undisguisable voice was used to narrate the documentary *Dale*, about racecar driver Dale Earnhardt, himself a superstar. Many know that Newman has been a racecar driver and enthusiast most of his adult life. He is also the narrator of the 2007 documentary *The Price of Sugar*, directed by Bill Haney.

Famous Voice Tones

One of the very first highly recognizable narrative voices used for a documentary was that of Sir Laurence Olivier, who narrated the British World War II documentary *The World at War*, a movie that demonstrates how a familiar voice can pull things together, and also the importance of fame in calling attention to a subject matter. In a positive way it demonstrated what I have come to believe is the chief contribution of the documentarians to be discussed in this chapter. The practices of these filmmakers seem at first to be diametrically opposed to those of Paul Rotha, who, in his discussion of documentary movies, insisted that they should have no entertainment value. Yet he does observe some other possibilities, in his *Documentary Film*:

> One method, the easier and therefore the most used, is to engage a well-sounding person—often with broadcasting or theatrical associations—and have him recite the written comment with one eye on the typescript and the other on the screen. This result is generally adequate to the type of film for which it is used: impersonal, without feeling, and, I suppose, to be regarded as inoffensive. The other, more experimental method, is to make use of people actually engaged on the work with which the picture deals—sometimes an engineer, perhaps a ship's draughtsman, possibly a miner, docker, postman, or journalist. I do not think the voice itself is of great importance. It is the sincerity and understanding and intimacy with which the words are delivered that is valuable.[1]

While the neutrality of the omniscient narrator is generally recognized as the standard, a door has been opened for a more involved commenter. By the early 1950s, certain other modifications started to come along, as exemplified by the popular six episodes of *Victory at Sea*, narrated by Leonard Graves and widely shown on American TV. Though not entirely recognizable (even if it may have become that way), Graves's voice and narrative did not hold back in underscoring certain moments. Currently, there is a resurgence of interest in *Victory at Sea*, perhaps due to our fascination with the "Greatest Generation," as Tom Brokaw has famously dubbed WWII veterans and the 1940s generation. The film also features—or "stars," as sometimes the Internet Movie Data Base describes the phenomenon—Winston Churchill, Dwight D. Eisenhower, Douglas MacArthur, Hirohito, Charles de Gaulle, William S. Halsey, and Louis Mountbatten, listing them as headliners in a film. Up until now, I never even knew the last listed had a first name, but such are the ironies of cast listings as given by the IMBD.

At the time, the series was so popular that it was consolidated into a feature film, and the following is a review of the movie when it came out in England from *Punch*:

> *Victory at Sea* is a ninety-minute documentary made by the American Producer Henry Salomon from the twenty-six half-hour episodes seen on B.B.C. television some time ago.... The music (Richard Rodgers) is no mere device for linking and accompanying the shots but is intelligently calculated to reinforce their effect and make others of its own and the commentary, though it is not free from those solemn rhetorical phrases familiar in declamation about the war, is made immensely more acceptable and impressive than

usual by the quite unemphatic almost gentle way it is spoken by Alexander Scourby.[2] [AU note: Scourby was the narrator in the British versions; Graves was used for the American.]

Like many of his generation, documentary director Ken Burns has said that he remembered watching *Victory at Sea* on television with his father in the 1950s and that as an adult—not that it was a direct consequence of that viewing—he had simply decided to make a film wherein the grittier realities of the daily life of World War II were presented more realistically. Burns has also said in numerous public talks about *The War* (the title that film eventually took) such as the one at the New York Public Library in the fall of 2007, that he wished to disparage the belief that it was a good or wonderful war, and so he decided to try to show it from the point of view of those who were actually there, in the trenches.

Hollywood Narrators

Today, the best-known super-presence of the contemporary documentary, former Vice President Al Gore, functions as both narrator and subject of the film *An Inconvenient Truth*.

Truly, though, the cinema may have conferred as much fame and glamour on Gore as he did on it. Director Davis Guggenheim agrees with the assessment, saying that these days the documentary can make a subject famous, but it goes the other way as well.

Showing once more that the apple doesn't fall far from the tree, *Arctic Tale* was released in the summer of 2007, cowritten with a script by Kristin Gore, daughter of Al Gore, and with a narration by Queen Latifah, another very familiar voice. It is a documentary tracking the lives of a polar bear cub and a walrus pup, as their mothers are raising them. But in their environmentally-challenged world, they have to contend with a foreshortened winter, thinning sheets of ice that will no longer support their weight, and the disappearance or shrinking of the ice floes that have in the past served as diving platforms and safe havens.

And, of course, Morgan Freeman provided an incalculable service in expressing the narrative shape of the story in *March of the Penguins*. To think how effective Freeman is, just imagine what the film would be like without his reassuring tones explaining the journey of family, fatherhood, and the battle against the elements. Freeman is known as one of the most consistently employed actors in the business, but his narrations have really stood out. Demonstrating this, a spoof appeared on the Web site

Hollywood.com, with the title: "Morgan Freeman Enters Rehab" [to quit narrating]. Here is the bit.

> Morgan is not only refusing to appear in films that don't include him narrating, but he 'simply can't stop narrating in real life,' said a family member. Freeman has already narrated *March of the Penguins, War of the Worlds, Million Dollar Baby, The Shawshank Redemption*, and dozens of documentaries, including *The Hunting of the President* and *The Long Way Home*. 'It's really sad because Morgan is such a wonderful actor, but he just can't kick this narration problem,' said a close friend. 'I hope he gets the help he needs.' Freeman's last public interview was two weeks ago on *The Charlie Rose Show*. When Rose asked him about his family life, Freeman got a blank look on his face and went into narration mode.

They're Family Too

March of the Penguins became the second largest grossing documentary of all time, after *Fahrenheit 9/11*, probably due to the fact that the more jejune voices of the three penguin characters in the French version that made the film seem more like a cartoon and less like a family drama were replaced by the gravelly, recognizable, and reassuring tones of Freeman. Also, the electronic soundtrack in the French version was dropped in favor of Alex Wurman's softer symphonic score. (The original French production was directed by Luc Jacquet, and based on a story by Jacquet and Michel Fessler. The production and its crew were beset by troubles throughout the film's creation, especially in Antarctica, and the entire project was stalled for a good while.)

Yet it did eventually make it to the Sundance Film Festival, where Warner Brothers president Mark Gill saw the film and called writer Jordan Roberts to ask if something could be done to make the film more appealing to American audiences. Jordan wrote a new narration, hired Wurman, and suggested Freeman for the narration. According to Adam Leipig, president of National Geographic Films, which distributed the movie, "Going from the voices of a mommy, daddy, and baby penguin to a story-teller telling a story is a significant shift."

Jacquet, however, defends his version: "There are millions of people around the planet who like the French version, my version, saying that the American version is a little less creative."[3]

But why the strong appeal and success of the film, which is, strictly speaking, not a documentary? "A few documentaries have been made on this species, but I had no desire to approach this film from a scientific point of view. There's a very simple reason for this. Everything we know about Antarctica is scientific. My feeling when I went there was that I saw very beautiful things, very moving things, very strong things. [But] I had the feeling that something was lacking artistically in the French version," says Roberts.

He also says, "I'm very proud to have been able to work with Morgan Freeman. It was Warner Independent who suggested working with him because they already had a friendship with him. But frankly, the day I was told that Morgan Freeman could do the narration, I said yes immediately. You can understand why."

And who can really calculate just what proportionate impact his tones had on the ultimate success of the film, and the setting up of the anthropomorphic narrative, which led to such success? Still, even Freeman does not escape the occasional quibble; some critics objected that, in *March of the Penguins*, the phrase "the worst is yet to come" was repeated by Freeman a number of times, though it should have been obvious that, as the narrator and not the writer of the movie, this is not a sentence he created; its doomsday quality might have been more so with another narrator.

Clearly, Freeman's success as a narrator comes from the layerings accumulated from years of his wise cinematic omniscient narrators and what we the audience bring to our viewing from those memories. As critic Peter Martin wittily observes about Morgan's omniscience on the Web site *Cinematical*, "Before he was God, he was a telephone lineman. Ever since *The Shawshank Redemption* in 1994, Morgan Freeman has become the go-to guy for voice-over narration, his calm, deliberate tones lending an air of authenticity to the proceedings. When he's not narrating, he's mentoring, fathering, or advising, usually playing some kind of wise authority figure, which helps explain why it was so easy to accept him as God in *Bruce Almighty*."[4]

In his documentary on the Civil War, Ken Burns employed celebrity voices in another type of narration[5]: It was the reading of the letters of his long-dead subjects and by the voices of well-known actors. His highly successful *The Civil War*, first shown on PBS, was initially disparaged by some history buffs because of the narrative it imposed on historical facts; it was not a serious, historical record it was said. And some documentary filmmakers dismissed the series for having too much of a point of view.[6]

Though the narrative voices are not identified in the film, but rather listed in alphabetical order in the credits, there can be little doubt to anyone who has watched television's *Law & Order* that it is the voice of Sam

Waterston that is used, to theatergoers that it is Julie Harris, or that it is Freeman as noted above, and so forth. Altogether, over forty distinguished actors—and their highly distinctive reading styles—were used, including Jason Robards, Jr. and Colleen Dewhurst. In a kind of narrative-within-a-narrative, the historian David McCullough was the frame, or overall narrator.

Burns has said on many occasions that that this original inspiration for his use of actors' voices to read letters came from watching actors reading the correspondence of Gertrude Stein in Perry Miller Adato's film *Gertrude Stein: When This You See, Remember Me*, during which he wondered how it would be if he put the actors off-camera. (See especially a detailed interview, "Capturing the American Experience: A Conversation with Ken Burns," in *Weber Studies*, Fall 2006, Vol. 23.)

Adato is one of the few female documentary filmmakers of the 1970s and a director-producer known especially for her work on artists, particularly women artists. In *When This You See...*, Adato also used interviews with Janet Flanner, Virgil Thomson, Bennet Cerf, and Mrs. Chapman, the woman who brought Gertrude Stein to America. (Other films of Adato's are *Dylan Thomas: The World I Breathe, Mary Cassatt: Impressionist from Philadelphia*, and *Georgia O'Keeffe*.) Adato worked as a film coordinator and researcher for CBS and then joined Channel Thirteen. Prior to this she was film consultant to the United Nations, where she forged the Film Advisory Center with—significantly—the help of Robert Flaherty.

Intriguingly, Adato told the *New York Times* in 1977, "I have to start out with a story. I'm interested in extending the areas of people's cultural experience, and to do that you must entertain and be lively; you have to involve them emotionally in the story. You can't do it with the work alone."[7] So even in 1977 there is some acknowledgment from this well-known television documentarian that a certain kind of narrative is highly important.

To Re-enact or Not

In his storyline for *The Civil War*, the most watched opening episode of a series ever to play on public television with 14 million viewers in 1990, Burns did not use the device of re-enactment as is sometimes done in historical documentaries, but instead showed battlefields at the hour of the day on which the engagements took place, mixed pan shots and zooms, and then occasionally cut to a photograph of the carnage. According to the May 1992 *Current Biography*, Burns finds re-creations "abhorrent," and he is quoted as saying "I don't think re-creations do justice to the people who died."

At a panel moderated by Janet Maslin, then-*New York Times* critic, Burns said, "For an artist as exceptional as Werner, it was all right to fake stuff. But most of us would have a great deal of difficulty doing this. When we begin to manipulate images, nothing is true" ("Visionaries With Their Eyes on the Truth," Sunday, May 2, 1999). The most he has ever used re-encactments is for a two- or three-minute sequence in *Lewis & Clark*, his film about the adventurers/discoverers.

Yet the following description from an academic article seems particularly applicable to Burns's work.

> Documentary cinema is intimately tied to historical memory. Not only does it seek to reconstruct historical narrative, but it often functions as an historical document itself.... These strategies are based on a desire to enlist the audience in the process of historical reconstruction. The documentary film differentiates itself from narrative cinema by claiming its status as a truth-telling mode.... The documentary calls upon its audience to participate in historical remembering by presenting an intimate view of reality. Through cinematic devices such as montage, voice-over, intertitles, and long takes, documentary provokes its audience to new understandings about social, economic, political, and cultural differences and struggles. The films actively engage with their world; however, often viewers respond to the same devices motivating classic Hollywood narratives.[8]

And from the other end of critical commentary, a gentle-spirited 2004 mockumentary called *The Old Negro Space Program* parodies Burns's filmmaking, relying heavily upon so-called "Ken Burns effect" shots, Burns-style plaintive piano bridges, and letters home read by a narrator, to the image of photographs. The opening credits even announce "A film not by Ken Burns," in case you missed the point.

Burns's first documentary for PBS was *Brooklyn Bridge* in 1981 and it also made use of a narrator: Pulitzer Prize-winning historian David McCullough. In fact, McCullough narrated Burns's films *The Shakers: Hands to Work, Hearts to God*, *The Statue of Liberty*, *Huey Long*, and *The Congress*. *Thomas Hart Benton* and *Empire of the Air* were both narrated by Jason Robards, Jr.

McCullough's voice is familiar to many (not just intellectuals or PBS viewers) and Robards's voice is also recognizably unique. For his 2004 documentary on the prizefighter Jack Johnson, *Unforgivable Blackness*, Burns used Samuel L. Jackson to read the words of Johnson.

Mark Twain was narrated by Keith David, using Kevin Conway for the voice of Twain. David was also the overall narrator for the 10-part series *Jazz*. As fine as these narrators may be, their voices are not necessarily familiar to the public ear. But in *The Civil War*—the work that brought Burns to the mainstream consciousness—it was the highly recognizable tones of celebrities reading letters which is, in this critic's opinion, his unique contribution to the form. In *The Civil War*, according to Erik Barnouw, Burns told his actors to "inhabit the words" of the letters.[9]

In an interview, "The Postbellum Ken Burns," in the April 1992 issue of *Emmy* magazine, Burns said, "Basically we begin with a stable of voices that we've used since the beginning—Paul Rochling, Julie Harris, Arthur Miller, and Kurt Vonnegut. With each film we've expanded, adding more and more people.... And all that has to do with the frequency of the appearance of the voice, how well they read [the script] and the life that they give to it, and the interpretation of a particular quote.... So we might say, 'Gee, I think Jason Robards would be a good Grant.' And you discover he is."[10]

Creative Narration: Hearkening Back to 1985

Incredibly, from the perspective of the subjective documentary so popular today, Burns, and his then wife and partner Amy, were moving in this direction even as early as 1985. (The couple are now divorced and Ken Burns has remarried. His ex-wife, now known as Amy Stechler, wrote and edited *The Life and Times of Frida Kahlo*, a television documentary, in 2005.) Though we may think of Burns as a traditional documentarian, perhaps because of his infinite and painstaking patience in researching, he was distinct at the time in stretching the boundaries of the documentary. In August of 1985, he and Amy Stechler Burns spoke of their "new" method to Leslie Garisto in a *New York Times* feature about *The Shakers*, about to air on PBS.

"In *The Shakers*, the Burnses employed actors, including Julie Harris, to speak for long-dead historical figures. The actors are never seen; instead, their voices are used to embellish the visual imagery, much of it consisting of etchings, engravings, and still photographs. In the words of Ken Burns, it was a way of 'penetrating the two-dimensionality of the photograph.'" According to Garisto:

> The couple admit that their unconventional approach to the documentary takes some of the 'vérité' out of their cinematic efforts. 'We use an incredible amount of poetic license,' Mr. Burns said, but he noted that history—whether written or filmed—is always

'an interpretive process.' He feels as strong a kinship with dramatic filmmakers as he does with other documentarians ('We share the common objective of manipulating images to evoke an emotional response,' he said), and he describes what he calls the '60 Minutes' approach to documentary filmmaking: 'They want it in 20-minute segments, they want an issue—the aesthetic doesn't matter at all.'[11]

Never Pay to Play

In his documentaries, Burns, like Frederick Wiseman, Albert Maysles, and numerous other documentary filmmakers, adheres to the well-established rule that people who are interviewed should never be paid or rehearsed. The model here of course is journalism. Burns has said that he does pay his narrators some amount, but that even big names like Tom Hanks (used for the voice of newspaperman Al McIntosh in *The War*) receive only the SAG minimum. In *The Civil War*, even highly recognizable superstars such as Gregory Peck and Paul Newman were paid union minimum day rates.

An interesting case in point to illustrate some of these distinctions is the memorable interview in *Unforgivable Blackness* with Stanley Crouch, the musician, now newspaper columnist. Another twist on fact-based "reality" in the wild and wonderful quote given by Crouch in the film about why white women like black men. "Because they eat cold eels and think distant thoughts." This is one he says he can't remember first hearing, or who said it. Yet Crouch disagrees with Burns's rule about never paying his subjects. He said he believed he "ought to be paid for his appearances in Mr. Burns's films," but that he participated in them "out of respect for the filmmaker and a sense of moral obligation." He goes going on to say, "From my perspective, the humanity of the negro is so infrequently achieved that you can say, on principle, 'I'm not going to appear in this,' but if you don't appear, you always run the risk of paternalistic lunkheads and ethnic paranoids distorting the whole subject."[12]

Making Memorable Pictures of Our Vanishing Planet

One of the most urgent if poignant motivations for the popularity of nature documentaries is the undeniable reality of our rapidly disappearing plant and animal species. For instance, in the highly popular *Planet Earth* series, the BBC documentaries narrated by acclaimed naturalist David Attenborough, the issue is brought to dramatic life, both on the earth and below water. The subtext may be the potential destruction of the planet, or of global warming, but it is driven home by the images of nature, underscored by the voice of Attenborough, a voice so familiar that it has been parodied by Michael Palin in *Monty Python's Flying Circus*, searching for the legendary Walking Tree of Dahomey. The hushed but excited delivery style has also been mimicked by Spike Milligan, Marty Feldman, *The Goodies*, and *South Park*.

Attenborough has also written and/or presented other, shorter productions. One of the first was *Tribal Eye* (1975), and others include *The First Eden* (1987), about man's relationship with the natural habitats of the Mediterranean, and *Lost Worlds, Vanished Lives* (1989), showing Attenborough's passion for discovering fossils. In 2000, *State of the Planet* examined the environmental crisis that threatens the ecology of the earth. *The Blue Planet* and *Planet Earth* in, respectively, 2001 and 2006, have been spectacularly successful.

Planet Earth is the first natural history series to be made entirely in high definition, and the genuine compliment of imitation is given now by Sigourney Weaver, who narrates some of the series in the American version. So add Attenborough and Weaver to the list of those who have become famous from or lend fame to the doc.

The Performing Narrator

While images of the natural world (frightening ones, for the most part) are smashingly effective in *An Inconvenient Truth*, it must be said that their force is very much underscored by the film's narrator and chief "performer."

I was one of the few fortunates to get to talk to Al Gore after his appearance at the Tribeca Film Festival in the spring of 2007, when he and producer-director Rob Reiner were on hand to introduce and make comments about many of the environmentally conscious films that were shown at the TFF.

In a miniature send-up of Gore's newfound status and underscoring his new role as the lead of a documentary, Mayor Michael Bloomberg introduced Gore as "Oscar winner and matinee idol Al Gore." He then asked the former vice president for his autograph to give to Bloomberg's mother, since Gore was "the hottest leading man of the moment."

"At first I thought it was a terrible idea to do my slideshow for *An Inconvenient Truth*. I had to be talked into it," said Gore, after a general discussion about a possible backlash about Hollywood types being involved in environmental causes. (Don't worry about it, reassured Reiner, in his

Hollywood producer persona and trying to defuse worries. "The world is just now catching up to Hollywood.")

"But," said Gore, "very soon into the production, the director, Davis Guggenheim, had earned my trust. By then I had seen enough to gain a tremendous respect for his skill and sensitivity. And he said that one of the huge differences between a live stage performance and a movie is that when you're in the same room with a live person who's on stage speaking—even if it's me [self-deprecating laugh]—there's an element of dramatic tension, a human connection that commands and keeps your attention. And in a movie, that element is just not present. He explained to me that you have to create that element on screen, by supplying a narrative thread that allows the audience to make a connection with a character."

Then the zinger: "'*You've* got to be that character.'"

"So we talked about it," Gore continued, "and as I say, by then he had earned so much trust from me that he convinced me. And he was a very skillful interviewer. What you hear in those biographical segments is literally one percent of the interviews he did. I began to suspect that his basic technique involved getting me so exhausted that I didn't care what I said anymore. [Laughs.] Still, it was a collaborative process. I don't want to step on the creative role that the moviemakers played. It's their vision. It's their movie, particularly Davis Guggenheim's. But at every step he asked me, What about leaving this in or taking that out? We had a mutual agreement on every aspect of that; there was not a single point where we had any serious disagreement at all."

There are also the scenes that make Gore much more accessible than the aloof, easily parodied campaigner we may remember. There is the sequence with Gore at his family farm, explaining how his own dad shut down the farm when his daughter (Al Gore's sister) had lung cancer; watching Gore make his lonely, frequently late-night airport connections, going from place to place with his "slideshow," as he calls it.

"The very things that turned off the public when he was campaigning— like the use of his son's near-death—audiences responded to in the film. People had a hard time buying into Al Gore's personal anecdotes when he gave them in his political speeches because they were skeptical hearing this in a political venue, but they accepted them when done in documentary form," said Davis Guggenheim when I spoke with him.

"Also, the way I interviewed and shot him helped show another side to Gore. Instead of the standard interview process, I used only audio interviews. I noticed that when the lights were on, he'd be different, but when the official interview lights were off, he'd be much more intimate."

Davis Guggenheim directs former Vice President A1 Gore for the film *An Inconvenient Truth*. Photo courtesy of Paramount Pictures.

Still, some critics didn't care for Davis Guggenheim's dwelling on the hospital scenes when Gore was worried about his son's near-death. To them, the movie seemed to indicate an overly simplistic connection between that experience and Gore's motivation to save or fix the world for the next generation. Unwittingly or not, journalists were commenting on a documentary as if it were a feature film, thereby merging and blending the boundaries between a feature and a documentary even more.

Guggenheim said one of the things that worried him the most during the making of *An Inconvenient Truth* was how to cut between a shot of a natural disaster, and then back to Gore, and then to his personal life or intimate scenes of him. Of course, it did work, and Guggenheim credits focusing on the personal, claiming that it is still the best way to make a documentary work. It is an approach learned in part from his documentary filmmaker father: "My dad [Charles Guggenheim] was getting increasingly personal in his films toward the end of his career."

A Director's Motivation

Davis Guggenheim was not at the Tribeca Film Festival, but he spoke with me by telephone from his office in California, where he lives and works. He had just come back from Toronto, where he had been shooting and editing a new documentary about three different musicians from three different

118

Davis Guggenheim, director. Courtesy of
Paramount Pictures.

generations. He directs features as well as documentaries, though he says docs
are his favorite form. "I also work for television [he has directed episodes of
"Deadwood," among other shows] as a way to feed my habit [of docs]," he says.

"My father made social justice documentaries," says Guggenheim. "I
used to hang around and look in wonder at the whole enterprise: the cables,
the lights, the coal miners, the political candidates. One clear memory was
when I was five. My father woke me up in the middle of the night. 'You want
to come to work with me?' We boarded a plane to cover Robert Kennedy's
presidential campaign. And my father made the Academy Award–winning
film *Robert F. Kennedy Remembered* from the footage he shot on the
campaign. I was hooked forever."

Here is *his* version of the origins of *An Inconvenient Truth*: "Laurie David
and Lawrence Bender [the producers] brought the idea to me. They said,
'Gore's got a slideshow on global warming. We want to make a movie of it.'
At first I didn't think it would work, a slideshow, starring a former politician.
But when I did finally see the show, at one of Gore's talks, in this case at the
Beverly Hills Hotel, it blew my mind. I was shaken to the core. I had no idea
how to make the film, but I just knew I had to try. And five months later, we
got it into Sundance and Cannes, and Paramount picked it up.

"Of course there were challenges. I would say the biggest one was finding a way to make a scientific slideshow full of charts and graphs into a movie that could entertain people. I had to find a way to personalize Gore's journey. To make the audience invest in his quest."

The narrative that Guggenheim did use—watching Al Gore's sometimes lonely journey, watching him working on his presentations, and soldiering on—is one way, and of course there are scenes of him relaxing in Tennessee, too. One thinks here of Barbara Kopple's comment that "what people often are hoping to see with these behind-the-scenes glimpses are the ways in which celebrities are normal people. Empathy is the most important tool in a documentary filmmaker's toolkit and genuine passion for a connection with your story and your subjects." [Kopple was replying to questions I had given her, and on the eve of the opening of *Shut Up and Sing* at the Toronto Film Festival in the fall of 2006. *Shut Up and Sing* had been awarded Gala (opening) status, the first doc to be so honored there in ten years.]

Yet paradoxically, and curiously, the charts, graphs and statistics that worried Guggenheim in their "transferability" to cinema may have been more palatable, presentable, and even interesting than he predicted. Such evidence—yes, let's call it documentary evidence—not only lends credibility, but we've gotten used to it by now. Sometimes it seems we've even come to expect it. Americans in particular like to have things proven to them, albeit if only in a quasi-scientific way. We've seen stats, figures, and charts used amusingly and effectively in films of Michael Moore and Morgan Spurlock; we don't turn off when they turn up.

And in the time-honored right-place/right-time mode, Guggenheim remembers: "We were supposed to shoot in New Orleans the night before Katrina hit—Gore was giving his slideshow to a group of insurance adjustors and we wanted to do a piece about sea levels rising because of the levees. We got a call about the hurricane. 'It's too dangerous. Don't go.' We didn't realize then what was about to happen—the event that would crystallize for the country what the real threat of global warming would be—and would be the pivotal event of our movie. It was truly amazing. The things we were dealing with in theory—like threats to polar bears—started to happen in real life, in front of us."

Even so, Guggenheim says it was quite a while before he realized how successful the film was going to be. "When the film was finished, it was shown to a key figure in the industry. I won't say who. And he said, 'It's a feathered fish.' That is, it can't swim and it won't fly."

As of this writing, a sequel to *An Inconvenient Truth* has been reported in the trade papers such as *Variety* and *The Hollywood Reporter*, and while Guggenheim says they were premature, it certainly is a possibility. An opera of the film has also been announced.

Guggenheim says he believes that docs are the most exciting form right now for any number of reasons. Feature films are subject to so many different levels of approval; even a test audience can negate an entire project. He also says docs interest him the most because there are so many different ways a doc can be made, and there is much more creative control than in film features or television.

"When I graduated from Brown [in 1986]," he says, "I was so worried cause I felt it was all over. The Ken Burnses and other documentarians had already done everything. I thought I had missed the boat. I do credit Michael Moore with turning things around. Of course, I have a love/hate relationship with his films, for all the usual reasons. Plus," he continues, "I truly believe audiences have learned to distrust the news as we receive it on the nightly news and the usual places. Documentaries may be one place that presents the truth. And [to this interviewer, here was the key to the mystery of Gore's new charisma] I came to believe that was the reason for the re-embracing of Al Gore. It was because his revelations were in the documentary format."

Unlike other documentarians interviewed for this book, Davis Guggenheim says he never writes a script or works with a script at all. Clearly, though, he is actively involved in the editing of his films (compare with a filmmaker such as Maysles, who often uses on- or off-site editors). When I spoke with Guggenheim it was at the very end of his day spent in editing facilities. He says that he is just finishing a television pilot as well as putting the finishing touches on *It Might Get Loud*, the doc about the three guitarists: Jack White, Jimmy Page, and the Edge.

Fame Transforms the Form

One of the most innovative ways in which the fame of a narrator has been used was in the documentary *When We Were Kings* by Leon Gast, the 1996 film about the "rumble in the jungle"—the much-anticipated and wildly publicized fight between Muhammad Ali and George Foreman in Zaire, promoted and brilliantly so by Don King, who had offered each $5 million, fronted by Mobutu Sese Seko, Zaire's dictator-president.

Through interviews and commentary by George Plimpton, Norman Mailer, and Spike Lee, the film takes on deeper, funnier, and much more socially significant ramifications. Yes, the movie would have been enticing without their recognizable tones. But unquestionably these highly distinct voices resonated in many ways.

"There was a time when you'd call a black person 'African,' you'd better be ready to fight," is one such contributing comment, by Spike Lee, a latter day "add-on" narrator in the film. Lee also says "Very few black athletes had ever talked the way Muhammad Ali talked without fear of something happening to them or their careers," repeating Ali's oft-quoted remark about Vietnam that "No Viet Cong ever called me 'nigger.'" Another editorializing voice giving narrative tension to the film was that of Howard Cosell. "I don't think Ali can beat George Foreman. Maybe he can pull off a miracle. But I can't conjure that."

There is no doubt that these highly distinct voices made the film stronger. And very few resonate as much as George Plimpton's, not coincidentally himself a practitioner of the New Journalism: a participant journalist in his articles and novels, in which he himself takes part in the activities of his subjects.

"I'd seen Foreman fight before," says Plimpton. "I saw him destroy Frazier. One thing I always remember is, a beaten fighter, all of a sudden, he just diminishes in size. Frazier became a pygmy while Foreman suddenly became this gigantic figure." As Ed Kelleher observed in his review of *When We Were Kings* in *Film Journal International*, "Looking startled at his own recollections, Plimpton tells of meeting 'a woman with trembling hands,' who assured him, before the fight, that a succubus would get to George Foreman. 'That impressed me enormously,' Plimpton admits. Mailer, true to form, muses about Zaire leader Mobutu's women and analyzes the title fight, which, he points out, was won not just by Ali's celebrated 'rope-a-dope' technique, but by his throwing of a daring 'right lead' punch, which the champion hadn't anticipated. Lee sees the fight in larger terms, as a pivotal event in black history."[13]

And leave it to that one-time pugilist himself, Norman Mailer, to penetrate the psyche of his subject. "I think Ali got scared as he got closer and closer to the fight. With his ego, he could keep telling himself that he would dominate Foreman, that he would dance, that he would make a fool of him…[But] in his private moments he had to know that he had not done nearly as well against two fighters—Joe Frazier and Ken Norton—whom Foreman had demolished."

This type of narration by famous people, putting it in the most simplistic terms, tells us how and what to think about events, a conceivable byproduct of the old journalism (though certainly not the BBC model of disinterested observation) though used here in the service of the new doc.

But even more significantly, and like the "New Journalism" that both Mailer and Plimpton were practicing, it mythologizes its heroes and perhaps the commenters, too, in the way that a fictive world can. We come to identify with not only the commentators but sometimes more readily with their subjects.

Good Luck Follows Bad Luck (Gypsy Proverb)

The fact that subsequent, non-contemporaneous interviews were edited in later, stemming from a lag due to initial problems in getting the film funded, turned out to be a good thing.

Director-producer Leon Gast was born in Jersey City, New Jersey, and went to Columbia University, where he studied dramatic arts. He dropped out just before graduation to take a job on the television program *High Adventure with Lowell Thomas*. The program featured filmed expeditions by the famous newsman in exotic locales and inspired the future documentarian to see the potential of nonfiction filmmaking.

Intermittently working as a still photographer as well as a filmmaker, Gast managed to direct and fund other films, including *Hell's Angels Forever, Salsa,* and *Our Latin Thing*. According to the documentarian, *When We Were Kings* took twenty-three years to get to the screen for he had difficulty getting funding to actually make the film after shooting 300,000 feet of footage about the fight.

In the end, the delays may have worked to the film's final aesthetic advantage, for it became a movie with much more historical perspective. It was thanks to the intervention and deal making ability of David Sonenberg, Gast's former attorney, that the film—which was stalled for years—ultimately got made at all. The history of the production of the film is, of course, a cautionary tale to those who seem to think that documentary filmmaking might be a quick and easy route to fame and fortune.

"Every time we made a cut, I'd show it to Ali," says Gast. "He was tremendously supportive. When you're dealing with hundreds of hours of material, you can make several different films. Originally, the film was conceived as an Afro-American *Woodstock*. But as interesting as that might have been, it didn't compare to a film centering on Ali." At this juncture, Gast and Sonenberg decided to add fight footage and archival clips to build the film around the champion.

Gast also credits Taylor Hackford, the director, who shot the new interview footage in the film and helped edit the interviews into the final product. One obvious lesson here concerns the importance of collaboration, but that point is always made about filmmaking. For our purposes, it is that the new doc format—mixing in out-of-sequence archival footage, interviews, latter-day information— has enriched what might have been a straightforward documentary of the old style. Leon Gast told Jack Mathews, "Taylor looked at the footage and said, 'You have to bring it into the nineties,'" Gast recalls. "He said, 'We need interviews, narrators.' I never wanted to do that. I figured if I couldn't tell the story with 280,000 feet of film, there was no point. But I was wrong. The interviews elevate the film to another level."[14]

Back to the Present

The 2007 documentary *Crossing the Line* used a celebrity narration not just for exciting or glamorous emphasis, but also to tie together a complicated, disparate story line. The voice of Christian Slater is mellifluous and pleasantly pours over some of the potentially confusing series of events. And Slater's voice—while recognizable—is not so distinct as to add another to-be-processed element to an already loaded scenario.

Crossing the Line tells the complicated, decades-long tale of four deserters from the American Army during the Korean War who defected to North Korea by way of the DMZ. The film is directed by thirty-four-year-old Brit Daniel Gordon, who for the majority of the film follows the story of Comrade Joe Dresnok. The stories of the other three—their American background, current Korean wives, and half-American children—are worked in a kind of subplot line B, C, and D. In June of 2007, in New York for a special event promoting the film, Gordon told this interviewer that Slater, known for his support of liberal or left-wing causes, worked for free on the film. Gordon said, "When people go to the film, and they hear Christian Slater's voice, they say, 'Oh!' in recognition. Or a similar reaction when they first hear about the film and that he is going to be the narrator. This is especially true for a younger crowd."

Ultimately, though the topic is highly controversial, and perhaps because of the amount of time that we spend with the more jocular Comrade Joe, our sympathies lie with him and actually not with the defector who reversed his position and came home after forty years, doing some jail time as a token retribution, with a sentence lessened by George W. Bush.

Crossing the Line is what one might see as an old-fashioned or Grierson-esque documentary. It carefully gives all sides, there is archival and background information presented, and the viewer is theoretically left alone to make up his or her mind about where the truth actually lies. Yet Slater's tones seem to smoothly move us into some preference for Comrade Joe, deserter that he may be. We are given some moving details of his hardscrabble upbringing in the United States, and Joe, despite being overweight and clearly a bit unstable, is rather likable, even being charismatic enough to work as a part-time actor in his adopted homeland. You might call it the "charisma factor," an element that up until the new doc was never really an issue for those who appeared in or narrated documentaries.[15]

• • • • • • • • • •

Endnotes

1. Paul Rotha, *Documentary Film* (New York: Hastings House, 1952), 165.

2. Richard Mallett, "At the Pictures," *Punch* (February 26, 1958).

3. Lepig and Jacquet, quoted by Doreen Carvajal in "Compared with Their Filmmakers, the Penguins Have It Easy," *International Herald Tribute*, in the *New York Times*, September 28, 2005.

4. Peter Martins, *Cinematical.com* (November 6, 2007).

5. For another point of view on this, see See John Tibbetts's excellent study, "The Incredible Stillness of Being: Motionless Pictures in the Films of Ken Burns," *American Studies* (Lawrence, Kansas: Spring 1996).

6. For a full discussion of this issue, see *Ken Burns's The Civil War: Historians Respond*, edited by Robert Brent Toplin, Oxford University Press, 1997. Another take on poetic license is given on www.twainquotes.com, an online source referencing "a list of mistakes and misrepresentations in Ken Burns's film *Mark Twain*." The main issue is that "accuracy has been sacrificed to artistic license." Examples given are mismatched images and quotes, incorrect or out-of-place quotation attributions.

7. Adato Profile, "An Artist on Film—and Behind the Lens," Grace Glueck, *New York Times* (November 15, 1977).

8. Rabinowitz, Paula, "Wreckage Upon Wreckage: History, Documentary, and the Ruins of Memory," *History and Theory* 32:2 (May 1993): 119–137.

9. Barnouw, *Documentary: A History of the Non-Fiction Film*, 283.

10. *Emmy* 14:2.10, p. 50.

11. Garisto, "Documentarians with a Difference," *New York Times* (August 4, 1985).

12. Virginia Heffernan, quoting Crouch, "Ken Burns: America's Arty History Teacher," *New York Times* (September 11, 2004).

13. Ed Kelleher, *Film Journal International* (December 9, 1996).

14. Jack Mathews, "Finally, a Knockout," *Newsday* (February 12, 1997).

15. One fascinating aspect to the relationship between fame and the documentary—possibly due to the genre's new eminence—is that it can confer fame (or notoriety) on some of its subjects, or in the case of Comrade Joe, upgrade the subject's reputation. Some of the subjects of docs don't actually like this: Two of the original seven subjects of Michael Apted's "Seven Up" series have dropped out of the series, one being the upper-class fellow who became first a journalist, then a media producer. One of the three upper-class friends who has remained a part of the series, now a barrister, says in the film that every seven years he has to let this "bit of poison" into his life again.

Others clearly enjoy the attention, even fame, that has come their way. Significantly—and in some ways this makes director Apted's point(s) about social class—one is from the working class (Tony), and the other an academic (what Paul Fussell in his book *Class* calls "category X": an academic, with bohemian but "classy," elegant taste), in this case originally from the Dales, a beautiful rural area in England.

The extroverted Tony, now the owner of a fleet of cabs, admits that he enjoys being recognized, and even came with Apted to the New York Film Festival in the fall of 2006 for a panel discussion on that most recent film. The professor, now a transplanted Brit at the University of Wisconsin in Madison, says only half-ironically to Apted (and we hear this in the movie, and in yet one more instance of acknowledging a director's presence), "My original ambition was to be more famous than the series. But unfortunately, Michael, that's not going to happen."

chapter six

THE DOCUMENTARIAN GETS TO STAR: MORGAN SPURLOCK, SYDNEY POLLACK, MARK WEXLER, ALAN BERLINER

· · · · · · · · · ·

When the documentary filmmaker decides to use himself as a guinea pig, a new kind of documentary is formed. Part personal, part sociological, and sometimes disparagingly called a stunt doc, the most successful of this mode to date has been Morgan Spurlock's 2004 *Super Size Me*, the eighth largest grossing documentary as of late 2007. *Super Size Me* is sui generis, therefore the first. A riff on the kind of journalistic experiment that resulted in *Nickel and Dimed* (Barbara Ehrenrich's book about trying to survive on minimum wage jobs across the country working as an unskilled laborer), Spurlock was quite clever in transferring this "stunt" approach to the documentary form, a simple but wonderfully effective idea.

His unique concept was to eat only Supersized McDonald's meals for thirty days.

Spurlock performed this feat by traveling across the country, because, as he says, there is not that much restaurant variety outside of certain urban centers where people walk a lot less and are, therefore, more susceptible to the connection between fast food and obesity. Spurlock told me, "McDonald's is everywhere. I really wanted to show that everywhere you go, this food is there. But it was also important for me to show how this is a nationwide issue. I live in New York City, where you walk everywhere. I came to Texas, where I walked just over half a mile a day in those three days."

Yet Spurlock went beyond a simple transference from writing to cinematic model. He integrated both Web and MTV editing styles to the documentary format, thereby ensuring an appeal to the younger set while retaining the intent of social good, a progressive one usually, with a built-in appeal for a slightly older audience.

Though he did not employ the flashy editing and stylistic techniques of Spurlock, Woody Harrelson followed suit in a smaller, though thematically similar, way in his documentary *Go Further*, which touted the values of health foods, yoga, and marijuana. Harrelson says of Spurlock's film, "There were times when I was disgusted watching Morgan eat those burgers. But I loved his film. In *Go Further*, quitting fast food is the fundamental first step. You have to free your body." Harrelson also said, "It makes sense to me that many celebrities are health nuts. You can't play a leading man if you're fat with acne, which is in part how I got into all this. I used to have terrible acne on my face, and also I was constantly blowing my nose. Then one day I was riding the bus and a woman came and sat next to me and told me I was probably lactose intolerant. Of course, she was right."[1]

In Harrelson's case, he was already a star before casting himself in his own doc, but point made about the attraction between the doc mode and stars, and using your own body and person as an example.

The question is: Will the stunt doc be repeatable? Or is it a one-trick pony of sorts, no matter how spectacular? Many proclaimed 2004 as the year of the food doc, and Morgan Spurlock seemed to realize the validity of this, shifting his gears to make *Where in the World is Osama Bin Laden?* a few years later.

The Innovator

Morgan Spurlock, because of the incredible success of *Super Size Me*, is now a recognized face and force across the world. Calorie and fat counts are now *de rigueur* in many restaurants—and legally enforceable in the United States— though the Paris McDonald's may have been the first one to ban some of its offerings. He has his own production company, Warrior Poets, which carries other socially progressive films under its umbrella, and he is into his third season with other stunt episodes in his series on the FX television channel.

I met with Spurlock in his Soho office, which is filled with worker bees running errands, answering telephones, and looking like the hip downtown New York young film crowd they are. The Manhattan office of Warrior Poets is modeled—whether intentionally or not—after the prototype of Maysles Films, and similarly the staff seems to genuinely like their boss.

Yet the style is different. It's hip, it's casual; but minus its patina of boho chic trappings, the setup could be that of any small manufacturing center. Spurlock has his own separate head office, whereas Albert Maysles has a desk not distinguished in any way from those of his staff. Spurlock's workers have desks in the outer room, which can be shut off by a framed glass

Morgan Spurlock when he is not conducting an experiment.
Photo credit: Robert Zuckerman.

door if needed. Spurlock's private office is casual Southwestern in its feel and look: Mission-style furniture, leather couches, a big, chunky wooden desk.

And a second egress is possible. Though this writer did not see it, there appears to be an editing facility available through a second door to Spurlock's office; when our very cordial interview was over, he suddenly vanished like a magician into that back room.

Our interview took place on one of those spectacular autumn days of crisp air and clean blue skies that New York City can occasionally produce, and Spurlock had just returned from Los Angeles, where he films his series *30 Days* for FX, in what must be kind of a killer schedule: three days in L.A. every week, then back to New York, where he was putting the finishing touches on his upcoming film about Osama Bin Laden. Plus, home is not actually Manhattan, but Brooklyn's Park Slope (by subway—he proudly declares his car-less state), where he lives with his wife, Alexandra Jamieson, and their new son.

Yes, Alexandra is the same Alexandra who appeared in his film *Super Size Me*, and who has taken part in some of his *30 Days* experiments. In *Super Size Me*, Jamieson is still a girlfriend, not yet a wife, but she has a rather large part in the film: preparing the last healthful meal Spurlock will eat for a while before he embarks on his program, and, generally speaking, worriedly clucking away at his project. Jamieson is a vegan chef, and Spurlock says he met her while she was waitressing at an Irish bar right around the corner in Soho. In Spurlock's words, "She picked me up."

Spurlock, now in his mid-thirties, looks, nevertheless, absolutely fit and rested though he says he has been up the entire night before, editing the new film. "I work out every day," he says, "and I run. And every morning I ask myself exactly what it is I want to accomplish that day. What is my intention for that day? It's a trick I learned after a month-long visit to a Navajo reservation in New Mexico."

Indeed, whatever the secret is, it seems to be working, though one guess is that Spurlock is simply, and by his own declaration, a focused workaholic. "I work twelve- to sixteen-hour days," he says. This admittance is quite unexpected. In his movie persona, Spurlock appears to be a causal kind of laid-back, blue-jeans-wearing guy with a down-home twang, though he never hides the fact that he lives in New York.

For my meeting with him he is in the formal version of that attire: black (not blue) jeans, black short-sleeved jersey top. New York black? Downtown black? His health has completely returned from his *Super Size Me* experiment, he says; upper-body muscles are well defined, and the sandy hair of the 2004 film has receded by just an inch or so. Just a regular guy. But he's always aiming for something.

"Every New Year's I write my year-ahead plan, five-year, ten-year. Then I check back. My goal of the moment is how to find time to be a better father and husband. I guess it's a byproduct of the role model I had growing up, for good and for bad. My dad was a kind of an entrepreneur, and while a lot of his projects failed, he never gave up. Then, too, I really love what I do. I work six days a week, no matter what."

My Big Break

Spurlock says that for two and a half years he took a break from the usual mode of trying to get in the movie business by working at whatever jobs were around—gaffer, rigger, truck loader—all in preparation for being a director and having his own company. "I was working and one of the guys—Peaches, I think it was—said to me, 'Well then, quit and become a director,' when I told him that was what I really wanted to do. He said he once had that ambition, too. It really made me think.

"Another thing that was helpful was working for the Sony corporation as one of its spokespeople. That's how I learned a little bit about marketing and about other aspects of the business. Working with executives, I found out about branding. And how to make use of it."

Good lessons, as it turns out. Public relations. Branding. How to present. This may be one reason why Spurlock is so comfortable in front of as well as behind the camera, why his narrative voice seems to so easily pull together some of the *30 Days* episodes, providing a framework for those in which he does not appear. Spurlock is a natural performer, as is Michael Moore, and this quality of being an entertainer has unquestionably loosened and lightened up the form.

He won't talk about the then-upcoming film, nor even reveal its title, except to say that, yes, he is in the film, and that it involves his traveling to a number of countries. That it is somewhat about Osama Bin Laden. That's as far as he will go.

It is in the doc mode of traveling to foreign spots, to find and/or explore, and in the new tradition as well of a star of sorts taking us there.

Not so by-the-by, the movie has been purchased by the Weinstein Company. Spurlock says, "Harvey Weinstein has been so helpful from the start, taking and giving notes, making suggestions." Whether this is a good or a bad thing, only time will tell. But it is a sure sign of success, if perhaps a bit too reminiscent of the committee mentality that doc filmmakers have been avoiding. (And in this way it is counter to the notion of the individual voice of the doc form, which is part of the heritage of the form, at least since the 1960s.)

The two seemed to be especially preparing for the film's unveiling at the Sundance Film Festival in January of 2008. "If the movie gets in," says Spurlock with a bit of faked modesty, "you'll know the title at that time." He said that for him, Sundance is the "Super Bowl of film festivals," and when *Super Size Me* won, took off, and became a rage at Sundance, it was "the greatest day of my life. [Self-conscious beat.] I mean my professional life, of course. The birth of my son was the greatest day of my life."

Of course, the film did get accepted at Sundance, but this one did not win. And the title of the movie is *Where in the World is Osama Bin Laden?*

The Eureka Moment

Spurlock is originally from West Virginia, and studied filmmaking at New York University's Tisch School of the Arts. As he often recounts, he had been rejected by USC's film school five times, and so after NYU he stayed in New York.

"I had wanted to make a feature film for quite a while," he says. "I had a play produced, which won a prize at the Fringe Festival in New York. But the more I saw of plays made into movies, the more they felt like plays that were made into movies. It wasn't what I wanted my first film to be."

"I first got the idea for *Super Size Me*," he says, "after I saw a news item about two obese girls who were filing lawsuits against McDonald's, blaming them for their extra weight.

"The trigger came one fall as the holidays were just beginning. I was at home visiting my parents and watching television when I saw continual coverage about the lawsuit. At that time, you couldn't open a magazine or turn on a television without hearing about the obesity epidemic in America. People were always pointing the finger at the fast food industry, and though I had always believed that really nobody was forcing you to eat the stuff, that maybe there was something there.

"The more I thought about it the more I realized that they don't make, or anyway at the time didn't make, the content of the food known—how much fat and sugar was in it. And when I heard the lobbyist saying, 'You can't link our food to these two girls getting sick or being obese; our food is healthy,' I really began to wonder. That's when the whole idea got formed. I thought to myself, Well, if it really is nutritious, I should be able to eat it for thirty days straight, for breakfast, lunch, and dinner. And it was a perfect idea for me. It was a eureka. As soon I got the idea, I turned to Alexandra and said: 'I've got a great idea for a movie!' and I told her and she said, 'You are not going to do that!'"

But he did, the rules being:

1) He could eat only what was available over the counter.

2) No Supersizing unless offered (but it always was).

3) No excuses: He had to eat every item on the menu at least once.

"I'd worked in the [entertainment] industry for about ten to twelve years at that time and had just finished a series on MTV called *I Bet You Will*. It started as a Web show, and it was the first show to make it from the Web onto television," says Spurlock. The Webcase, as he called it, featured five-minute episodes of ordinary people doing odd or embarrassing stunts in exchange for money, such as eating a full jar of mayonnaise for $235 or a worm burrito for $265. It's not, of course, the food commonality that is so striking here, but rather the fact that these are stunts—silly ones, if you will. People performed them, and other people wanted to watch them. Surely this provided some sort of example, or potential pattern, for Spurlock.

For though his overall intent may have been one of health consciousness, with a countercultural edge and social slant, his Web site and MTV work gave him the commercial sensibility to create a highly entertaining film, in part by figuring out what might appeal to a youth market.

Super Size Me, it would seem, is the first Web-inspired documentary. (For the use of the Web for marketing, that kudo goes to *The Blair Witch Project*.)

New Techniques and the New Technology

And Spurlock is the first to tell you that Web editing is fast, cheap, and effective. Yes, he nods, the superimposed repeat images in *Super Size Me* were a Web style he consciously used in the film. It's all accomplished with the clever, mainly fast (Internet-influenced) eye and editing of a practiced filmmaker. As they do on the Web, images pile upon each other, superimposed, and not canceling others by a wipe or cut. "Let's face it," he says, "I'm from a remote-control culture. So my movies are frenetic, very quick in their rhythm. [Laughs.] Maybe I just have ADD or a short attention span."

(Curiously, this is a supposition about himself that Al Maysles made, deciding that he became a documentary filmmaker because he was so quiet. He had to really listen to people and learn to take mental notes in order to be able to focus, he says. For him, what he called his ADD became his ability to tune in to his subjects. Maysles keeps a journal these days of his daily activities to "cure" his ADD.)

The film has a recurring motif of cartoonlike images as well. Particularly effective are the increasingly ghoulish and gothically shot Ronald McDonald images that pop up periodically. While Spurlock could take credit for these, he doesn't.

Instead, he enthusiastically gets up to grab a nearby folder and pull out some of the paintings used in the film. One is "The Last Supper," a take on the Biblical image but with Ronald McDonald at the center; another is of the young child made out to be a cigarette-smoking and car-driving Ronald McDonald; and, of course, the dark, demonic image of Ronald McDonald, which comes up as a leitmotif throughout the film. These paintings are the product of New Jersey artist Ron English, who was already fairly well known for his work when Spurlock tracked him down. And, gesturing to the glass door that separates his office from his staff's, Spurlock indicates that the film's very witty chicken cartoon was created by one of Spurlock's staff who calls himself simply "Joe the Artist."

Of course, in the film, Spurlock does fully employ the conventions of the documentary mode: traveling, testimonials, charts, and graphs. The movie begins with rapid superimposed cuts of a map with obesity trends shown state by state, growing year by year, and identifying flags of where McDonald's are located in New York, and around the world. Spurlock's three doctors, who will monitor his physical condition throughout the thirty days, are identified by doc-like IDs on screen. And, most amusingly, we have the measuring and recording of Spurlock's own condition at the beginning and at the end of the movie.

As the filmmaker found out, a straight diet of McDonald's resulted in weight gain, mood shifts, and more serious problems: liver enlargement, sexual dysfunction, and hypertension. According to both the film and what Spurlock told me, some of the effects of this straight diet may be irreversible: "At the time, I just didn't know I was going to sustain liver damage and have my cholesterol and sodium levels at critical levels."

Spurlock claims that neither he nor his doctors had any idea how things were going to turn out after the thirty-day diet: "Perhaps nothing significant would happen. We didn't know." In this, he is within the doc tradition of going where the film and its events take you. Spurlock's more spontaneous methods are not the same as Moore's, who, audacious as he very well may be, still follows a classic (if degenerated, as some feel) model of a documentary with a specific social intent. Even when it appears to be the kind of Gonzo journalism that Hunter Thompson employed, it is still a social intent documentary, working toward ameliorating a wrong.

And while Spurlock's overall intent may be benevolent in the familiar socially progressive mode of the doc form, the guinea-pig model is a new one. (To make the point, we don't, for instance, see Michael Moore trying to survive on unemployment in Michigan.) Both may be in the picaresque or travel tradition, but then, this is an element of the documentary, no matter what.

Spurlock disavows any specific agenda or script. "I don't map it out. Who knows where it will go? Once we begin, then we start writing. And in the edit too there may be hundreds of renditions of the script."

Accordingly, Spurlock says he rejects any kind of manipulation of reality. And about the term "stunt doc," he says: "You can call it whatever you like, but at the end of the day you're not seeing anything false in what I do. It's a real journey. Nothing is constructed. There is no false environment. I didn't build something to make something else happen.

"I am capturing an action as it unfolds. That, to me, is the definition of a documentary.

"I never know how it's going to end. How we will get to point Z. That's a great journey we go on together. For instance, in *Super Size Me*, I didn't come in to prove anything. Remember, I had three doctors who didn't know what was going to happen either."

Whether or not there will be a cinematic follow-up of matching proportions, the effects of Spurlock's film have been spectacular. In his own words: "Yeah, they've completely done away with 'Supersize' options. It's a huge accomplishment. [But] for me, the film is not an indictment of McDonald's; it's an indictment of fast food culture. It's an indictment of the food industry as a whole. It's an indictment of a food industry that sells gigantic portions, that sells food that is filled with fat and sugar, that markets to kids."

Spin-Offs Don't Bother Me

And stunts spawn other stunts, which, of course, can only bring more attention to the original stunt. A Canadian teacher decided to prove Spurlock wrong by eating McDonald's but exercising the whole time. He did lower his blood pressure and did lose weight. However, he ate McDonald's salads too.

Spurlock brushes off these kinds of films, and with a laugh. "For me, McDonald's is iconic. It represents the 'everyfood.' They are the biggest chain in the world, and by being the biggest chain, they're the ones that most easily can institute a shift. And that's what's happening. Now they've said, 'We're a part of this problem. We're a part of what's going on, so we're going to change our menu.' By them doing this, it will happen across the board. It will happen at Wendy's, Taco Bell, Burger King. All of them will now say, 'You know what, we need to do this as well because we care about you.' They don't want to be seen as the guys who don't care about you now. They want to say they care about you as much as McDonald's. So they're all going to follow, one into the other. So as McDonald's introduces public health into [its] menu, so will everyone else.

"Once you leave the cities, your healthy food choices really become limited. If you're only eating at restaurants, you won't find many healthy options. It's really a chain mentality, and that's what the film is examining. We've really become a chain culture. It's not just fast food. It's not just McDonald's. It's all of these chains. You think you're getting better food, but the portion sizes are massive. You get this plate of pasta at Olive Garden that's 1,500 calories by itself. People really need to examine these choices.

"In Texas, for instance, there were definitely big people, and in West Virginia, where I grew up, there were definitely big people there. This isn't a picky epidemic. It isn't choosy where it strikes. It's pervasive across the entire United States. It's really enveloped our entire country, and so that's part of what we wanted to show. It's not just here and there. I mean, in New York City, where people walk all the time, there's still a 25 or 30 percent obesity rate now."

All fine enough, but what drove the message home was Spurlock's witty use of doc film techniques. He has interviews with the three doctors who monitored his downhill slide, and they give facts, figures, statistics in quasi-documentary style. They seem to tell the truth.

My Doctors, My Stars

For instance, the highly credible Dr. Darryl M. Isaacs, Spurlock's internist, is hilarious in his perfectly timed response to the question, "Should people eat fast food?"

Ironic hesitation for effect. "Uh ... [more hesitation] ... no."

"Audiences love Dr. Isaacs," Spurlock laughs. "He's a really cool guy. He enjoyed doing some of the promotion for the film. And, no, there were no financial tie-ins, ever.

"Dr. Isaacs is right around the corner on Mercer Street, one of the three doctors who monitored me. And he's still my doctor. So from the film I got both a real good character and also a doctor."

The movie includes testimonials from his girlfriend about his failing sexual prowess, and Spurlock told me that he was deliberately not present when the scenes with her were shot. "I let Scott, my DP (director of photography), shoot those sequences so she could feel free to say what she wanted," Spurlock said. There are pictures of how he looked when started the 'Supersized' diet, and how he progressively looks fatter and less muscled, as well as side-by-side charts indicating how his erection declined too: Photos of Morgan in a bathing suit with a condemnatory, cartoon-like arrow pointing to the offending spot.

Fat, calories, and grams are weighed and recorded. All of this lent a kind of *gravité* to the experiment, broken by an occasional tongue held firmly in cheek. And it is to the investigative, data-oriented form of the documentary that the film's success is at least partially owed. Because otherwise, the humorous tone of the film, while wonderfully entertaining and fun to watch, would have been just and only that—just another MTV sketch or hip Web site prank.

Something Old, Something New

Yet while there is no question that McDonald's is the enemy here, along with Burger King, Taco Bell, and all the chains that Spurlock mentions, *Super Size Me* is not an entirely one-sided presentation. And in this sense the film imitates—if in a highly pop way—the old-style balanced documentary. For instance, Spurlock decides and shows that because a fast food chain like California's In-N-Out actually makes its food fresh, it's as good as it can be (the film shows real potatoes being peeled at the restaurant) and is not as meretricious as the other fast food spots. For more factual backup, the DVD includes a conversation between Spurlock and Eric Schlosser, the author of *Fast Food Nation*, and they discuss the slaughterhouses, packaging, and delivery of stale food across the country.

In a follow-up to the successful thirty-day motif, for the FX channel Spurlock filmed his and Alexandra Jamieson's attempt to live on minimum wage for a month; they picked what they thought would be a typical American city: Columbus, Ohio. The story begins with the couple locking up all of their savings and credit cards, to force them to not tap into other resources and to start with only one week of minimum wage ($5.15/hour) savings, totaling around $150 each. Spurlock got a job as a construction worker, while Alexandra found work as a dishwasher. Though they did scrape by, at the end of a month they were in debt, partly because Spurlock had hurt his wrist on his construction job.

Other thirty-day experiments were conducted: working at Wal-Mart, being incarcerated, living with a gay person. All for thirty days. Though Spurlock told me that after their stint in Ohio in the dead of winter, his wife told him: "You're on your own from now on."

Still, the question remains: How many stunt docs will a filmmaker be able to undertake in his or her working lifetime? While the McDonald's idea was a good one that really caught on, the minimum wage concept has already been made use of in print by Barbara Ehrenrich. And on film—a riff on this topic by Lynn Hershman Leeson, an experimental filmmaker and professor in Northern California who went on the road pretending to be an itinerant worker and filmed her experiences.

The Sincerest Form of Flattery

A recent entry in the stunt doc category is *King Corn*, a movie directed by Aaron Woolf, which tracks two twenty-two-year-old real-life friends,

Ian and Curt at the harvest of their crop in *King Corn*. Courtesy Mosaic Films, Inc.

Ian Cheney and Curt Ellis, to a tiny town in the middle of Iowa, where they plant and grow an acre of corn and follow its growth and journey for a year.

The 2007 documentary has a number of elements reminiscent of *Super Size Me*, including an expert in the field. *King Corn* includes an interview with Michael Pollan, whose book, *The Omnivore's Dilemma*, deconstructs the average meals of Americans. Where *Super Size Me* was backed up by Eric Schlosser and *Fast Food Nation*, at least in its DVD, *King Corn* has Pollan.

Similar to Spurlock's journey, the two pals, Ian and Curt, take a cross-country road trip and keep track of their meals. They run their hair through a spectrogram, which determines what they've been eating, and it seems that it is mainly corn. They decide on Iowa because both of their great-grandfathers came from the same town there. They follow their crop to see how modern farming is contributing—not necessarily deliberately—to the obesity crisis of America. What they find is both hilarious and horrifying: genetically modified seeds and home-brewed corn syrup, a bumper crop of obesity and diabetes, and a government paying farmers to grow what's making us fat. According to the movie, high-fructose corn syrup sweetens our sodas, corn-fed beef makes burgers fat, and corn oil crisps our fries.

But the film, unlike *Super Size Me*, does not point the finger at any corporation or particular group. Rather, it is a system, not one particular individual, responsible for the problem. In this way its tone is much less histrionic than the documentaries of a Michael Moore, or even the one-sided presentation of a Spurlock.

Luminaries Work the Form

The autobiographical narrative, whether or not it uses stunts, has become so appealing that even big-name directors are working, and working in, the form. For instance the highly regarded director Sydney Pollack (*Tootsie, Out of Africa*, to mention just two) chose to do a film about a friend of his, Frank Gehry, the very successful, if sometimes controversial, architect (the Bilbao Museum, the Walt Disney Concert Hall, and the Staples Center in Los Angeles, among many others).

The film is structured on the matrix of a two-person conversation, with about 40 percent of the film focusing on Pollack who, of course, does the narrative voice-over as well. So the new formats for docs were open-ended enough to attract Pollack. As he said, "Since I'm not a professional documentarian, I didn't really attempt what I would call a traditional documentary. I was trying to satisfy my own curiosity about Frank's creative process. So for me, it was a perfectly selfish exercise in trying to understand what went on in Frank's head when he created something as beautiful as the Guggenheim in Bilbao. I became obsessively curious. Though I must admit, when I first saw it myself, I was stricken by it. I didn't get it. I kept thinking it was as if Don Quixote got stoned.

"What I learned in the course of making the film was a reaffirmation that the creative process in all of us is terribly dependent on keeping the child alive in all of us. You have to be in touch with the playful part of your nature. What you see in the film is Frank playing the way a child might, with blocks or toy soldiers. It was also somewhat reassuring to see that the anxieties, concerns, highs, and lows are similar in all creative people," Pollack said after screening the film in 2005 at Symphony Space on Manhattan's Upper West Side.

Including himself.

Pollack laughed about this aspect of the film. "I realize it's a bit narcissistic. I mean, who is this guy [me] shoving himself into the movie?"

Birds of a Feather

Not that it's uninteresting, but a great deal of *Sketches of Frank Gehry* brings up comparative insights between Gehry and Pollack on what it is like to be Jewish, go through therapy, and to be in charge of creative projects. These activities are not necessarily connected though it sometimes does seem so in the movie business. The film does, of course, show examples of Gehry's work, and in doc mode, it travels to places where his buildings have been erected, and includes interviews with locals about how they feel about the buildings. And there are also one-on-one interviews with Michael Ovitz, Michael Eisner, and Dennis Hopper (who lives in a Gehry-designed house). We travel to visit doyen Philip Johnson to get the revered architect's opinion of Gehry's work. (He likes it.) There is even the time-honored doc tradition of giving a bit of the other side—an architect who is critical of Gehry is interviewed.

The movie's structure is reminiscent of *My Dinner with Andre*, Louis Malle's 1981 film about two old friends discussing life and art. Similarly, Malle's film was considered too static by many critics, and yet for Pollack's film, the doc format has solved that problem through its use of travel and interviews.

Pollack, who appeared at times in his own feature films, was already in the auteur, Hitchcock-derived tradition of what you might call self-cameos. Pollack's background was in acting, having studied under Sanford Meisner, before he eventually moved to directing and producing. So it seems natural that he took small parts that came his way, roles such as a partner in a law firm in *Michael Clayton*, the agent in *Tootsie*, films he also produced and in the case of *Tootsie* directed. A much admired and widely liked figure, Pollack died of cancer in the summer of 2008.

But he is also in the reflexive—some call it the self-reflexive—mode of the new documentary, inserting himself in his pictures. Happily for him and his films, he was used to being on camera. (Gehry too seems quite comfortable in his own skin and at ease in the limelight. This is surprising, for Pollack told me Gehry is very shy in person.)

Contacts, and Using Them

"I actually met Frank at a party in the early eighties, not quite thirty years ago," Pollack said when he was in New York City two years before his death. "And I suspect we were drawn to each other because we were both big complainers. We were complaining to each other about the difficulties of working in fields where you have to be validated by masses of other people. The world of commercialism, if you will. I had done the film *Tootsie*, so I had some standing. Frank was the up-and-coming, avant garde, interesting, anti-establishment guy. He had not attained anywhere near his present stature, but he was a guy to watch."

Pollack said he worked on the project off and on for a number of years until "an artist who adored Frank's work put up the seed money for the film," and that it was actually Gehry's idea for Pollack to be the director. "Frank said to me, 'Have you ever done a documentary?' and I said, 'No.' At which point he said, 'That's why I think you'd be good at it.'" It's pretty clear that the freshness of vision, or a "new look," is what Gehry had in mind, and it seems born out of what Pollack said he experienced. "You don't know what the hell you're doing. It was like making a documentary in relation to classical documentaries, like Frank's work relates to classical architecture."

Overall, and responding to the new creative opportunities of the newly formed neo-doc, Pollack said, "I found the experience of making a documentary very liberating. There's a marvelous freedom to trusting your impulses. I wish I could find a way to bring some of those techniques into the making of fiction films."

Pollack was not the only filmmaker—though he may be one of the more recognizable names—to comment on the opportunities for improvisation and creative input in the doc mode and to observe that feature filmmaking is by comparison these days a huge and unwieldly behemoth. Add Pollack to the list of doc filmmakers who fulfilled the doc form's capacity, even requirement, for improvisational techniques.

The obvious danger to this is that with the great new success of the doc mode, it too will become subject to the pitfalls of its more structured brother/sister, the feature film. Potential case in point is the overseeing of Morgan Spurlock's "Bin Laden" film by Harvey Weinstein of the Weinstein Company. Whether or not Weinstein made good suggestions, it is still another editorial hand in, and potentially not just the vision of the documentarian. And where a filmmaker like Spurlock could go on the road with only a director of photography, and shoot and complete a film for $65,000 (other documentary filmmakers question this figure, which Spurlock cited to me), once success enters the picture, a film can become—if the filmmaker wishes, clearly—subject to the same advice dispensed from the money men that independent filmmakers used to complain about.

By taking such advice, the filmmaker risks moving away from the kind of personal documentary to which it is indebted.

Whose Idea Was It, Anyway?

Perhaps reflecting the temper of the times, the personal documentary became popular in the 1980s, growing out of film societies and film festivals. Ralph Arlyck's *An Acquired Taste* (1981) has the filmmaker ruminating about the highly competitive media world (the film begins with an Academy Awards ceremony he is not part of) and about his own lack of a killer, competitive instinct.

In 1986, Ross McElwee shifted to the personal or autobiographical documentary and made some connections between his own experiences and that of society at large. In *Sherman's March*, McElwee tells of his decision to trace Sherman's route through Georgia. McElwee starts out visiting historic sites. But having just broken up with his girlfriend, he is intent on finding a new one. History and his personal needs run parallel, and as he travels he meets and has some off-the-wall experiences with women, accompanied by some deadpan comments that our later generation of film watchers might see as resonating with the ironic commentary of Morgan Spurlock in his fast food journey. McElwee follows his route and also finds a girl. In his next film, *Something To Do With the Wall*, completed in 1990, the couple has married and pay a visit with their child to the Berlin Wall in its final stages of disintegration. (Just so, *Where in the World is Osama bin Laden?* ended up including the pregnancy of Alexandra, by that time married to Spurlock, and the birth of their child.) The personal and the political have merged for McElwee, and hopefully for those watching his films.

It turns out that many of the luminaries in documentary filmmaking credit and admire McElwee, who now teaches at Harvard. He says he takes a long time between films and is modest about the praise from other filmmakers.

McElwee also seems to have elicited a positive response in some of today's younger filmmakers. Celia Maysles, for example, spoke enthusiastically of his work, how it had touched and influenced her own.

I Did It My Way

Alan Berliner is a relatively well-known New York filmmaker who has been working in this form for a number of years, as shown in his films *Intimate Stranger, Nobody's Business, The Sweetest Sound,* and *Wide Awake.* I spoke with Berliner just after *Wide Awake* aired on HBO for the first time. He says he sees his movies as a mix of documentary and avant garde film.

Even as early as 1997, the marriage of fiction and documentary comes up in comments about his films. In the January 12 *New York Times*, Phillip Lopate notes that Richard Pena, program director of the Film Society of Lincoln Center, said of Berliner's film *Intimate Stranger*, a movie about his maternal grandfather: "Mr. Pena compares *Intimate Stranger*, with its own multiple, contradictory narrators, to *Citizen Kane*. Mr. Berliner agrees that *Citizen Kane* was an influence. The point is that Mr. Berliner's storytelling may have more in common with the subjective psychology of characters in fiction films than with the traditional documentary's display of fact as objective truth."[2]

But Berliner, though working in the confessional, even the artistic, mode, is nevertheless using documentary conventions. While historically this is traceable to the cine clubs and art films of the very early doc movement of Europe in the 1920s, for today's watchers this kind of doc may seem to have as much in common with the New Journalism. It is impressionistic, self-involved, and full of personal pain and pleasures.

For example, *Wide Awake* examines, quite wittily, the filmmaker's insomnia, and its possible genetic/family origins. It shows the effects Berliner's insomnia has on his immediate family, work, and domestic schedule. "It would be nice, Alan," says his wife plaintively at one point, "if we could go to bed at the same time."

"I received so many e-mails about the movie from other insomniacs after the HBO premiere," Berliner proudly observed to me over the telephone in the summer of 2007, just after the film aired.

The doc format is in use—archival footage, sometimes from his own family files, and interviews with members of his family. And bits about New York City, the city that, like Berliner, never sleeps. Berliner is perhaps making a lighthearted homage here to the great city documentaries of the 1920s, the subgenre started by painter-documentarian Walter Ruttman in, for instance, 1927's *Berlin: Symphony of the City*, directed and edited by Ruttman and photographed by Karl Freund. Aesthetically sophisticated and painterly, Ruttman's film started a wave of city symphonies including tributes to Düsseldorf, Stuttgart, and Hamburg.

Berliner's nighttime footage of his insomniac's view of New York is cleverly intercut with clocks and nocturnal elements, visually stunning in an art-for-art's sake way. No surprise here—Berliner is clearly an intellectual, and he studied filmmaking at SUNY Binghamton, a place he praises for its program stressing the relationship between filmmaking and the other arts.

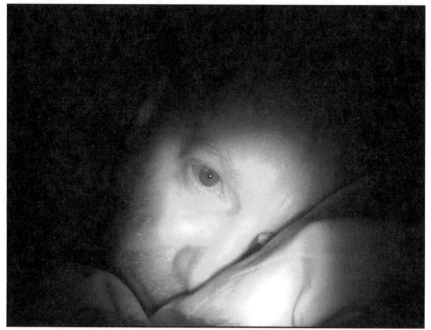

Alan Berliner has trouble sleeping and makes a documentary about it in *Wide Awake*. Infrared image from the film, courtesy HBO Documentary Films.

He adds that he had initially wanted to go to the University of Buffalo, also known for its progressive approach to film and the arts, but that his New York businessman father, the subject of Berliner's documentary *Nobody's Business*, felt it was too far away, so they settled on SUNY at Binghamton (literally half the distance). Berliner grew up in Queens, New York, and now works in his downtown loft in Manhattan. He and his wife, an economist, and their son, live uptown.

One of his earliest films is *The Sweetest Sound*, a doc about twelve people he has rounded up who have his name. How strongly did this influence a contemporary film such as *The Grace Lee Project*, a clever film about how one's name can influence behavior, made in 2005 by twenty-seven-year-old documentarian Grace Lee? The Harvard grad and doc filmmaker decides that her own name—Grace—encouraged certain "good girl" behaviors, and she set out to determine if there are some Grace Lees out there who broke the mold. (She finds some.) How indebted was Lee to Berliner, or was she simply making use of the new autobiographical forms of the neo-doc? She answers some of those questions in chapter 9.

Father Knows Best

In 1996's *Nobody's Business*, which is about Berliner's father and the filmmaker's attempts to get his dad to tell his own story, the generational differences are explicit; it's a kind of feisty, intellectual tête-à-tête between father and son. Contrasting lifestyles, including the son's need to find out about his roots, something not shared by his father—"Who cares?" is the senior Berliner's constant refrain throughout the film—are illustrated by basic doc techniques: archival footage, trips to Poland to try to find his ancestors' graves, and interviews with his own family members, both close and only recently discovered. The film was well received when it was shown at the Lincoln Center Film Festival, and Berliner *père* was on hand. Still, to this viewer, some of the funniest lines are when the senior Berliner says, "You have one bad habit and you best get over it. You think that if something is important to you, it's got to be important to somebody else, but everybody has his own sense of values. It's important to you, great, it's not important to me. I don't care about it."

It leads one to wonder what the elder Berliner would have to say about the films of Morgan Spurlock, who proved that what is important to him may have turned out to save the lives of thousands of Americans.

What Dad Hath Wrought

Mark Wexler is another documentary filmmaker who makes mainly personal documentaries. The son of famed cinematographer and director Haskell Wexler, Mark spent ten professional years of his life as a magazine photographer before becoming a full-time filmmaker within the personal mode.

Wexler spoke with me about his work in the fall of 2007, by telephone from his office in Santa Monica. He was frank about his career, his films, and his feelings about his father: much-improved relations, he says, via the making of *Tell Them Who You Are*, his film about his father. And himself.

The title of the film, by the way, comes from the proddings of his father when the younger Wexler would first show up for work on a photography shoot.

Wexler, who is fifty-two, says, "For any number of reasons I didn't want to be necessarily associated with the movie business. I didn't want to trade on my dad's name. Yet since he and my mother, who was a painter, were both such visual people, it was inevitable that I would end up doing something in the visual arts."

A scene from *Tell Them Who You Are* from the Wexler Family
Archives. Courtesy Wexler World, Inc.

After a bit he started making movies, documentaries as personal if not as
flamboyant as those of Michael Moore.

The younger Wexler says that he had to either make a film about his
father, Haskell Wexler, or go into therapy. And making a film seemed
cheaper.

Wexler has made other docs, however. One is about twins, another about
a Jewish matchmaker who was trying to get him, Wexler, married. He is
currently working on a project about health and longevity. He explains: "One
of my films, though I wouldn't call it a personal documentary, was about
twins because my first serious girlfriend was a twin, and I became interested
in the twin phenomenon. My second film, *Me and My Matchmaker*,
was about a Jewish matchmaker who complicated my personal life." He
laughingly says he has a friend who refers to three of his movies—*Me and
My Matchmaker, Tell Them Who You Are*, and his current health and longevity
project—as "The Wexler Trilogy."

"My love of flying was one of the main reasons I chose to produce a
documentary about Air Force One—perhaps the only film I've done that
wasn't in the first person. We were granted rare access to the plane and had
the opportunity to interview both Presidents Bush as well as Clinton and
Carter." (In one of the sequences in *Tell Them Who You Are*, you can't help
but observe that Haskell Wexler shows his most sardonic side as he makes
fun of Mark's relationship with these "power figures.") "I would say, though,

that the film I'm most well known for is *Tell Them Who You Are*, and it's true that it has definitely helped my relationship with my dad, who, of course, has been so very brave in letting me film him."

Let Me Entertain You

"I've always felt that entertainment is the key to making a great film. It's also essential that the filmmaker be passionate about his or her subject. Most documentaries take several years to finish, several years in which you essentially live with your subject, so you'd better be passionate about it," he said. "Because you are not doing it for money. I've always been interested in father/son relationships, particularly my own, since it's been complex. I wanted to explore our relationship. As the subject's son, I was always a participant in each scene we were filming, but during the lengthy editing period, it was interesting to be able to step out of the situation and observe the interplay between my father and me as though I were just an outsider. As Jane Fonda says in the film, it's the child's duty to go to the parent before it's too late to work out any difficult relationships."

Wexler says, "Jane knew I was making a film about my dad, but I think she probably thought it was more of a tribute film. And halfway through the interview, she just stopped and started crying and said, 'I didn't know we were gonna get into all this.' Because I think she had a lot of feelings about her dad, similar to mine. And she also made the movie *On Golden Pond*, also to reconcile with her dad. There were a lot of parallels, I think, in our lives."

In *Tell Them Who You Are*, there are doc-style interviews with Fonda as well as with Milos Forman, Dennis Hopper, George Lucas, and Martin Sheen, people who know and have worked with Haskell Wexler throughout his career, and some of whom know of the not occasionally strained Wexler family set-up. "My dad's an artist, so he's an opinionated guy sometimes, so I didn't think it would be any different onscreen. I hoped that the film would be a way of reconciling with him and bringing us together, which it has."

Family First

"In the film, I'm filming him, he's often filming me. And I think we felt more comfortable with each other sort of hiding behind the camera. The camera was sort of a shield for me, anyway. So I think the film was a real way to go about reconciling with him. And that's what I had hoped the film would be. I know he loves me and I love him.

Haskell Wexler in foreground, Mark Wexler looking
at him, both "hiding" behind their cameras.
Photo credit: Douglas Kirkland

"I can't tell you the number of e-mails I've gotten from people who say things like, 'I haven't spoken to my father for ten years, but now that I've seen your movie, I'm going to call him tomorrow.' It doesn't get any better than that."

While there are elements of the film-within-a-film, and the insider industry movie, as well as the autobiographical/personal film, what seems to make the doc form especially appropriate here is the sense of really being there. Family photographs, home movies from Haskell Wexler's own childhood, and interviews with family friends—albeit those friends may be the likes of Michael Douglas. Old photographs are layered together in ways that mimic three-dimensional space and shift in interesting ways according to different camera movements. Without these contributions from the documentary form (as well as the fame of the subject of the movie), it would be just another father/son exploration, as interesting as that might be. There is even a bit of voyeurism, as you wonder about the personal lives, even the aging process, of some really talented and famous folks. Haskell Wexler does allow his son to give a warts-and-all portrait with personal as well as professional probes.

Wexler says he was first intrigued by the autobiographical mode of filmmaking because he was moved by the work of Hunter S. Thompson as a practitioner of the New Journalism. There was no eureka moment, just a gradual realization that although he may have resisted filmmaking for a while, it simply became an inevitability.

He used his own money, approximately $300,000, he says, to make *Tell Them Who You Are*. And while he thinks it's terrific that equipment is now so inexpensive that many try their hand at documentary filmmaking, he cautions against unrealistic euphoria: "Unless you can get people to work for free, or for some sort of barter—and it's great if you can—you still have to pay people to do work, especially if you want professional help." This is probably a realistic warning note in a movement that a lot of people may find more time-consuming, and more expensive, than they had first hoped.

So add Mark Wexler to the canon of filmmakers freely mixing in some of the new documentary film techniques with the old. *Tell Them Who You Are* is full of self-references, placing it firmly in the reflexive doc mode while simultaneously being in the framework of a personal doc.

"For me as a filmmaker," Wexler observes, "one of the more interestingly difficult aspects was that there were scenes in which I was in a conflict. For instance, the scene with my mother—who is in a nursing home now with Alzheimer's—when my father visits her. Some things were revealed that I just had to get on camera because they were so dramatic. But as a son I was reacting in quite another way. I was in a raw emotional state. So that was quite a challenge. To flip back and forth between filmmaker and participant is an interesting dance."

Curiously (or maybe not), Haskell Wexler has spoken many times about a similar sort of conflict. In making *Medium Cool*, he has often been cited as saying he felt he had to choose whether or not to actively participate in the Chicago riots going on around him—or to keep his cool and get it on film. For the most part, he stuck to his role as filmmaker.

This much, at the very least, Wexler has inherited from his father.

Generational Drift

Today's documentaries do seem to be yielding a number of father/son explorations, not just in structure, but on a thematic level as well. This may be because the woman's movement has already tapped the vein of mother/daughter connections, at least for now. These days, it's men who seem a bit more confused, and the "truth-seeking" but newly personal doc form may hold a strong appeal. The personal doc can use archival family photographs and interview family members, and it can travel to family places of origin. And, of course, it is subjective, or emotional, though in the "butch" informational documentary format.

For men, it's a safe way to get emotional.

And another irony of the personal film is that currently there is a family struggle concerning the rights to the footage of *Blue Yonder* (to be distinguished from *The Wild Blue Yonder*, Werner Herzog's movie), the David Maysles film that was unfinished at his death. The film is in the vaults of Al Maysles, and Celia Maysles, David's daughter, says her uncle will not give her access to the footage. One of the reasons Al Maysles gives for refusing—and it becomes a sequence in Celia Maysles' film *Wild Blue Yonder*—is that he, Albert Maysles, may make an autobiographical film some day.

While it certainly may be the case (and the 1970s *New York Times* coverage of the Maysles brothers by Vincent Canby discussed in chapter 2 indicates that autobiography had been in the back of the brothers' creative minds for quite a while), it is a high irony that the purist Al Maysles should now advance his plan to make a personal film as a reason to not yield footage. Direct Cinema, as Maysles is so fond of saying, insists that the director have nothing to do with the subject.

• • • • • • • • •

Endnotes

1. A dual Q&A conducted by Logan Hill for *New York* magazine, "Woody Harrelson and Morgan Spurlock" on November 15, 2004. Harrelson gave nearly identical quotes on MySpace and YouTube.

2. Phillip Lopate, "American Family Life Wittily 'Revealed,'" *New York Times* (January 12, 1997).

chapter seven

THE DOCUMENTARY FILMMAKER
IN THE ROLE OF SPOOFMEISTER:
ROB REINER, CHRISTOPHER GUEST,
MICHAEL RITCHIE, ALEX KARPOFSKY,
SACHA BARON COHEN

• • • • • • • • • •

When *This Is Spinal Tap* was first shown to preview audiences in a Dallas shopping mall, according to Rob Reiner, "A small section of the audience laughed. The rest asked why we would make a serious documentary about a terrible band they had never heard of.

"It was alarming initially, but then I thought about what I had learned about the difference between satire and slapstick," says Reiner, in reference to his years on *All in the Family*. "Satire in general is a much more difficult style and form for audiences to grasp. It takes a certain sensibility and a certain amount of intelligence to appreciate satire. It's not really for everyone."[1]

Things have changed quite a bit since then—or perhaps audience awareness has—when a spoof movie such as 2007's *Walk Hard: The Dewey Cox Story*, will appear and everyone seems to already know that it is a send-up of biopics, in this case the recent film about Johnny Cash, *Walk the Line*. And the doc form has now become so much a part of our cinematic reference point that it is not only in the reflexive but also a referential mode, at least for sophisticated viewers. Some of *Walk Hard* is set in the style of director D.A. Pennebaker's black-and-white footage of Bob Dylan in Pennebaker's acclaimed 1967 doc about Dylan, *Don't Look Back*. It may also remind audiences stylistically of director Todd Haynes's take on that same period (and on Bob Dylan), in Haynes's film *I'm Not There*. One way of seeing this is that audiences have become so aesthetically knowledgeable that they know the difference, and, of course, advance publicity has made things clear in any case.[2]

But it was an entirely different situation in 1986, with Marty DiBergi (Reiner) appearing in the film as part of its framework, conducting interviews with the band members and commenting on Tap's history. Most of

The group Spinal Tap as they appear in the seminal, if not quite the very first spoof documentary: the rockumentary. Courtesy StudioCanal.

This Is Spinal Tap was originally shot on 16 millimeter and blown up to 35 millimeter, giving an even more exaggerated graininess reminiscent of vérité. In one scene, the group is seen performing on TV during the mid-1960s, captured with the quality of a kinescope recording of the live transmission, complete with a stretched horizontal plane and vertical transmission lines. In the words of critic Dan Harries, "It mimics the technical codes associated with … cinéma vérité—i.e., the mishaps associated with being at the moment of the happening—by using whip pans, shaky handheld camera movements and uneven lighting to create the look of a 'camera in the field.'"[3]

Standard documentary conventions are used obviously and well: black-and-white photos of the childhood of David and Nigel (Michael McKean and Christopher Guest), captions both to show the concert locations (with conventional establishing shots of various theaters) and to identify (fictional) figures within the recording industry.

Actors' Rules: Never Drop Character

And the put-on did not end there. Even the press notes to the re-release of *Spinal Tap* kept the literal tone:

Rock and roll is here to stay, and no one has done more staying than Spinal Tap!

Spinal Tap, the world's loudest band, set the rock world aflame when their comeback tour supporting their controversial twelfth album, *Smell the Glove*, was chronicled by rockumentary auteur Marty DiBergi.

Critics said their final tour would be the end of Spinal Tap. But over a quarter century, countless unfortunate drummers, and two additional final tours later, like a phoenix rising from the ashes, Tap has emerged triumphant for its newest comeback blitz: a new, special-edition DVD release, with commentary from the band, of DiBergi's seminal film that chronicles the sights, sounds and smells of Tap, *This Is Spinal Tap*.

The group—composed of lank-haired lead singer David St. Hubins, pseudo-poetic co-lead guitarist Nigel Tufnel, firefly and funny bass player Derek Smalls, catatonic keyboard wizard Viv Savage, and the band's fifth drummer, the late Mick Shrimpton—are captured here, raw and uncensored, in a defining moment in their development, the early 1980s. Documentarian and lifelong Spinal Tap fan Marty DiBergi gave up a lucrative shot at directing Wheat Thins commercials to fulfill his dream of following the fabled five across the American heartland, recording their electrifying, if badly attended, concerts and off-stage adventures.[4]

As with some other mockumentaries to come, including *Borat*, the publicity does not break tone or character.

Making things even more confusing by erasing the line between the spoof or goof and reality is the real-life extension of the rock group Spinal Tap, spun off from the film. Although the film refers to numerous phony Spinal Tap albums, the "band" since then has actually released five albums: *This Is Spinal Tap* (1986), *Christmas with the Devil* (1984), *Butch School* (1992), *The Majesty of Rock* (1992), and *Break Like the Wind* (1993). It has also conducted two national tours, produced several videos, and even created a corporate endorsement for IBM. By then, of course, everyone was in on the joke.[5]

The parodic form of the spoof documentary became such a recognized phenomenon that several recent academic books have come out, finding a pattern within the syndrome. One cleverly presented thesis comes from Harries, about *Spinal Tap* and *Zelig*, Woody Allen's faux documentary (another term used for the format): "Both [*This Is Spinal Tap* and *Zelig*] employ the conventionalized technique of interviewing people who are either related to the film's subject or called upon as experts in their field. In *Zelig*, real contemporary cultural heroes (including Susan Sontag, Saul Bellow, Irving Howe, and Bruno Bettelheim) are interviewed and offer their interpretations of the Zelig phenomenon. ... The fact that they are famous people playing themselves also adds an element of similarity to the parody. The transformation occurs in the role they serve as commentators on a fictional person, thus disrupting the level of validity aimed at the character's credibility."[6]

Schtick

Improv was a natural for Reiner, son of Carl Reiner, who grew up around Mel Brooks and Norman Lear. "Norman is responsible for the two big breakthroughs in my life," Reiner says now. "*All in the Family* and *This Is Spinal Tap*, which he convinced the studio to back." As a student at UCLA, Reiner founded the improvisational comedy group The Session and also had a stint with the famed improv group The Committee.

When *This Is Spinal Tap*—or *Tap*, as it is referred to in in-jokes—came out, Reiner was a thirty-seven-year-old television director. An accident was the catalyst for the movie, said Reiner, who now heads Castle Rock Entertainment. "As I remember it—and I probably do since I've told the story so many times—during the taping of a segment we had a breakdown in a special effects machine we were using. Chris [Guest] and Harry [Shearer] and Michael [McKean] started schticking around with these British rock 'n' roll characters. I remember thinking to myself, 'We should find a format for these characters.' And since I was the only guy who couldn't play an instrument, I got elected to direct."

"I did a late-night special for ABC called *The TV Show*," said Reiner. "One of the things we did a takeoff on was *The Midnight Special*. I played Wolfman Jack and introduced Spinal Tap. Chris, Harry, and Michael played three of the guys in Spinal Tap."

Thus the mock rockumentary as we know it was born. Still other earlier prototypes for this have been catalogued, such as a short piece on the *Swiss Spaghetti Harvest* that appeared as an April Fools' joke on British television. Critics and historians like to cite that brilliant if sometimes pernicious prankster Orson Welles and his radio broadcast "War of the Worlds" in 1938 as being the very first mockumentary, but Simon Callow's biography of Welles has pretty much dispelled the myth that the sensational impact of "War of the Worlds" was anything but an accident, as much a surprise to Welles as it was to everyone else. Welles announced on air that the show was a theatrical presentation, and it was only by the curious fact that some of the audience had tuned in late that they missed this disclaimer. According

Rob Reiner stays in character as director Marty DiBergi (a wink at Martin Scorsese's documentary about The Band) while making a mockumentary about the group Spinal Tap. Photo courtesy StudioCanal.

to Callow, and his very rigorous research supports this, Welles's thoughts were actually on his Broadway show, which was not doing that well—another reason why he couldn't have been focusing on perpetrating a hoax. Initially, he tried to disavow responsibility for the show when the hysteria and threatened legal action began, only later deciding to (successfully) use the publicity for his own ends.[7] "War of the Worlds," as much as it ultimately did for Welles, is simply not a deliberate mockumentary in the category of *This Is Spinal Tap* or *Borat*.

Plus, *Tap* makes full use of documentary conventions. There is the trip (here, a road trip), the interviewing of the band personnel, and a setting up of the historical background of the group with some quasi-archival footage. And there is the device of filming-within-the-film, in the persona of as Marty DiBergi (an homage to Martin Scorsese, for his documentary *The Last Waltz*, about the last days of the group The Band) using his own version of cinéma vérité to capture *Tap*. The year was 1986.

Shared Sensibility

Though Rob Reiner has not written or directed another mockumentary (or rockumentary), *Tap*'s co-writer Christopher Guest has. Two of his most popular are *A Mighty Wind* (2003) and *Waiting for Guffman* (1996). In fact,

Guest has become so well known for his documentaries, or mockumentaries, that the Museum of Modern Art held a retrospective of his work in 2005. Guest's other films include *The Big Picture* (1989), *Best in Show* (2000), and *For Your Consideration* (2006).

Some of the signposts of his films—aside, of course, from the extreme wit—are "relatively static one-on-one interviews with the subjects (i.e., talking heads), not totally unlike the so-called 'confessional' featured on some reality TV shows, and 'live' background noise on the soundtrack, such as the lovers in Mitch's motel in *A Mighty Wind*," says critic John Kenneth Muir, in his book *Best in Show: The Films of Christopher Guest and Company.* "There is even the sense that the camera is capturing life as it unfolds before us, not re-creating dramatic moments or conflict that happened once in a character's life." And though Guest himself rejects the term mockumentary, he says, "one can detect a context in which the descriptor 'mock' fits rather appropriately without connoting any hostile or ugly intent on the part of the filmmakers."[8]

In May of 1993, Guest told Louis B. Hobson, the entertainment writer for the *Calgary Sun*, "Our films are created in much the same way as a real documentary, in that we shoot eighty hours of film for a ninety-minute movie." But, like Frederick Wiseman, Guest rejects any fancy terms or categories: "I call it comedy that's done in a documentary style. People have adopted that term [mockumentary] because it's easy to use and say."[9] And to Mikes Standish in *MovieNews*, "I personally don't think you can do it outside of the documentary concept. I think [the format] sets the perfect structure to hang this on, and without that, you're lost."[10]

Another hallmark of Guest's films, placing them in the documentary context, is that many of them end with a coda accompanied by a tagline, such as "Six Months Later." However, he has said that the mockumentary form he helped create is not one with which he wishes to be identified exclusively: "It's a term I don't like or use. I think it's a bit cheesy. The last three films I've done have been in a documentary form. The next one, in fact, will not be," he said after a retrospective of his films at the Museum of Modern Art.

Many feel that it was Guest's creative oomph that was the driving force behind *This Is Spinal Tap.* When people are co-writers, and in the film business in general, it is practically impossible to figure out exactly who wrote what, whose idea was the original one, and so forth. But here is a brief description of Guest's creative background, which may help the reader draw her or his own conclusions. (Note that he has worked with another writer, Eugene Levy, on most of his other films.)

Guest, a Brit entitled to sit in the House of Lords, met Michael McKean when they were at New York University's Tisch School of the Arts and became roommates. A number of years later, McKean was a co-star on television's *Laverne and Shirley* with Penny Marshall, married at the time to Rob Reiner. Guest made appearances on *Laverne and Shirley* and *All in the Family*.

His sensibility is most perfectly on display in *Waiting for Guffman*, a film about an acting troupe waiting for the arrival of an influential critic. Guest takes the role of St. Clair, with stereotypically gay mannerisms. He supposedly has a wife, although no one has met or seen her, and for Guest aficionados, St. Clair is a role that they love to refer to. Of course, the influential critic Guffman never turns up. Here, as with *Tap* and with *Zelig*, and even *War of the Worlds* after the public's initial overwrought reaction, there is no doubt that something, someone, is being set up. This is the clever compartmentalization found by critics Roscoe and Hight in *Faking It*: "Like drama-documentary, mock-documentaries are fictional texts, but they position themselves quite differently in relation to the discourses of fact and fiction. In sharp contrast to drama-documentary, they tend to foreground the fictionality (except in the case of deliberate hoaxes). Whereas drama-documentary attempts to align itself with documentary in order to validate its claims to truth, mock-documentary utilizes the aesthetics of documentary in order to undermine such claims to truth. To play with, undermine, or challenge documentary, rather than to seek validity through an association with the genre."[11]

Guest himself does not have kind words about the chief proponents of some current documentarians. "You could do a parody of a Michael Moore movie. But I don't know what the point would be. I love documentaries. My problem is when the filmmaker becomes the star." He will not contribute to a theory about comedy, or the creation of his films, except to say that something is either funny or it isn't: "I find it really appalling when people talk about comedy." Nor does he have much regard for reality shows: "I've never seen a reality show. I don't watch television. The fun part about doing our movies is that you're creating something using the talents of people, rather than finding these pathetic people who are thrust into these situations. That to me is completely artless."[12]

And in an online interview with *The A.V. Club* about form and structure, he said:

> When I did *Waiting for Guffman* and the next two, those were done like documentaries. This current movie [*For Your Consideration*] is in narrative style—we dropped that whole documentary template. *Waiting for Guffman* was different right away from *Spinal Tap*,

because we didn't show the interviewer. That person became invisible immediately. That created a different way of tuning it and ultimately editing it. There was no person to cut to, to react to the person doing interviews—merely the people being interviewed. So there's an evolution through all of these movies, and now the biggest evolution by moving to narrative.

AVC: Why did you want to move away from that style?

CG: Well, we had done three, and we thought it was time to do something different. To take on a different kind of challenge. It is quite a dramatic difference in the way you construct a movie. With a documentary, you can cut away, you can do jump cuts, cut to a photograph at any point to bridge two scenes. And in *For Your Consideration*, you go from scene to scene the way you would in a typical movie.[13]

Where to Draw the Line? Is There a Line?

Spinal Tap was preceded by the difficult-to-categorize but nevertheless witty early mock-doc, *Smile* by Michael Ritchie. A satire of a beauty pageant which has actual stars as well as real people in it, the sly send-up rings true. "Everything in *Smile* is true," Ritchie told *American Film* when *Smile* came out. "I got the idea when some Jaycees showed me 16 millimeter home movies of their last Exhausted Rooster Ceremony. The guys cracking eggs on each other, the goosing with beer bottles, all came out of that little 16 millimeter film. We showed *Smile* in Norfolk Virginia to a group of Jaycees. They came up afterward and said, 'Wow, that was terrific. You know, we do our Exhausted Rooster Ceremony a little differently, but from now on we're going to do it the way they do it in the film.'"

The viewers' belief that what they were watching was "real" is similar to the initial reaction of the first watchers of *This Is Spinal Tap*. Still, there are enough big names in the film—Barbara Feldon and Bruce Dern, to name a few—that you might think some folks would have caught on. For this viewer, the moment when Barbara Feldon as the housemother/coach of sorts says, to encourage her girls, "Beauty knows no pain," will forever rank as one of the great lines of satire, wonderfully delivered.

Some of the verisimilitude and the inspiration for the film was explained by Ritchie (now passed away): "I'd been a judge at the Junior Miss Pageant in Santa Rosa. While all the guests thought I was taking notes about them, I was in fact taking notes on all the great things that were being said and the talent acts. Then came a moment of horror. The night before the final elimination, the head judge said to me, 'You're all going to be turning in your judge's books tomorrow. We have to destroy them so the girls will never see what's written about them.' And I had all these notes for the movie in my book! I frantically rushed back to my hotel room and stayed up all night copying down all the notes."

Making the Audience Complicit

The following statement is curiously prophetic of some of the manipulations that the current phenomenon of reality TV is employing. "To get reaction shots from an audience," Ritchie said, "we staged a real pageant, which contained a lot of stuff that we never filmed, just to keep the audience entertained. . . . We put on this two-and-a-half-hour show, which was like a beauty pageant. We kept the actual winners of the contest secret even from the girls who were acting in it. . . . They were real beauty pageant acts. For instance, the girl packing a suitcase was used in the Miss America finals in 1947. The Sincerity Strip, the girl that starts off with the wig, the fancy dress, and all the jewelry, and peels it off down to the simple leotard and holds the lilies at the end, is a standard beauty pageant routine. We copied it almost verbatim off the national films of Miss Teenage America. I think Miss Utah did it."[14] Big Bob Freelander is played by Bruce Dern, Brenda DiCarlo played by Barbara Feldon, Miss Anaheim was Annette O'Toole. The script was by Jerry Belson, directed of course by Ritchie, and the year was 1975.

What makes *Smile* different from director Ritchie's *The Candidate*, for instance, is that we know that *The Candidate* is about a fictionalized campaign: Robert Redford's presence forces us to acknowledge this, and the same thing with Ritchie's *Downhill Racer*. We are fully aware that those films can't possibly be real. Yet there are enough unknowns, or not-yet-knowns, in *Smile* to keep us guessing.

Even a latter-day viewing pulls you into the film, I think, as an "Is this for real?" feeling takes over.

The use of recognizable actors in the lead may be one factor which makes things obvious. Consider, for instance, the 1992 fake doc *Bob Roberts*: The film is a sophisticated blend of the full range of documentary codes and conventions, circling around the conventional expositional narration provided by the character of a journalist named Kerry Manchester, combining Manchester's coverage of Roberts (Tim Robbins) with documents such as photos of his childhood and early life, most notably

Roberts's music albums and videos. And even though the film was a satire a few people tried to vote for Bob Roberts as a write-in candidate, possibly because the star, Tim Robbins, was not well-known enough at the time to tip them off (though the character Bob Roberts was an odd duck of a guitar-playing, folk-singing, conservative—albeit corrupt—candidate).

A closer look would have indicated that Robbins was the writer-director as the well as the star. Of course, there is no obedience here to the rule that the film must make its intent known.

Kids Do Mock

In 1994, student filmmakers Heather Donahue, Michael Williams, and Joshua Leonard traveled to Burkittsville, Maryland, to film a documentary about a local legend known as the Blair Witch. They hiked deep into the woods, where unusual and frightening events took place, and then they disappeared.

The movie, of course, was *The Blair Witch Project*, directed by first-timers Daniel Myrick and Eduardo Sanchez. The entire film was a brilliantly successful hoax, even on its actors, who did not know that the people they were interviewing were in on the joke. Still, the movie used many doc techniques successfully: the handheld cameras (so successful that some viewers claimed they got sick watching the film), the trip to Maryland to explore the mystery, the interviews with the locals. To maintain the improvisational quality of the film so many documentarians have spoken of, the actors were given only a thirty-five-page outline of the mythology behind the plot, so all the spoken lines were impromptu. About this, Daniel Myrick told *Filmmaker* magazine that he was used to shooting movies in a traditional way due to his work as a cinematographer, but that he wanted "to combine narrative and improvisational modes using the fact that the expressions on the actors' faces were unrehearsed."[15]

A teaser poster and other advertisements for the film were designed to reinforce the "documentary" concept, leading many people to think the film was an actual documentary, and that the three really had disappeared in the woods. Following up, the Sci-Fi Channel aired a fake documentary, *Curse of the Blair Witch*. The program contained interviews with friends and relatives of the missing students, paranormal experts, and local historians. To this day, the hoax is still maintained on the Internet (see "The Aftermath" on the Web site for *The Blair Witch Project*, with a car of one of the "lost, presumed dead" actors supposedly found in the woods).

The Blair Witch Project was a huge financial success, making $250 million worldwide to date. Yet unfortunately, none of the principals involved in the film have managed to repeat any part of their successful formula.

In terms of film history and the mock-doc subgenre, *The Blair Witch Project* has a unique place, presciently spotted by Bernard Weinraub in his column "At the Movies": "By all accounts, what has made the film so successful is the Internet. Its Web site, *www.blairwitch.com*, blurred the line between reality and fiction. It displays 'police reports' and newsreel-style interviews that make the movie seem real. . . . The reaction to the Web site has been powerful; there have been nearly 80 million hits on it.

"'There was a young Internet audience out there that hasn't been tapped,' said Mr. Block [Bill Block, a partner at Artisan Entertainment, which presented the film], a former talent agent. 'This movie converges with that audience. They've embraced it. All the kids have seen it on the Internet. In some ways it's the first Internet movie.' Weinraub also quotes Amir Malin, another of the partners at Artisan, as saying that the *Blair Witch Project* found 'a niche the way *Easy Rider* tapped into a niche in the 1960s. It taps into an audience that's been weaned on television and the Internet.'"[16]

Myrick himself confirms this in a contemporaneous interview given to *Time.com*: "The Internet was early on our way of raising awareness about the film. It was an inexpensive way to promote the mythology and backstory associated with the movie. And that, in turn, generated a loyal fan base, which created a lot of buzz and word of mouth going into Sundance. And that's where it all started. The Internet was integral to all."[17]

This is distinct from the faux documentary aspect and the fact that Eduardo Sanchez, the other filmmaker responsible for the film, has said in every interview given about the film that "we wanted it to look like a documentary [handheld jiggly cameras and the like] because we had no money." Myrick has said so many times that he kept even the actors in the dark about plot developments for much of the film so they would retain their documentary-like freshness of response.

But beyond this, photographer Joshua Leonard, who worked on the film, told Brett Mannes of *Salon.com* that, "before we got out into the woods, we'd go into a restaurant. Now, we knew we were supposed to go into a restaurant, and we knew that we were supposed to stay in character. Now, this is a regular restaurant with regular people in it, but invariably inside there are one or two people who are plants. So what we've got to do is walk into the situation and, by process of elimination, figure out who's gonna give us our next plot point to get to the next person who we're gonna interview to continue the story. So we walk in and we start interviewing people about this bullshit myth, about the Blair Witch, who doesn't exist in the first place, and funnily enough, by power of suggestion, some people [who had nothing to do with the film] are like, 'Oh yeah, I have heard of that.'"[18]

This is a primitive prototype for the spoofy scenes that Sacha Baron Cohen and company have set up: It's a goof, it's a lie, and who is kidding whom? Yet because it is the formerly reputable truth-based doc mode that is being employed, it manages to both blend and challenge our notions of what is real and what is fake.

Though the *Blair Witch Project* did not have a successful follow-up, it still managed to 1) make a breakthrough in the mockumentary mode, which seemed to have reached a "you couldn't top this" apex with *This Is Spinal Tap* and the films of Christopher Guest; 2) use the Internet for marketing (if not style—for that we must acknowledge Morgan Spurlock); and 3) create the kind of unannounced use of plants that Cohen has so cleverly employed.

Cohen won't talk about the creation of those setups—always citing legal reasons—but Myrick, Sanchez, and Leonard did. Their "getting over" on people seemed a point of pride and part of their game plan.

The Highbrow Version

Another interesting case is *The Battle of Algiers*, a great and important film, but a faux documentary nevertheless. Here the filmmaker Gillo Pontecorvo always made it clear that he had fictionalized the film based on events that took place during the National Liberation Front's guerrilla war in Algeria. And though it makes use of documentary aesthetics, it is generally categorized as a drama-documentary. Still, Pontecorvo was so certain of his film's documentary look that after the credits, he informed his audience no newsreel footage was used in the making of the film.

According to Roger Ebert, "Pontecorvo's film remains even today a triumph of realistic production values. Filming on location in Algiers, using the real locations in the European quarter and the Casbah (which sheltered the FLN), he achieved such a convincing actuality that he found it necessary to issue a disclaimer: There is 'not one foot' of documentary or newsreel footage in his two hours of film. Everything was shot live, even riot scenes in which police battle civilian demonstrators."[19]

And, in fact, the film is so effective that prints subsequent to the 1965 film included the disclaimer. Still, the film seems so authentic that it is hard to keep the disclaimer in mind when you see it. For, by drawing on nonactors and locals (with the exception of Jean Martin, a professional actor, as Colonel Mathieu) and what seems to be shooting events in real time, with a documentary style, it presents a convincing on-the-spot account of the historical sequence of events; even including torture sequences.

Much has already been written about this classic 1965 doc, and it is not the purpose of this book to elucidate those comments any further. But it is worth noting that what made the film so effective was the typically cinéma vérité cutting, with dramatic juxtaposition, hand-held mobile cameras, overexposure, and shooting against the light to give the effect of on-the-spot reportage. There is also commentary briskly interpolating chronology, facts and figures, and brief biographies. As such, it has a newsreel authenticity captured by Marcello Gatti's grainy, black-and-white photography.

You might say it subverts cinema vérité to make a propagandistic film. Or you might observe that it is the ultimate in reconstruction, an entirely reconstituted film. Surely not a spoof, but just as certainly designed to make some comment by pulling the wool over the eyes of its audience.

My Midwest Winter

Though not as commercially successful as *This Is Spinal Tap* or *The Blair Witch Project* (that would be hard to top), Alex Karpovsky's 2006 *The Hole Story* is a mockumentary that similarly blurs the distinction between reality and fiction, though it also has elements of the personal or autobiographical film. It is confessional and intimate, and—taking things to the ultimate personal moment, perhaps, as does Alan Berliner in filming his wife on the toilet in *Wide Awake*—the most blatant of the narrator's confessions come as he is seen in three progressively close-up shots in his bathroom.

In fact, Karpovsky actually *is* a filmmaker based in Boston, who has been editing karaoke videos to support himself. And in *The Hole Story* he plays himself—a wannabe TV documentary director. In the film, he has given up his editing job to pursue his dream of selling a pilot to cable television. The pilot will be called *Provincial Puzzlers*, and the premise is that a number of small towns around the country have some similar riddle. First stop is Brainerd, Minnesota, in the middle of the winter, famous—at least locally—for a hole in the ice that spontaneously opens and closes every year. The director and his crew decide to film this phenomenon but in spite of temperatures well below zero, the hole is just not forming on North Long Lake. With his small crew (some of whom deserted the project throughout the making of the film), Karpovsky, appearing "as himself" in the film, assiduously searches for the hole, tries to figure out the reasons for its nonappearance, and conducts interviews with various laconic townsfolk who are in ironic contrast to his own highly voluble, introspective, even self-absorbed persona. The hole's nonperformance seems to have some cause-and-effect relationship with global warming, but the filmmaker's frustrated search also becomes a metaphor for his own sense of futility.

(Not that he necessarily had this in mind, but it is quite similar to Werner Herzog's trip to a Caribbean island to shoot a volcano about to erupt in *La Soufriere* in 1977, except that the volcano remained dormant.)

Ultimately, when it seems the event and his film are both doomed, Karpovsky has a kind of breakdown, which he includes in the movie. As in *Super Size Me*, there are scenes in which his doctor (the head of an institution into which the filmmaker has committed himself), is interviewed. We are present at group therapy sessions, where Karpovsky talks about his disappointment and receives advice for recovery.

Throughout *The Hole Story*, Karpovsky addresses the camera, in the tradition of the personal or autobiographical film, culminating with the chatting-on-the-toilet scenes in a series of increasingly detailed close-up shots, a kind of low-level confessional intimacy.

Alex Karpovsky, "playing" himself, goes on a rant in *The Hole Story*. Courtesy Spot Creative.

But it is the documentary outlines which are used the most effectively: the travel to a desolate place, the interviewing the townsfolk as if they were natives or at least ethnologically very different from the director-star, the loss of his crew in difficult conditions, and of course the coverage of an event (or in this case, non-event) in nature.

When I interviewed Karpovsky, he was living in a sublet apartment in Brooklyn's Williamsburg, and about to take off for an early summer shoot in Austin, Texas for a small acting part in a friend's film. "I am not one who craves the energy of Manhattan as so many do," he said, explaining that the Brooklyn proximity was plenty close enough for him to avail himself of Manhattan's numerous editing and technical facilities. "As you see," he says gesturing around, "I don't live luxuriously." And he described a bit about his ongoing deal with an independent film production company, but understandably declined to give financial details. When I talked with him, Karpovsky was working on his next movie, *Woodpecker*, about "America's fastest-growing recreational activity: birdwatching." Just completed as this book goes to press, the film is described by one critic as a unique combination of narrative and documentary.

Persona Plus

It took until 2006 for a spoof to be as commercially successful as *Spinal Tap* eventually became. Of course, I am speaking of *Borat: Cultural Learnings of America for Make Benefit Glorious Nation of Kazakhstan.*

"I admire the way he looks in a bikini," said Werner Herzog of Sacha Baron Cohen. "I wouldn't have the nerve to do that kind of thing myself." So much for Cohen as a serious filmmaker or a persona to be dealt with—in Herzog's opinion, anyway. Herzog is referencing Cohen's appearing at the Cannes Film Festival in May 2006, promoting his film in a high-cut bathing suit, a take-off on the old-fashioned early-twentieth-century men's bathing suits with straps (and a version of which you can order on one of the film's Web sites). Of course, while staying in character, Borat says it is the uniform of the Kazakhstan running team.

Nevertheless, and even if you wish to see the film as only a send-up, *Borat* (for short) is a great homage to the doc form. Recognizable documentary elements are used within the film: for instance the picaresque or travel tradition: going to another land to examine another culture. "I intend to take back the lessons about America to Kazakhstan," says Borat. Maps of Kazakhstan detailing Borat's trip are shown in the film, not dissimilar to the kinds of cartoonlike maps that Michael Moore uses in *Roger and Me* to find Roger Smith.

There are only four actors who actually take part in the film, and all the rest—from Senator Bob Barr to Alan Keyes to Pamela Anderson (and all spots in between, including the racist South Carolina frat boys)—are real-life people. With the exception of Anderson, the others had only partial awareness of the purpose of their interviews. They signed releases that declared, according to various reports, that the interviews were to be shown for limited audiences, or at the very least not in the US. Cohen defends this practice as being ultimately in the service of a "higher cause": "People were a lot less careful about making anti-Semitic or racist remarks if they thought the film wasn't going to be shown in the US, and this is exactly what we wanted."

Senator Bob Barr, for instance, knew his interview was being recorded; he just didn't know Borat was a made-up character—though the mention of the offered cheese as having been made from the breast milk of Borat's sister might have given him a clue. Too late by then, though. Yet to politician Barr's credit, he is rather cool about it.

Whatever one thinks of these practices—including the small fees paid to some of the subjects—it still brings up some hot documentary issues: how much warning to give a subject and whether an adversarial relationship should be maintained. In some odd and subversive way, *Borat* is actually using the older form of guerilla cinema vérité with a specific end, which precedes the softer personable interview Errol Morris developed, or the personal parallels Werner Herzog finds with his subjects. For Sacha Baron Cohen, it is one way of getting to his version of a higher morality, or so he says. And the end will justify the means.

Plus, for Borat—or rather, Sacha Baron Cohen and company—the controversy around the nondisclosure, and the lawsuits filed, were used to good publicity effect. For this film, anyway.

And it's not only when the frat boys from South Carolina turn on Borat that it's "real;" at the recent film festival promoted by Michael Moore in Traverse City, Borat's director, Larry Charles, showed another scene from the movie, shot in Texas, that didn't make it in. Borat goes to the door of unsuspecting locals, trying to sell them a newspaper subscription. When they let him in, he asks to use the bathroom, then emerges wrapped in a towel after taking a shower. The Texans politely ask Borat to leave, lock him out, and then call the police.

Will the Real Sacha Baron Cohen Please Stand Up?

Was all of this the brainchild of Sacha Baron Cohen? Not entirely, though he hedges this in my interview with him. That is, he drops back into character when a question comes up that he would just as soon avoid. The only way I got to talk with Cohen, and some of his writers was by being part of a Writers Guild of America West event in Los Angeles. For the most part, Cohen's public appearances are limited to strictly keeping in persona. The nuts-and-bolts stuff comes from the three writers who have worked with Cohen over the years—Peter Baynham, Dan Mazer, and Anthony Hines. Baynham says, "We've done this character for quite a long time, and Sacha is so in the mindset of Borat that he just knows instinctively what Borat will do in any situation. Which means that he can react and he can go with it, and it's beyond an acting job; it's a complete immersion."

The team does admit to imposing some narrative structure on *Borat*. Dan Mazer, who is the executive producer on *Borat*, says, "We were aware that you have to really like Borat and feel for him in order for you to go with him through the movie." This is, of course, contradicted by press notes to the film, which say: "There was no script. The movie is an experiment—a new form of filmmaking for an age in which reality and entertainment have become increasingly intertwined. Real events with real people push the film's fictional story, [especially] when scenes played out in unexpected ways."

Mazer has been around Cohen the longest. They met in school in England when the two were eleven years old. He describes the school as "basically a factory of comedy." In high school, Baron Cohen spent much of his time with a Jewish youth group, Habonim Dror, where he started acting. When he graduated, he took a year off to live in Israel at the Rosh Hanikra Kibbutz, then on to Christ's College at Cambridge University to study history, ultimately performing in productions including (but of course) *Fiddler on the Roof* with the Cambridge Footlights.

As is true of a lot of comics, when he does finally drop character or persona, he is earnest, often worried about work issues, and looks—without his Borat mustache—like any young professional on the Upper West Side of Manhattan or in Westwood, California. There is a vaguely intellectual air about him; Cohen, as is apparent from his educational credentials, is highly analytical, and was just on the verge of throwing in the towel and becoming a lawyer when he finally hit it big as a comic in England with his character Ali G.

Borat plays, too, with the spoof form: there's just enough reality in the movie to bring everything into question. It is, after all, the real Pamela Anderson in the film, and as an article written around the time of the movie's release queries, "On the way out of the theater, many of them [the audience in the theater] most likely cleared their hoarse-from-laughter throats and then asked: Who was in on the joke?"[20]

Pamela Anderson isn't saying, of course, though the publicity about her subsequent divorce papers (from Kid Rock, who said one of the reasons for their separation was that he didn't like her being in the film) did not hurt the movie's profit potential.

As broad as the satire is, the film is a spoof of ethnographic filmmaking, though this time the "natives" are Americans. There are unarguable observations. We are (still) racist, we do (still) idealize blond, big-breasted women, we are (still, probably, and in spite of everything) homophobic and antifeminist. And even if one prefers the more sophisticated humor of *Spinal Tap, Borat* is actually a mockumentary of social intent.

For instance, in the admittedly over-the-top nude scene between two men, Borat being one, the blubbery body and belly of Borat's would-be seducer is quite disgusting. We are left with little choice but to turn ourselves off, aesthetically. But in doing so, we encounter our own homophobia, acknowledged or not.

This spoof, these tricks, all depend on Cohen's highly developed and various personae. Besides Borat, of course, there is Ali G., who, though originally only available through English television, can now be seen worldwide on YouTube. If there is any question that Cohen is politically left-wing, or wishes to use his characters to make those points, his interview with Pat Buchanan about President Bush settles it. Buchanan answers the "stupid" questions in a straightforward way, demonstrating both his own gullibility in taking these questions literally, as well perhaps as a bit of racism. He never once questions the questions, implying perhaps that a "dumb" African-American interviewer like Ali G. would ask such questions, or that his audience would buy in.

The zinger is about the weapons Saddam Hussein supposedly has. "And does he have BLTs?" asks Ali G. "Yes," says Buchanan, "He used BLTs to bomb the Kurds in the north." Ali G.: "Was it worth fighting a war over BLTs?" Buchanan: "Yes, as long as they weren't nuclear weapons."

If you look closely you can see a small but knowing smirk on Ali G.'s (Cohen's) face. But he never really drops persona. And, of course, Buchanan doesn't catch onto the game.

How in the world did Cohen get Buchanan to not only be on camera and be interviewed, but to also not catch on? This is always a first question to Cohen, but he will never answer, because he says he is legally bound about revealing the methods used to entice people onto a show, or to be filmed. Compare here the makers of the *Blair Witch Project*, who kept up the artifice for their "actors" only while the film was being made.

Now that Cohen's identity and look are more well known, people will be chary about being interviewed by him (though obviously one should never discount his ability with disguises), and possibly this is why he is currently in features, rather than other satires. The moment has probably passed when he can get away with telling a NASA officer who he is quizzing, but who starts to wonder about Cohen's credibility, that it's the other guy who's imitating him, and he has hired a lawyer to deal with the imposter.

In his turning conventions inside out and upside down, Cohen may be seen as a kind of Jonathan Swift for our age. His modest proposals are as mind-blowing for us—anti-Semitism, for instance, being a moral equivalent of Swift's baby-eating.

One writer/critic, Neil Strauss, in *Rolling Stone* magazine, has decided that *Borat* has permanently changed the documentary form: Only a small cadre of central actors is used and all else is impromptu, he asserts, using real-life people, whether or not they know they are being so used.[21]

Future film historians will figure out whether or not the documentary form has been permanently altered by such tongue-in-cheek activities. Perhaps Cohen's *Borat* will remain only a riff on a more serious form. But on his own home turf, Cohen is taken quite seriously. He was given the *Evening Standard* (the highly regarded newspaper) Award for Best Comedy in 2006 along with—in their categories—such respected figures as Dame Judi Dench and Peter Morgan.

• • • • • • • • •

Endnotes

1. Interview with Rob Reiner, press junket for *This Is Spinal Tap*, Los Angeles, 1986.

2. This obviates the need some academic theorists have insisted on; namely that the spoof film be upfront about its intentions. An interesting comparison here can be made with Orson Welles's 1974 *F for Fake*, in which the very last bit of the film has a brief spoof—a kind of film-within-a-film—of what would have happened if Picasso and Oja Kodar had had an encounter. But then Welles comes on screen to say that this just-viewed sequence was a put-on.

3. Dan Harries, *Film Parody* (London: BFI, 2000), 53.

4. Press notes to the DVD release of *This Is Spinal Tap*, collected at the Billy Rose Theatre Collection of the New York Public Library for the Performing Arts at, Lincoln Center. Reprinted by permission of Embassy Pictures.

5. Scott R. Olson, introduction to *Parody as Film Genre*, by Wes D. Gehring (Greenwood Press, 1999), xiv.

6. Harries, *Film Parody*, p. 45.

7. Simon Callow, *Orson Welles, Vol. 1* (New York: Penguin/Viking, 1995).

8. John Kenneth Muir, *Best in Show* (New York: Applause Books, 2004), 6, 5.

9. Bob Strauss, "Extended Play," *Los Angeles Daily News* (April 13, 2003).

10. Mikes Standish, "Interview: The Cast of *A Mighty Wind*," *MovieNews* (March 10, 2003).

11. Roscoe and Hight, *Faking It, Mock-Documentary and the Subversion of Factuality* (Manchester and New York: Manchester University Press, 2001), 46. They preface this observation with the comment that "reflexive and performative modes of documentary are the factual precursors for the mock-documentary. Parody, irony, and various dramatic codes and conventions are utlised [sic] in order to make less familiar the documentary genre. Here forms have significantly expanded the documentary repertoire, yet crucially, while they have challenged the assumed boundaries of 'fact' and 'fiction,' they have nevertheless effectively left the foundations of documentary intact." p. 36.

12. Adam Sternbergh, "Wit," *New York* magazine (April 11, 2005).

13. Tasha Robinson, "Interview with Christopher Guest and Eugene Levy," *AVClub.com* (December 14, 2006).

14. "Interview with Michael Ritchie," *American Film* (November, 1997).

15. Stephen Gallagher, "Into the Woods," *Filmmaker* magazine (Winter 1999).

16. Bernard Weinraub, "At the Movies," *New York Times* (August 13, 1999).

17. "Transcripts," interview with Daniel Myrick, *Time.com* (August 11, 1999).

18. "Something Wicked," July 13, 1999.

19. Roger Ebert, "The Battle of Algiers," *Chicago Sun-Times* (October 10, 2004).

20. Larry Carroll, *MoviesonMTV.com* (November 6, 2006).

21. Neil Strauss, "The Man Behind the Mustache," *Rolling Stone* (November 14, 2006).

chapter eight

HAPPY HYBRIDS: KEVIN MACDONALD, JASON REITMAN, PETER MORGAN, ROY FRUMKES

· · · · · · · · · ·

S ome believe that the most creative, the most exciting, of all films being made today are those that mix documentary techniques and standard feature film methods (and setting aside for the moment the notion of the documentary filmmaker starring in his/her own film, the stunt doc, the biopic, or any of the fairly easily characterized subgenres). They are hard to categorize and even harder to describe, but that makes them no less compelling or successful.

There have been a number of such successful hybrids in the past few years; *Good Night and Good Luck*, probably because of the superstar status of George Clooney, comes to mind first. But there have been many others; for instance, the highly sensationalistic, high concept imagining of the British documentary, *Death of a President*, showing a digitized but very real-seeming assassination of George Bush. A less controversial hybrid is *The Last King of Scotland*, directed by Kevin Macdonald, who was up until that point mainly identified as a documentarian; he directed the Academy Award–winning documentary *One Day in September* in 1999, about the assassination of Israeli athletes by Palestinians at the Olympics, narrated—significantly for this study—by Michael Douglas, himself a superstar actor/producer and, of course, one more unmistakable voice narrating.

Recasting a Tyrant

The Last King of Scotland, about the final days of Idi Amin, was a huge success due in no small part to the highly praised and multiply—awarded performance of Forest Whitaker as Idi Amin, for which he won an Oscar. I spoke with Macdonald, a Brit, about the film and his directorial methods in the fall of 2006, when he was in New York City for the film's promotion.

His overall goal in filmmaking, he told me, is to go back and forth between feature films and documentaries. He was quite specific about how his background as a documentary filmmaker affected the shape of *The Last King of Scotland*. The well-spoken Macdonald sees his place in the history of film and filmmaking quite clearly: "I've got a theory of filmmaking, which is that there are two types of moviemaking. One is coming from the Hitchcock line, if you will, where people control every aspect of filmmaking, and the other is from the Rossellini/De Sica neo-realist line, which is, 'Let's capture real life, because real life is more amazing than anything you can come up with in your head.' And I come from that tradition."

This sounds remarkably similar to the way Kopple, Maysles, and other "old-style" documentary filmmakers characterized their successful filmmaking methods. The ability to let it happen, recognize it, and get it on film or tape is a key ingredient in documentary filmmaking.

True to what he says he has hoped to do, the director's most recent film was a documentary: *My Enemy's Enemy*, an official entry in the 2007 Toronto International Film Festival. Macdonald is in his mid-thirties and is in possession of twinkly blue eyes that flash with humor and elegant manners. For instance, when he accidentally opened the door to the (unlocked) hotel suite bathroom at the press junket for *The Last King of Scotland* just as this writer was leaving, he politely and laughingly took the blame on himself for bursting in at the wrong moment.

And while there is nothing new, really, about using historical or archival footage in feature films, by now we are starting to accept another refraction of this practice. Audiences don't challenge Forest Whitaker's Idi Amin, even if we have a very different memory of Amin. I'm going to guess here that this is a whole new concept for presenting historical figures. It is different from a star "turn" as historical figure, or an actor's highly realistic recreation of a famous person—not to take anything away from an extraordinary performance such as Philip Seymour Hoffman's in *Capote*. Nor is it a docudrama—a simple retelling of events in a more dramatic form—though that too is a new concept (or category, at the very least).

Macdonald said, "I think our Amin is an example of lying to tell a greater truth. I think Forest is very authentic to what Ugandans experienced, but if you see Idi Amin on film, he's not the same person as Forest Whitaker is playing. Forest is a heightened, more real version of Idi Amin, if you want to put it that way."

So while *The Last King of Scotland* was based on a novel, the research for the film also used a documentary, *General Idi Amin Dada*—a sort of turning to one version of reality, if still a version.

"We looked at as much footage as we could get hold of, and the Barbet Schroeder documentary is one of the best things out there—it's particularly good because it's in color and so you can see the colors and architecture of the place. That film really helped the set designer."

Macdonald also observed, "It's hard to be in Uganda without meeting someone who hasn't been touched by Idi in some way, getting people jobs and so forth. But then they might go on to recount the horrors of the killings. It's a much more complicated story than just the fact that he was a brutal dictator. He did change the country tremendously."

Theory into Practice

The Last King of Scotland was the director's first feature, and he was very clear about his documentary-derived work habits and how they impacted his debut feature. "I take each day new, without a grand master plan. That way you can be more spontaneous and respond to what is actually going on around you. I like to work in an atmosphere of controlled chaos. I think it's more open-ended.

"I also insisted on going to Uganda to film. For instance, the historical buildings of the 1950s and 1960s still standing give a special texture to the film. Some of the buildings were around when Amin was, so that was perfect. As a documentarian, the specifics are always more interesting to me. You should always go to the actual place to film.

"My technique, if I can call it such a thing, was basically to let things happen, and then to film them. Make the environment right so that the actors felt they could go way off script if they wanted to; try to film every scene in one take if I could, even when loads of it is useless because they've got their backs to you—just keep shooting, keep shooting, and then accidents happen. The actors do something different, or something different happens in the background, and you think, 'That bit of spontaneity is really nice, let's keep that.' That is my modus operandi."

He also credits the documentary form with having taught him flexibility during the shooting of a movie. "Directing a feature movie is like dragging a huge boulder around behind you. How to change directions?"

Macdonald, a highly literate fellow, once worked for the BBC as well as the publishing house Faber and Faber (and, in his authors' notes to a book he co-edited on the documentary, *Imagining Reality*, he makes reference to the fact that he also does/was doing documentaries. So here is a case, like the famed documentary filmmakers Paul Rotha, and Grierson, and now Errol Morris, of practitioners writing about their form). "I had read the novel on which the film is based when I worked at Faber and Faber, so when I did get the offer to direct, I was able to say yes right away," he says.

It's not surprising, then, to find his quite witty piece about his Oscar win in the British newspaper *The Observer*, called "'Errr. . . Thanks, Uma," a blow-by-blow reminiscence of his (unlikely as he presents it) win for best documentary picture of 1999 for his film *One Day in September*. The article has some choice bits. Upon entering the United States, a customs official tells Macdonald "Oh yeah. You don't stand a chance of winning—*Buena Vista Social Club*'s gonna walk it, although to my taste, *On the Ropes* sounds a better film. But have a good stay anyway." And it concludes:

> Suddenly it's upon us. Uma Thurman and Ethan Hawke are the presenters. Just as they start giving their naf [sic] little introduction about 'what a documentary is' ('A film without any actors—gee, we might all be out of a job!'—who writes this stuff?), a camera comes down into the audience where the documentary nominees are sitting. We'd been told in advance that the camera moves to the winner—and there it goes straight to Wim Wenders[director of *Buena Vista Social Club*]!

> Then Uma opens the envelope and says those magic words: 'And the Oscar goes to... *One Day in September!*'

> I feel the way you're supposed to feel in a car accident—utterly, irrationally calm.[1]

A Doc That Didn't Take

Richard Linklater's fictional *Fast Food Nation* is adapted from Eric Schlosser's nonfiction book of the same name and uses some documentary footage, such as shots of the kill floor in a meatpacking plant. It has a narrative three-act structure, with fictional yet based-upon-fact characters. Though it was not a great success at the box office, it does raise the consciousness of the viewer as social issue documentaries do; in the film, a group of college teens have their eyes opened as they turn into pseudo-activists after learning about the cruel practices imposed on cattle. Yet for some reason, the film loses steam narratively.

My guess is that, because there was no one in the movie with star quality, the feature film structure that was imposed on the facts of the book wasn't well enough fleshed out in the film. When I asked Morgan Spurlock

Kevin Bacon and Frank Langella bring star quality (something that was arguably lacking in *Fast Food Nation,* Greg Kinnear notwithstanding) to *Frost/Nixon.* Courtesy Imagine Entertainment.

his theory about the movie's lack of commercial success (Schlosser is a friend of his and, as noted in chapter 6, he appears in an interview on one of the DVDs of *Super Size Me*), Spurlock simply said he had no idea. In this critic's opinion, it turned out to be an awkward chimera of sorts, to take the stem cell analogy about combining forms.

Though it does not pretend to be a documentary, George Clooney's *Good Night, and Good Luck* takes much of its strength not just from authenticity and replication—although there is plenty of that—but from re-telling and recasting history, and with social intent. The 2005 film, directed by Clooney and co-written by Clooney and Grant Heslov, incorporates chunks of vintage footage, including some of the real-life Senator Joseph P. McCarthy himself. "We realized that whomever we got to play McCarthy, no matter how good they were, nobody was going to believe it. They were going to think the guy was overacting, so we decided to use the real footage," said Heslov. Clooney says that Heslov, who plays Don Hewitt in the film, watched "footage for thirty-five days straight to find what we needed, which was all in CBS archives. Some was kinescope, some 16 millimeter, some 35 millimeter. We intended to shoot black and white but didn't want matching film stock—the way it is in *Forrest Gump* as though we were making what we shot look real. We cheated a bit in that whenever

McCarthy appears, he's projected on a wall or a television screen —further distinguishing original footage from ours." [2]

Just how much of the success of these creative hybrids is owing to audience familiarity with the new doc form? Probably quite a bit, as you've got viewers so used to the doc form that they can readily and rapidly shift between reality and fiction. It doesn't disturb them at all, or even seem remarkable enough for comment.

Breakthrough Bio Docs

One of the most sophisticated (and successful) practitioners of the new hybrid form is the British screenwriter and playwright Peter Morgan, who wrote the scripts for *The Queen* and *The Last King of Scotland*, as well as the play and film script for *Frost/Nixon*. "I like to take defining moments in recent history and allow drama to explore areas that have perhaps been neglected. I was inundated with scripts after I was nominated for an Academy Award," he told *New Yorker* writer John Lahr. [Yet] "None of them interest me, because they're all fact-based." Of this, Lahr observes, "He owns the franchise on a certain kind of scrupulously researched and astutely observed investigation into the emotional ructions behind contemporary events—neither documentary nor fiction, but an imaginative amalgam of the two." [3]

Whatever this amalgam is—if it exists at all—it sounds like the aesthetic and thematic space and place Werner Herzog has created and is describing in his films. In fact, as Peter Morgan has said about his play *Frost/Nixon*, "It may not be accurate, but I believe it's truthful," a quote perhaps worthy of Herzog.

Lahr calls the new category "ructions" (implying conflict, or emotional difficulties, the essence of drama); others call this new space between fiction and film interstices or a meeting place. Perhaps these are just overloaded terms to indicate that imagination is filling in some details in a fact-based but otherwise empty frame. This rarefied ether may be attractive to very smart people who—like artists in other realms starting with a structure like a canvas or a stanza—simply use this as an inspirational taking-off point.

For today's highly creative filmmakers and writers, that structure is turning out to be the documentary.

Mixing It Up

The documentary is now so popular as a genre that allusions to earlier docs are woven into new movies and docs. This may partly be in keeping with the *auteur* tradition of homages to other directors and their works, or it may simply be a case of the new importance of the doc form and nods being given from one filmmaker to another. Or to themselves. It is also a contribution to the reflexive or self-reflexive category of documentaries.

Les Blank filming Herzog eating his shoe is one obvious example, in the event of Morris finishing his film *Vernon, Florida*. So is Herzog's film of himself walking to Paris in *I Am My Films* to visit critic Lotte Eisner, a champion of new German filmmakers, hearing she might be on her deathbed (she wasn't), and the Les Blank film *Burden of Dreams*, described in Film Forum's summer 2007 program notes as "a riveting account of the crazed—even for Herzog—shooting of *Fitzcarraldo*."

References to others' work as well as his own earlier films are on view in the films of Roy Frumkes, a documentary and independent filmmaker who has been working in New York for many decades. Calling himself a "reflexive filmmaker," when I asked him if he fit into Bill Nichols's documentary categories, Frumkes says, "My latest feature, *The Meltdown Memoirs*, is my most personal film yet. I was wearing a *Street Trash* belt buckle when on camera [*Street Trash* is another Frumkes film]. The older I get, the more reflexive my films become. I'm more interested in highlighting my life and my friends."

This sounds a bit arrogant, but it is completely at odds with Frumkes the person. Casual seeming, although he is under constant deadline, as seem to be many of the documentary filmmakers I talked to, Frumkes made himself available for interview at his apartment cum editing studio cum editorial offices of the film magazine *Films in Review*, which he has owned and edited for a number of years. He was in the middle of editing a project in this base of operations on Manhattan's Upper West Side, in the 10024 area code, which he observes offhandedly he shares with Michael Moore.

Frumkes is from a family with a show-business heritage, if one takes into account that creativity sometimes skips a generation. His grandfather, Benny Burke, was Houdini's agent, Frumkes says. But he points out that his dad, who was in the garment business, always brought home the latest techno gadget (his term) when he was growing up, his family was the first on the block to have a television, and so on. And he credits his father with getting him "a 16 millimeter Bell & Howell camera when I was in high school. I was the only kid shooting film at Harrison High."

Yet Frumkes studied English literature and writing at Tulane University before coming back to New York, where he was raised, and becoming— inevitably, it now seems—an independent filmmaker. He has written, directed, and produced a number of docs as well as independent features.

He has had small acting roles in others' films, as well as bits in his own. ("That's to save money," he says. "I don't have to pay myself.")

Frumkes played a zombie in George Romero's 1978 *Dawn of the Dead*, and turns up in subsequent films that others are making, sometimes with footage edited in from the earlier films he has written and directed about Romero.

A recent project is an update of 1989's *Document of the Dead*, called *The Definitive Document of the Dead*. "That will be the last one," he says humorously, "as I'm going to retire from this chronicle." In 1979 he made the first installment of his film about Romero, and also, more recently, did the television special on the set of *Land of the Dead* called *Dream of the Dead*, which was shown on IFC in 2005. "I said to George, 'You can keep on doing this but I'm retiring. I don't want this to be the *Seven Up* series of horror.'"

Other films Frumkes has written and/or directed include the cult film *Street Trash*, his fantasy horror feature film, which inspired *The Meltdown Memoirs*, a documentary that Roy made about what happened to the people who were involved in the making of *Street Trash*, approximately twenty years after the shooting ended.

"Outside of the fact that *Document of the Dead* and *The Meltown Memoirs* are both grouped under the generalized heading of documentary, they're extremely different," says Frumkes. "In *Memoirs* I used the word 'memoir' because it's a personal film. It's very subjective. There are whole sections in the film about people like Victoria Alexander, who played a woman in a car in *Street Trash*. She was in that film for only thirty seconds and I give her four minutes in *Meltdown*. For *Meltown Memoirs*, I interviewed every cast and crew member of *Street Trash* I could track down and then edited them into some twenty-year-old behind-the-scenes footage."

Frumkes says: "What drove me to the documentary form was certainly not the promise of a retirement fund. I wanted to make teaching films for film students who had nothing indie to relate to. All the 'making of' films back then were about *Star Wars* or *Butch Cassidy and the Sundance Kid*, not stuff you could relate to while in college. That was how *Document of the Dead* evolved. Since then, I've returned to the genre from time to time, and I love it. It's very cheap, has infinite possibilities in most areas of production (narratives do not), and has a 'merc unit' sensibility while shooting—go in for the kill with your team, and then get the hell out."

Nor does he mince words when it comes to the Johnny-come-lately recognition of the form in the celebration of Frederick Wiseman's work as a documentarian in the fall of 2006 by the Lincoln Center Film Festival.

"Same thing with the Academy [of Motion Picture Arts and Sciences]," he says. "They were really paying lip service, and often to films about the Holocaust, which would make them feel good about themselves, until Michael Moore made docs commercially viable. They were only about twenty years late in recognizing the brilliance of Wiseman."

Frumkes, like Herzog and Macdonald, works in various features as well. He co-wrote (with Rocco Simonelli) and produced the romantic comedy *The Sweet Life*, with Joan Jett, which won the Best Romantic Comedy award at the Independent International Film and Video Festival, and he wrote *The Substitute*, a series of features (also with Simonelli).

Teacher Burt Raphael and pupil Heather Duff at the big race in *Burt's Bikers*. Courtesy of Roy Frumkes Productions, Inc. Photo credit: Robert DePietro.

Burt's Bikers is a docudrama (his denomination for it) that Frumkes made about mentally handicapped children, and as noted in the earlier chapter on narrative, he used the voice of Glenda Jackson to tell the story.

He teaches filmmaking at New York's School of Visual Arts, and has taught filmmaking at NYU, where Spike Lee once was his student. "He was a very good student," says Frumkes. "Very committed, sat in the front row, and always turned up whenever I had advisement hours." Some of Frumkes's advice to others is summarized in his book, *Shoot Me: A Guide to Making Independent Movies*, which he co-wrote with Simonelli.

Reflexive Realities

Jason Reitman, who directed *Thank You for Smoking*, is the son of the highly successful Ivan Reitman (*Ghostbusters*, among others) who—to take nothing away from his son—used a similar fiction/documentary paradigm quite successfully in his 1993 film *Dave*. Though both *Dave* and *Smoking* are, strictly speaking, not documentaries or fact-based except in the loosest way, they do still employ many doc conventions.

Dave is a political comedy based on impersonation and the confusion between authentic behavior and performance, a narrative about a presidential look-alike who has to perform as the real President (a dual role played by Kevin Kline). It features a number of cameo appearances by real celebrities, thus mixing it up even more. Appearing as themselves are Jay Leno and Larry King, the loudly bickering McLaughlin Group, the politician Tip O'Neill, and a number of well-known reporters, including Helen Thomas and Nina Totenberg. There is even the insider joke of Oliver Stone attempting unsuccessfully to convince others of a political conspiracy involving the President in an identity switch.

Somehow, though, the real celebrities are not used to authenticate the fiction, but to underscore the fact that it is not "reality."

And *Thank You for Smoking*, directed by Jason Reitman, has numerous documentarized elements in his version of the Christopher Buckley book. The film, though tongue-in-cheek from the start, still presents a straightforward series of events: the story of Nick Naylor (Aaron Eckhart), a lobbyist for the tobacco industry, often fighting with and frequently trumping such opponents as the granola-ish Senator from Vermont, Ortolan Finistirre, played by William F. Macy.

Thank You for Smoking is a mirage of what looks like fact and is actually fiction, but which is fact-based: the destructive power of cigarettes.

Here, statistics come in handy, as do the familiar charts and graphs of the documentary mode. And—thanks in part to our concepts of and awareness of mockumentaries and even stunt docs—it is accepted by the audience with ease. There is no longer any of the incredulity or misunderstanding that took place at the original screening of *This Is Spinal Tap*.

In October of 2006, Christopher Buckley was in New York (he lives in Washington, D.C.) and told me there had been a number of bids to make a film version of his cautionary tale and send-up of the tobacco industry, but that it was Reitman's script he liked the most. "It's a whole different skill set," he said, in answer to the question about why he did not do the screenplay. He said he is very pleased with the way the film turned out, though he admits that it hasn't had that much effect on his immediate family. "My daughter, who is in college, still smokes in spite of everything. She says it's to help her keep her weight down, even though I pointed out to her that her grandfather [William F. Buckley] always smoked and now has emphysema." (William Buckley died in the spring of 2008.)

Both *Dave* and *Thank You for Smoking* are cautionary tales, and both use documentary-like elements: hearings, irritated Senators, and statistical facts that cannot be disputed. These films are examples of the fact that we have learned to both believe and not believe at the same time, a feat of sophistication made possible by the developments of the new documentary.

Everything Old is New Again

But cinematic hybrids also have their precedents, and some respectable ones at that. According to noted film historian Kevin Brownlow in addition to factual films about the West, there were also numerous Western narrative films that incorporated significant amounts of factual footage, and in so doing, not only reconstructed Western history but also became an extension of that history. Brownlow also says that the directors and producers of many silent Western films worked with actual ranchmen, cowboys, Indians, and railroad men in their attempt to portray life and customs accurately. [4]

So, even back in the beginning, the movie business was liberally intermixing various real and fictional elements. And if audiences knew, they accepted it with ease. Over the years, as the definition of documentary has changed, there have been many discussions about how *Nanook of the North* influenced the form's development. But Flaherty's final film was even more prophetic of the movement's transformation in our time.

Elephant Boy was commissioned by Alexander Korda in 1935, after Korda decided that the Rudyard Kipling story would provide the framework for Flaherty's proposal to make a documentary about a boy and an elephant. Flaherty spent a year filming on location in India (the Maharaja of Mysore, profusely thanked in the opening credits, granted him access to his land), and then the footage was taken out of his hands and intercut with new material written by John Collier and shot by Korda's brother Zoltán. The film, which won the Best Direction award at the Venice Film Festival, falls between documentary and drama, with the star of the film being Sabu, one of the Maharaja's stable boys, and also the son of a *mahout* (an elephant driver). Like Nanook, the thirteen-year-old Sabu turned out to be a natural performer, and his onscreen relationship with the elephant Kala Nag displayed an enviable chemistry. The film went on to great commercial success.

It sounds as much like a fiction film as a documentary, or is it the other way around? The incredibly interesting cross-fertilization of the two forms may have been prophesied long ago.

• • • • • • • • •

Endnotes

1. Kevin Macdonald, "Errr. . . Thanks, Uma," *The Observer* (April 20, 2000).

2. Jennifer Merin, "'She's Dumb'—George Clooney Talks Politics," *New York Press* (October 5, 2005): 22.

3. John Lahr, "The Impersonator," *The New Yorker* (April 30, 2007): 34.

4. Kevin Brownlow, *The War, The West and the Wilderness* (New York: Knopf, 1979), 223.

chapter nine

THE NEW BREED SELECTS AND MIXES FORMS: AMIR BAR-LEV, SARA LAMM, GRACE LEE, CELIA MAYSLES

• • • • • • • • • •

Documentary filmmakers working today seem to approach their craft like cafeteria Catholicism. They take what they consider the best of the recent splashy innovations in the doc form, picking and choosing at will, while never giving up some traditional labels.

Nor, in most cases, do they seem to feel the need to overturn the work or stance of their immediate predecessors. (Here critic Harold Bloom's famous phrase "anxiety of influence" comes to mind.) There is definitely no movement to set forth any new dogma, as there was with some of the intense doc filmmakers of the mid-nineties, protesting against some of the more outré films of that decade in an effort to preserve the form. Or even to set forth a belief system, as Al Maysles does on his Web site. This is what Celia Maysles calls the "dogma" of her uncle, Al Maysles, and his take on Direct Cinema.[1] Or—to go back even further—like Vertov, Grierson, Paul Rotha, to mention some, in their proclamations about what they believed the documentary should be.

If the devil can quote scripture, of course, so too can film historians. Richard Barsam refers to the expressionistic Vertov to support his argument for a more traditional and realistic cinema,[2] while today filmmaker-critic Kevin Macdonald also cites Vertov, as do Errol Morris, Spurlock, and numerous others, to argue for a less stringent format.[3]

And very often this highly intelligent and aware (and often highly educated) generation of young filmmakers is clear about its position in film history, and the films and theory that have gone before. Some members of this generation have studied filmmaking—theory as well as technique—and most are very aware of their position in the history of ideas. Sara Lamm, for instance, the thirty-one-year-old former performance artist from North Carolina turned doc filmmaker, says her approach to filmmaking is based on bits-and-pieces: "It's not that I have anything against first-person

Sara Lamm, director of *Dr. Bronner's Magic Soapbox*. Photo credit: Matt Aselton.

filmmaking—in fact, I really enjoy the style—but in this particular instance it just didn't seem the best way to serve the story, which was already complicated and interesting enough," says Lamm. "I didn't feel that including more of myself would serve to clarify anything. That said, I was very conscious of allowing the filmmaking 'seams' to show through."

I spoke with the director just after her documentary *Dr. Bronner's Magic Soapbox* debuted last summer (as attorneys say, in the interest of full disclosure, I did the review of the film for *New York Press*).

Lamm uses family photographs, archival footage, and some historical documents to showcase the life of the manic nutcase, Dr. Emanuel Bronner, who created "Dr. Bronner's All One" soap, popular in the counterculture of the sixties and seventies and found in health food stores today. Though you never see Lamm on camera, there is some sense of her presence, particularly when she interviews Bronner's son, who is still very much alive and out and about.

She said: "None are exactly revolutionary, but by maintaining the reference to filmmaking in general, leaving shadows of mikes, including slates in the archival material, allowing my questions to be heard,

I hoped to in some way acknowledge the subjectivity inherent in the whole endeavor. I tried to reflect the experience that all of us might have had at one time or another of trying to piece together our own family narratives—speaking with our parents, aunts, uncles, grandparents. Often what we are left with is more of an impressionistic version of events, as opposed to a completely factual one, and so in the film I wanted to preserve the idea that each of the Bronners has his or her own version of Dr. Bronner's history."

Another refraction of subjective technique is expressed by Kim Longinotto, a British filmmaker and strong feminist who makes movies about women, their special issues, and sometimes exploitation, and whose 2005 film *Sisters in Law* received a great deal of positive attention in the world of women in film. Kim says, "I love the way Nick [Broomfield] appears in his films, but I don't want you to be thinking about me, or the camera, or the filming when you watch my films."

Without undertaking a full rundown of every important documentary out there, it's interesting to note that *Jesus Camp*, the much-praised recent film about the early training and camp experiences of young Christians, breaks its narrative into following three kids, with no insertions of the filmmaker. In this way, it is structured like a film very different in topic, *Working Girls* by Lizzie Borden, the 1978 documentary about prostitutes, which also follows three characters. It's standard, cross-cutting, fiction-influenced technique, but doesn't make us aware of the filmmaker.

Yet other young filmmakers, such as Adrian Grenier, are sticking to the purely personal film, the methods of Ross McElwee and Alan Berliner. Grenier's HBO documentary *Shot in the Dark* details the thirty-one-year-old filmmaker's trip to find and meet his previously unknown father. The travel elements often associated with the documentary are used; here it's on the road across America once again. So are interviews with people he encounters along the way in trying to find and find out about his father. Still, the film remains highly subjective, perhaps too much so for *New York Times* reviewer, Ginia Bellafonte, who decides that the movie is "tepid": "Sometimes Mr. Grenier just lets the camera linger on his face, as he stares out searchingly from behind his aviator-style sunglasses. Early on, the camera inexplicably points itself at a vast gray sky. Mr. Grenier doesn't quite know what to do with himself or where to go next, but he assumes that everyone he encounters must have some vested interest in his story and quest."[4]

Their Game Plans

Some young documentarians seem to slip effortlessly into filmmaking, as Sara Lamm did. After leaving North Carolina, she had been a downtown performance artist in New York when the doc form calling came to her. She says it was an easy transition, for if you have a background in the arts, the documentary filmmaking community in New York is open to you.

Others make a conscious, almost career-planned and studious choice. One of the most successful films of 2007 was *My Kid Could Paint That*, a movie that includes the filmmaker and his statements about his relationship with his subject. But on the whole, the film is primarily concerned with telling the story—not entirely conventionally but not in a stylistically edgy way either—of four-year-old Marla Olmstead, whose artwork drew attention to herself, her family, and the highly successful shows she had in Binghamton, New York.

Amir Bar-Lev, a thirty-five-year-old New York filmmaker, echoes Lamm's remark, saying he has been in New York City for five years, and describes what he calls the congeniality of the documentary world, referencing, apparently, academia. Originally from Berkeley, California, Bar-Lev graduated summa cum laude from Brown University, where he says he eventually got "tired of post-structuralism." At that point he decided to study filmmaking at the world

Director Amir Bar-Lev in 2008. Photo credit: Jason Blaney.

class FAMU, the Film and Television School of the Academy of Performing Arts in Prague, which claims Milan Kundera and Milos Forman among its graduates. And for some sense of how downright smart and intellectual he is—like many of the contemporary filmmakers—check out his comments in a piece called the "Golden Age of Documentary" he wrote for his very occasional blog on the *Huffington Post* Web site.

Out in the Field

Somewhat more intrusive than Lamm or Longinotto, even interacting at times with his subjects in *My Kid Could Paint That*, here is how Bar-Lev sees his role: "Not to place myself in the center of a film, but not to necessarily leave myself out either. I aim to say, 'This is what I think. This is how it affected me. But also, here is the evidence. You make up your own mind.'" Like Lamm, he says, "I love the films of Nick Broomfield. But he's front and center. I prefer to hover around the margins."

Bar-Lev says he sees especially 2003's documentary *Capturing the Friedmans* as a precedent for his work: The highly lauded documentary attempted to find the truth about alleged pedophilia by both father and son in this middle-class Long Island family. In the end, the film does not conclusively decide one way or another, but it is definitely a poignant examination of the issue, the people involved, and the legal system.

My Kid Could Paint That was a winner at Sundance. It is a film that tackles the difficult subject of modern art, its easily imitated look, and the fact that some people believe Abstract Expressionism to be a bit of a hoax anyway. Bar-Lev says he latched onto the idea for the doc by scouring newspapers, looking for a topic, and was relieved when he had read of Marla Olmstead, whose Jackson Pollock-like paintings were "selling like hotcakes." National media attention did (or did not) expose the art (and the artist, or, more correctly, her father, as the propagator) as a sham.

Bar-Lev, whom I interviewed in his West Village office, says that when he contacted the Olmsteads, Marla's family, they seemed eager to have him come to Binghamton to make his movie. Their hope was that he might clear up some of the exposés that were starting to take place on shows such as *60 Minutes*.

When he made the film, Bar-Lev had already made a highly praised film, *Fighter*, about two elderly boxers. To support himself, he says he worked in the cable industry, something many documentary filmmakers apparently do. Bar-Lev himself looks like a kid, or some universal graduate student

Marla in front of a canvas, working at home in the 2007 documentary
My Kid Could Paint That. Courtesy Sony Pictures Classics.

version of same. Rather short, the filmmaker has nice blue eyes that beam
out a preternaturally calm aura. Flannel-shirted and running-shoe shod,
and accompanied by his Blackberry, which he continually checked for text
messages, Bar-Lev lost his aura of "West Coast cool" only once when I asked
him about his trips upstate. "People ask me that all the time," he said a bit
testily, maybe defensively. "You know, Binghamton is only a hundred and
seventy miles from New York. It really wasn't an issue."

Bar-Lev was forthcoming in saying that while he still has an
intermittent relationship with the Olmstead family (in fact, one of the
more touching scenes of the film is when he asks the family's forgiveness
for having intruded upon their lives), the truth is that documentary
filmmakers do sort of move on to another subject once their film is
completed. For this reporter, this explains some of the comments made by
Maysles and Herzog, though not Morris, about losing touch with their
films' subjects.

Bar-Lev also had some incisive comments on a kind of symbiotic
relationship between subject and filmmaker. This issue also comes up in the
doc *A Summer in the Cage*, a film about a friendship begun one New York
City summer between the filmmaker, Ben Selkow, and his subject, Sam, a
then-resident of the City who has manic-depressive, or bipolar, illness.

A Summer in the Cage aired on HBO in the fall of 2007 and, while the majority of the film shows Sam and his daily life in New York and Los Angeles, where he returns to be with his family, there is a highly dramatic—even funny at times—sequence. Sam calls up the filmmaker with wild accusations about Selkow having invaded his life by filming it and decides that the filmmaker now owes him big time because of that.

For this viewer, the complicated relationship between the director and his subject was the most cleverly executed part of *A Summer in the Cage*, particularly the scene where the director allows us to listen to Sam's rant over the telephone about how the film has ruined his—Sam's—life, while providing the filmmaker with a subject. Focusing the camera on his answer machine, Selkow also shows himself looking at the camera—us—as he listens to the ravings. This bit is reminiscent of *The Thin Blue Line*, in the scenes where only the tiny Sony tape recorder is shown on camera, though in *A Summer in the Cage*, the director can clearly be seen reacting to the tape.

Both Bar-Lev and Selkow are using their own presence in their films—"in the margins," says Bar-Lev, though Selkow is on screen quite a bit. They are not the focus or locus of their documentaries, but they do use their own presence. Yet Bar-Lev, at least, says he would rule out neither a totally autobiographical film nor one in which he does not appear at all.

Down to Business

Like so many documentary filmmakers, Bar-Lev says he has made very little money from even his most successful film, *My Kid Could Paint That*, though he is clearly thrilled to have had it picked up by the Sundance Channel and by the Sony Corporation.

The Big Name documentary filmmaker whom Bar-Lev admires the most, he says, is Werner Herzog, for his creativity, of course, but also because "at times, Herzog does the 'stay-in-the-margins thing' really well."

Yet though Bar-Lev may have hit upon just the right idea at the right time, in the long run, perhaps his documentary *Fighter* will be considered the superior film. Winner of numerous awards, it was Bar-Lev's debut doc about two seventy-something friends taking a trip back to their past. Beginning as a historical biography, *Fighter* becomes a psychological drama, as the trip becomes a contentious clash of ideologies, personalities, and life paths. By the time the two pack their bags and draw a premature end to their road trip, what has emerged is a portrait of the last century's most horrific event, the Holocaust, recounted not through dry historical facts, but through an unlikely friendship brought to the brink of collapse.

By combining spontaneous action with reflective conversations and historical films, *Fighter* weaves a complex portrait, linking the two subjects with the stories of: their playing soccer while waiting to be gassed in Auschwitz, losing one's virginity the night before a transport to the camps, running toward the front rather than away from it in fervent desire to fight Hitler. For *Fighter*, Bar-Lev used rare archival footage never before seen by Western audiences, from the 1942 bombing of Yugoslavia with fleeing refuges to the kitsch Socialist musicals staged in technicolor power plants.

Back to Basics

Other filmmakers, however, seem drawn these days to more traditional formats, with just the hint of a subjective relationship. Lauren Greene's *Thin* visits a rehab facility in Florida and follows the narrative of four of its residents. Her film almost seems to be patterned after Barbara Kopple's *Harlan County USA*. And like Kopple, Greene says that the way she got good footage was by proximity to her topic for some long period of time and by gaining the trust of her subjects. This was similar to Rory Kennedy's approach in her film about Appalachia, *American Hollow*. Like the relationships with their subject matter described by both Kopple and Greene, Kennedy has said about *American Hollow*, "I ended up living with the family because the hotel was an hour and a half away. They invited us to stay with them; I think that made a big difference. The time you spend with the camera off is really important to what you get when the camera is on."

Some relationship is hinted at, if not on camera, then off. But Rory Kennedy's subsequent *Ghosts of Abu Ghraib* was even more restrained. Similarly, spartan is the approach taken by the more generally flamboyant Spike Lee, who also directed two major documentaries, *4 Little Girls* and *When the Levees Broke*. Possibly the subject matter of both is incendiary and significant enough to not warrant any kind of extreme directorial comment. "I have a great researcher," says Lee. "Her name is Judy Aley. For *When the Levees Broke* [Lee's documentary about the Katrina disaster], she made two trips to New Orleans before we got there. She just walked around and met people. So she would shoot me back e-mails with their stories. And I would make the determination as to whether or not we would interview them. When you're a director, you have many different choices.

"When we did the other HBO documentary, *4 Little Girls*, about four African-American little girls killed during the bombings of black communities in Alabama, once again Judy found great material: the postmortem photographs of the girls. And so when I got them, that decision of should we include these or not kept weighing on me. And I prayed on it. And I made the decision that we had to show what these hundred sticks of dynamite did to these four little black girls. And I knew I was going to show bodies, but it was a matter of how much. I wanted to show as much as I felt the audience could take. And in a way, I felt that it was paying respect to these bodies. Who knows whether they received a proper burial or if their remains were united with their families? So that's how we approached that."

Lee obviously also wrestled with the issue of audience manipulation. "But even for me, the hardest stuff that I knew had to go in *When the Levees Broke* was like the interviews with Kim Polk. I'm interviewing her and she's holding a picture of her five-year-old daughter. She was gracious enough to let us bring a camera to the funeral. But for me the most poignant shot in the entire four hours is the final shot of episode three. She completely breaks down. Then her little boy runs into the frame completely unaware—just a little kid—that his little sister is dead. And then we fade to black. That happened. We were just there. It was just one of those magical moments that we were able to capture."

Would a Bar-Lev have cut to his own reactions during the interview? Would some filmmakers avoid this for fear of being accused of sensationalism?

Those questions are impossible to answer. And now that the neo-doc has opened other doors (some like Herzog, Morris, and Corra would say re-opened them), there are just that many more possibilities to choose from.

More than Homage

Another film that made its own modification on the subjective or personal doc is *The Grace Lee Project*, a 2005 movie by Korean-American filmmaker Grace Lee, who explored the idea of finding those who have her name to determine the effect of being a "Grace Lee."

But let her tell the story, from her home and by telephone from Los Angeles: "Growing up in Missouri, I had no idea that Grace Lee was such a common Asian-American name. Nobody was named Grace [in Missouri] and there were also very few Asians around. Everything about my upbringing

Grace Lee (on the right) and Detroit activist Grace Lee Boggs, featured in *The Grace Lee Project.* Courtesy LeeLee Films.

led me to believe that I was a unique individual. After college, I left the Midwest and lived in Korea, and then New York and then California, where I would often meet people who would tell me about the other Grace Lee they once knew. When I would press them to tell me about this other Grace Lee, the answers would always be the same: nice, smart, violin prodigy, went to Harvard at fifteen, etc. . . . essentially the 'model minority' stereotype. I started feeling like a loser in comparison. The way people talked about Grace Lee sounded a lot like the way people might stereotype an Asian person."

She says that she has seen *The Sweetest Sound*, as well as other similarly structured names of films, but that she sees her film as taking a different approach. "I think there are several documentaries/same-name projects out there: Alan Berliner. Angela Shelton. Dave Gorman. I was never interested in just finding the people who share my name, however. That didn't seem very interesting to me. What was interesting was how 'Grace Lee' seemed to be a stand-in for the quintessential Asian-American female or the 'model minority.' I thought *The Grace Lee Project* would also be a humorous way to tackle an identity crisis." In the film, there are, of course, a number of serious identity issues, but there are many moments of absurdity as well.

In response to my question about the four, and more recently five, documentary categories set out by Bill Nichols, Lee said, "I usually call

GLP a personal essay, or personal documentary, but I suppose 'reflexive' [one of Nichols's categories] would also be an appropriate label. I think the film has elements of autobiography, but only superficially. I used my name/ story primarily as a through line or device to explore larger questions about stereotypes and our collective experience/identities as Asian-American women. The film doesn't really give a thorough understanding of my autobiography, although I think the women I chose to highlight hints at what interests me and what sorts of stories pull me in."

Her description of some of the other types of Grace Lees she found is humorous: "I still occasionally get e-mails from Grace Lees and I've met many more at screenings, including a performance artist whom I had heard about years ago but never could track down. She showed up at a screening in Philly and now we are Facebook friends. Ha! Also, last year, I was stopped by Homeland Security at LAX because my name showed up in the computer. The guy kept looking at me and then looking at the computer—I knew what was going on. Finally, I asked him what was wrong and he asked me to confirm my address. Apparently there is a Grace Lee out there who had a kilo of cocaine delivered to her apartment and she's on their list!"

The Grace Lee Project opened to very good reviews in the *Los Angeles Times*, the *New York Times*, and other major publications when it came out in 2005. Lee says she has slowed down a bit recently after the birth of her son in September 2007, but that she is now eager to get a film project going again; she is also developing some ideas for television shows.

Lee says she does not feel she must be in New York City to be a successful documentary filmmaker. "The beauty of documentaries is that you can be anywhere to make them as long as you have a compelling subject. I feel like I could make a couple of them here in my living room, with my hand-held high def camera and my laptop computer."

One film she finished before her son was born is what she calls a "fictional documentary or a personal horror film. *American Zombie* is about two filmmakers (one of them is called Grace Lee) who set out to document a community of high-functioning zombies in Los Angeles. I crudely refer to it as '*The Grace Lee Project*, but with zombies.'"

Pick and Choose

At this point, it seems the options for documentary filmmakers are wide and open, and they are taking them. The form and format of their storytelling seems to depend more than anything else on a personal choice, perhaps even one dictated by temperament. Congruently, it is reflected in their pick of role models. For Bar-Lev, it is Herzog and his expressionism. Yet Daniel Gordon, the thirty-something British documentary filmmaker (*Crossing the Line*; see chapter 5 on narration) happily accepted the description "Griersonesque" when I interviewed him in the summer of 2007.

For obvious reasons, her father David Maysles, who died suddenly and unexpectedly when Celia was seven, is Celia Maysles's hero. This becomes clear in her debut documentary, *Wild Blue Yonder*.

The much-discussed issue of the 2007 Amsterdam International Documentary Film Festival—the equivalent of the Cannes Film Festival, but for documentaries—was the controversy surrounding Celia Maysles's *Wild Blue Yonder*. It is a personal and autobiographical film, and in this way, goes against the dicta of the Maysles brothers. But more intimately, the subject of the film is Celia's attempt to gain access to film footage that David Maysles left unfinished, which is still in the vaults of Maysles Films, but which Albert Maysles won't release to his niece. As the saying goes, you've got to see the film for the full story.

In the fall of 2007, industry gossip surrounded the issue of whether or not the film, subsequently accepted at 2008's important Hot Docs festival, was going to be screened at all in Amsterdam. Celia, whom I interviewed at her working headquarters, Corra Films, says her uncle merely threatened to not show up to the Amsterdam Film Festival if the movie were shown there. However, her executive producer on *Wild Blue Yonder*, Henry Corra (a former protégé of the Maysles), said Albert Maysles tried to have Celia's movie suppressed. Given Albert Maysles's importance in the documentary world, perhaps those two come down to the same thing.

In the film, there are scenes where Celia is trying to talk her uncle into letting her into his film vault to borrow, have, or see the film. (Maysles says he let her see some footage.) And, of course, if it weren't the Maysles, who would care? But giving the film a deeper layer is that while it may be a family saga about wills, inheritances, and lawsuits, it is played out on the grid of the new documentary style against the old. Also, there are intellectual rights and personal feelings.

"I went in with high hopes," says Celia Maysles. "I thought I would get my family back. I wanted a relationship with my uncle and with my cousins."

But in the film we see Celia's hopes for this dashed, even as Al Maysles himself appears in the film and the film progresses. "I told him, 'Be a good guy. You don't look good in the film,'" she says. It would seem to be a simple matter for Al Maysles to let Celia have the movie, or at least see it, but both he and David Maysles's widow (Celia's mother) say in the film that after

Celia Maysles at her father's grave in *Wild Blue Yonder*. Courtesy Corra Films.

four and a half years of litigation there was a settlement, and the rights to *Blue Yonder* went to Al Maysles. Celia says that she and her mother never discussed the matter much, though some of that has changed because of her making of *Wild Blue Yonder*. The two branches of the family hadn't been in touch since the settlement.

To Maysles's credit, he does let her come to his office, he does let her film him and the discussions the two have about whether or not she can see or use sections of *Blue Yonder*. (And to Celia Maysles's credit, she shows some touching scenes with her uncle.)

But in the end, Al Maysles says, on film, that he wants the movie exclusively because he may be making an autobiographical film himself at some point. Presumably there is footage in *Blue Yonder* of the brothers' shared family experiences.

Family and/or Film Squabbles

Wild Blue Yonder, which takes its name from David Maysles's original film *Blue Yonder*, is a charmingly put together tale, and it does incorporate bits and pieces about the Maysles brothers' work. There are many scenes concerning *Grey Gardens*, and an intriguing segment Celia uses from an interview with Charlotte Zwerin, the Maysles' longtime editor, which was originally conducted for the Sundance Channel.

But of the sequences from *Grey Gardens*, and other Maysles films, Celia complained to me, "I had to buy *Grey Gardens* and other Maysles films in the store like everybody else."

Both Celia and her boss/producer, Henry Corra, reject the purity of Direct Cinema. "There's an untruth to the idea of unfiltered reality," says Corra, who allows that his company is modeled after the Maysles' (and that he himself trained with Albert and David in his early years as a filmmaker), and that the company makes both commercials and independent films. One he speaks of eloquently is his highly personal film, *George* (1996), about his twelve-year-old autistic son, which got very good reviews. The film is a touching evocation of George, including some scenes of the Corra family; using some cinéma vérité techniques and making effective use of color photography, occasionally intercut by black and white footage.

Henry Corra puts it right out there: "Albert's dogma is boring." And Celia Maysles interjects that her father didn't necessarily agree with the "dogma" either.

After I initially met Celia at the office of Corra Films, near Canal Street, she asked Henry Corra to take part in the interview. Whether this was because she wanted protection, or she felt unable to talk about her film herself (clearly not the case), or because she wanted to share some credit with him, was anybody's guess.[5] In any case, Corra, now in his early sixties, speaks for his own generation of filmmakers: "I was very influenced in the eighties by vérité and personal filmmaking. Not so much re-enactment or staging, but I don't have a problem with it. I simply wanted to take vérité to new places."

So while you wouldn't say the two have a particular axe to grind, it's obvious they share some very well thought-through positions on filmmaking, and what it should be.

"There are no rules," is Celia's insistent belief.

"Small, personal films don't have to be made in New York City, of course. But the talent pool here is very deep," says Corra. "What we don't want to make is the flat, vérité HBO-style of public television filmmaking. It's very good; don't get me wrong. But it's a little predictable by now, though it is an American, classic style.

"What we found when we went to the Amsterdam Film Festival was that there were no rules; there was fresh, creative, and exciting work being done."

Celia adds, "I'm not wedded to any one style—I'm drawn to certain characters, and depending on the character or person is how I come up with a shooting strategy or style for the film. I happen to really like personal films, but I think both of us are open to anything and everything that is character driven."

She says she intends to release the film commercially on TV and in a few theaters. "It will not have a huge theatrical release like some docs, but it is definitely being shown commercially. My movie asks a lot of its viewers. It's subtle." But she does say she is now hooked on filmmaking. "I was a social worker. I know my dad got interested in making movies because he was interested in people. In a lot of ways, it's the same thing. But I must admit that until I made the movie, I wasn't really intending to be a filmmaker."

For this viewer, one of the most poignant bits in the film is in the beginning, when Celia is shown about to embark on a trip uptown to visit her uncle, and in the favor-asking mode. She emits a plaintive little sigh, which seemed to this viewer to foretell and set the apprehensive tone of the film. And when I asked Celia about the decision to keep the sigh in the film, she was refreshingly honest in saying it was her editor's idea to use it.

An intriguing fact is that Celia Maysles may be herself a bit of a throwback. Most of the younger new generation of filmmakers refuse to become identified with any one approach to docs. They wish to keep their options open, whether making a straightforward documentary, a personal one, or presenting some combination of the two. For the moment at least, Celia Maysles and Henry Corra seem insistent on being identified with a particular kind of personal, revealing, even quirky movie. In their own way, they may themselves be practicing a bit of dogma.

• • • • • • • • •

Endnotes

1. See Al Maysles's principles of filmmaking, from his Web site, *www.mayslesfilm.com*.

2. Richard M. Barsam, *Non-Fiction Film: A Critical History* (Indiana University Press, 1992), 68.

3. Mark Cousins and Kevin Macdonald, *Imagining Reality* (London and Boston: Faber and Faber, 1996), 48–56.

4. Ginia Bellafonte, "A Dad Hunt that Ends in Ohio," *New York Times* (June 1, 2007).

5. A few months after I interviewed Celia Maysles and Henry Corra, I was informed by a third party that the two are a couple in real life; they are life as well as work partners.

chapter ten

IT'S A WRAP

· · · · · · · · · ·

S omewhere in the middle of writing this book, and in conversation
with Aviva Slesin, the Oscar-winning documentarian (*The Ten-Year
Lunch, Hidden Children*) who now teaches at New York University, Slesin
said to me, "I hope you're not going to just profile the big Fab Four of
documentary filmmaking [Burns, Maysles, Wiseman, Kopple]. There's so
much more, so many more, and of course nobody ever credits the editors and
cinematographers." She suggested I take a look at the Oscar-nominated docs
of the past few decades to get a better sense of the diversity of documentary
filmmakers. Not that the Oscars are the be-all and end-all, but still. So, in a
kind of shorthand, here is a list of winners.

2007   Taxi to the Dark Side
2006   An Inconvenient Truth
2005   March of the Penguins
2004   Born into Brothels
2003   The Fog of War
2002   Bowling for Columbine
2001   Murder on a Sunday Morning
2000   Into the Arms of Strangers: Stories of the Kindertransport
1999   One Day in September
1998   The Last Days
1997   The Long Way Home
1996   When We Were Kings
1995   Anne Frank Remembered
1994   Maya Lin: A Strong Clear Vision
1993   I Am A Promise: The Children of Stanton Elementary School
1992   The Panama Deception
1991   In the Shadow of the Stars
1990   American Dream
1989   Common Threads: Stories from the Quilt

1988 Hotel Terminus: The Life and Times of Klaus Barbie
1987 The Ten-Year Lunch: The Wit and Legend of the Algonquin Round Table
1986 Artie Shaw: Time Is All You've Got and Down and Out in America (a tie)
1985 Broken Rainbow
1984 The Times of Harvey Milk
1983 He Makes Me Feel Like Dancin'
1982 Just Another Missing Kid
1981 Genocide
1980 From Mao to Mozart: Isaac Stern in China
1979 Best Boy
1978 Scared Straight!
1977 Who Are the Debolts? And Where Did They Get Nineteen Kids?
1976 Harlan County USA
1975 The Man Who Skied Down Everest
1974 Hearts and Minds
1973 The Great American Cowboy
1972 Marjoe
1971 The Hellstrom Chronicle
1970 Woodstock
1969 Arthur Rubinstein—The Love of Life
1968 Journey Into Self
1967 The Anderson Platoon
1966 The War Game
1965 The Eleanor Roosevelt Story

I stopped with *The Eleanor Roosevelt Story*, as it seemed that the award-winning docs preceding it were also mainly biographies or foreign land explorations—nothing necessarily new there.

What was it I was looking for or expecting to find? I wasn't really sure, but a couple things struck me right off. The Maysles have never won an Academy Award. How could that be? (Though *LaLee's Kin: The Legacy of Cotton* was nominated in 2001.) Neither, somewhat unaccountably, has Frederick Wiseman. (For a fuller recounting of the Academy's retrograde stance about docs, see Carl Plantangia's article in *Wide Angle*.)[1]

Another thing that leaped out at me was the mention of the film *Best Boy*. I had casually met the movie's cinematographer, Tom McDonough, in the late seventies. The circumstances are a blur of friends of friends. Nice fellow, I thought, but a documentary? Who cares?

This attitude was perhaps best characterized by the film's director himself, Ira Wohl, and truly takes us back to a time before the documentary hit its stride as *the* hot format. The year is 1980, and the publication is *The Soho Weekly News.* "Saying a film is a documentary is one strike against it," said Wohl ironically. "Mental retardation is two strikes. But it's not a depressing film, as you would be led to believe. I think it's very entertaining and enlightening. I'm not worried about what's going to happen to people once they go in and see the film. It's got a very strong story line."[2]

Entertaining. Story line.

And the more I thought about it, *Best Boy* seemed prophetic of some of the super-docs to come. It *did* have a story line (i.e., narrative). It *was* entertaining (despite its downer topic). And the filmmaker had some part in the film, and influence on his subject. Additionally, the film was a great hit with critics and is a humane, beautifully detailed and never condescending portrait of Wohl's retarded cousin, the "best boy," and of his parents, the director's aunt and uncle.

Wohl may have picked a topic with some hint of sensationalism, an unusual subject. But just as intriguingly, it touched on the question of how the documentary filmmaker might be encouraging his aunt and uncle—by the very making of the film—to see that their best boy might eventually have to leave home and live in another facility, some kind of broadening out of the "Heisenberg principle" of changes in behavior when viewed by the camera or a potentially broader audience. It also indicated the kind of subjective involvement with subject matter that both Errol Morris and, increasingly, Werner Herzog subsequently demonstrated in their films. It did not, of course, have the announced social intent of a Moore or Spurlock film. But maybe it did, in a more subtle way. The film also makes an intriguing contrast to the current darling of the film circuit, Jennifer Venditti's *Billy the Kid*, which has a similar subject matter (no big deal to us these days) but which instead sparked some discussion about the filmmaker's treatment of her subject.

Reviewer Michael Koresky had this to say about the film: "Like its protagonist, Jennifer Venditti's acclaimed documentary *Billy the Kid* is both pretty hard to dislike and difficult to parse. It's already scooped up awards at the Edinburgh, Los Angeles, and South by Southwest film festivals, and it's easy to see why: This compelling, ingratiating portrait of some days in the life of a charming and troubled fifteen-year-old New Englander, with its canny intimacy and sharp editing, manages to be up close and personal as well as safely discreet. Venditti, following around the not-quite-outcast teenager Billy vérité-style, is inoffensive in her intrusion, yet also manages to make the boy a compelling screen presence. What the film lacks in painful revelation, it makes up for in the way it avoids exploiting its subject. Refreshingly, in these days, when most documentaries seem couched in meta-commentary, the film never falls back on the crutch of having the filmmaker's ethical dilemma as a pivotal plot thrust."[3]

This last sentence may have been a swipe at Bar-Lev's documentary *My Kid Could Paint That*, yet the *New York Times* is harsher in its condemnation of Venditti's approach, deciding that "as one candid confession follows another, the camera's role in their solicitation becomes difficult to overlook," and concluding that "the filmmaker's decision to eschew other viewpoints underscores the fundamental friction at the heart of the documentary process: the flattery of observation is difficult to resist. When Billy, after persuading a shy waitress to be his girlfriend, is loudly applauded by a clique of town hangabouts, he is pleasantly surprised. 'The years of loneliness have been murder,' he tells them, and the men collapse with laughter. Whether a blurted confession or a line to the gallery, we'll never know."[4]

So it would seem that the question of the "Heisenberg Principle" that Frederick Wiseman and others have declared settled—that objects (or cinematic subjects) do not change when being looked at, or in the case of documentary, that people behave differently because cameras are around—is still open, after all.

And though Venditti is not in any sense a narrator or a participant in the film, the fact that she elicits confessions from her film's subject—someone who is a bit maladjusted—seems to make the director and her methods suspect, according to some.

Still, a film like this might never have been made or been as well received as it has been, historically speaking, if it were not for *Best Boy*.

In Wohl's case, a cheerful umbrella covers all this, and he said he wasn't worried about the film's fate due to its very strong story line. Perhaps that was why *Best Boy* had some reverberation for me. Story line. Narrative. What the breakthrough docs of the 1980s have in common.

Reports are that some of the negative comments about Venditti's movie took her aback. My guess is this reflects some current backlash against the inserted narrator, autobiographical film, and any kind of manipulation of the topic. But these things—as I have attempted to show—do seem to go in cycles.

It's the Story, Stupid

For yet another perspective, I looked to the picks of an Internet Web site, *Kino-Eye.com*, and its Ten Best Documentary films. After a first choice for the 1929 Vertov film (Vertov seeming to become the Flaherty of our age), *Kino-Eye.com* lists:

Don't Look Back (D.A. Pennebaker, 1967)
Titicut Follies (Frederick Wiseman, 1967)
Werner Herzog Eats His Shoe (Les Blank, 1980)
Notebook on Cities and Clothes (Wim Wenders, 1989)
Dialogues with Madwomen (Allie Light and Irving Saraf, 1993)
When We Were Kings (Leon Gast, 1996)
Buena Vista Social Club (Wim Wenders, 1999)
A Kalahari Family (John Marshall, 2002)
Bowling for Columbine (Michael Moore, 2002)

All these films have a strong narrative story line, some have a strong presence of a narrator or autobiographical superstar, and many have some witty and baroque stylistic flourishes. And as with all film history, especially in the development of a new form, the influence of one filmmaker on others comes up. In *When We Were Kings*, for instance, Al Maysles was a cinematographer. Taylor Hackford, who did the film *Chuck Berry Hail! Hail! Rock 'n' Roll*, the classic doc about Chuck Berry, shot the later footage for *When We Were Kings*, which was incorporated in such a way as to extend the narrative, and the cinematic layers, over twenty years. (Chapter 5 has tracked this enhanced narrative more fully.) Al Maysles, working as a photographer, even captured and kept a bit of photographer Richard Leacock in the classic and breakthrough film *Primary* about John F. Kennedy's Presidential run. How many of them thought about the positions they might have taken on ideas about movie-making, or their works in progress? How many had their work changed or influenced by the others? These are fascinating questions that are impossible to conclusively decide.

Some probes into these questions are taken up today in a wonderful intellectual sideshow. A conversation between Herzog and Morris where the two discuss their friendship, each other's work, and the doc form in general. Originally published in the magazine *The Believer*, it is reproduced on Errol Morris's Web site, *www.errolmorrisfilms.com*. (Quite intriguingly, Herzog is identified as a filmmaker, Errol Morris is identified as a documentarian. You'll have to ask them.)

Still, even they do not have any doctrine or code they are formally promoting in the organized way that Direct Cinema once did. Yet this once-familiar format, which the New Documentarian has been working against, is under constant and current revision by theorists today. It is, for instance, cleverly, if a bit wickedly, summarized by the eminent documentarian and critic Brian Winston:

1. The filmmakers, having arranged for their presence, should then say nothing further to the subjects of the film, certainly never ask them to repeat actions or do anything for the camera, least of all interviews.

2. The filmmakers should never use artificial lights, but rely on the increasing sensitivity of film stocks, further enhanced by forced development.

3. They should never add sound—neither effects, nor music, nor, most importantly, 'voice of God' commentary.

However, Winston observes about Robert Drew and the Direct Cinema Group that "they immediately cheated." According to him, these "purists" added music and light, their editors manipulated footage in order to create narrative, and their backers (the network) forced them to add commentary. Most tellingly, Winston declares that editors, particularly Patricia Jaffe and Charlotte Zwerin, manipulated the footage in order to "release the meaning of their long shots and create the necessary stories audiences expected from a narrative." And he suggests that there is much more attitude expressed in a Maysles brothers film than they ever admitted to. *Salesman*, Winston observes, is a "feature cut for theatrical release by Zwerin, the inadequacies of the central figure are as ruthlessly exploited by the filmmakers (Al and his brother David on sound) as are Willie Loman's in Arthur Miller's fictional *Death of a Salesman*." Ultimately, Winston decides that in his later years, Al Maysles insists that he is lovingly sensitive to his subjects, but that is not so. "In old age, Al Maysles has taken to insisting that the clue to his cinema is his sensitivity to his fellows, but this is simply not on view in his masterworks, such as *Salesman* or *Grey Gardens*, which equally unkindly and unsympathetically probes the lives of two extremely eccentric, reclusive distant relatives of the Kennedys."[5]

Still, Winston concludes this article by saying that Direct Cinema is far from dead, and is still a reference point for contemporary documentarians.

A Seismic Shift

It's always fun—if often wrong—to pinpoint a turning year as a fulcrum or watershed. To hazard a guess for the official appearance of the new doc form, 1988 seems like a very good possibility.

Though I cited *Medium Cool* in the opening pages of this book to indicate a seedbed of cross-fertilization from fiction film to documentary, other commentators and filmmakers, including Slesin and Henry Corra referred to the decade of the 1980s and the personal films of Pincus and McElwee.

"Ed who?" said this writer-as-ignoramus when first hearing the name Pincus. But a probe here and there and some difficult-to-find films revealed Pincus's significance in two incredibly important parts of the movement toward the neo doc: he kept some possibly vérité inspired elements in his movies, and he also included scenes of himself and his family. The press release for his 1980 film *Diaries* picks up on Pincus's sense of humor. Here is a clever mini-treatment of the film, taken from the Pincus folder at the Billy Rose Theatre Collection at Lincoln Center:

Diaries:

The Main Characters:

Jane, age 34–39. Ed's wife and mother of two. A co-author of *Our Bodies, Ourselves*: does batiks and works in the women's health movement.
Sami, age 6–11. Ed and Jane's daughter.
Ben, age 2–7. Ed and Jane's son.
Ed, age 33–38. The filmmaker (see attached biography).
Tapper. Their dog.
Ricky Leacock. A filmmaker. Ed's colleague at the MIT Film Section.
Other characters.

Pincus embarked on his *Diaries* after becoming disillusioned with standard documentaries and their (in his words) "peculiar distance between filmmaker and subject." To correct that, *Diaries* is shot by a single person, who happens to be the husband, father, or pal of everyone in the film. Pincus had the breakthrough thought of leaving certain "mistakes" in the film. For instance, he told G. Roy Levin, "One time Jane and I were having an argument—it was about me filming all this personal stuff—and it ends with her telling me to fuck off, and just as she says that, the light starts coming on and disappearing. Well, that stays in."[6]

And 1988 was also the year of *Driving Me Crazy* and *The Thin Blue Line*, followed by *Roger and Me* in 1989. In this year (and the next) it seemed that documentary filmmakers were there to mix it up, to force us to rethink things. Not just the state of the documentary, but the state of the world. A fancy way to classify what these filmmakers were documenting might be the deconstruction of reality in the postmodern world. And one of the easiest ways to do that—just ask Eisenstein and D.W. Griffith—was by using fiction tactics.

Detractors to such a broad generalization will say that there has always been such a mix, citing *The Great Train Robbery*, based on real life events and shot in 1903.

Yet from lowbrow to highbrow and everything in between, films of the past thirty years have picked up on or blended the new doc form and formats, from *Crumb* to *Hoop Dreams* to the lesser-known *Night and Fog* (the Resnais film about the concentration camps that mixes black and white newsreel images, color photography, and archival footage with classical music and a calm but truth-telling narrative voice).

There is the ready movement between fact and fiction (thank Perry Miller Adato, Peter Davis, Herzog) the inserted narrator or star (thank Moore and Spurlock), an intimate interviewing style that reflects our view of people as being both or neither good or bad (kudos to Errol Morris), and a continuing exploration of the personal voice and experience (thank Berliner, McElwee). Even so, the documentary is retaining some social, or in any case humane, goal (credit here to Kopple, Maysles, Wiseman). This is beginning to sound like an Academy Award acceptance speech, which, of course, in some ways it is. And as if to take an additional poke at reality, some postmodern documentarians include self-reflexivity in their works, making evident the subjectivity that shapes their representations of reality.

Television: The Democratic (or is it the Documentarian's?) Art

The way I see things shaking out, today's generation of documentary filmmakers is in a somewhat more conservative mode than the expressive documentarians who preceded them, and yet are not limiting themselves or strictly harkening back to the methods of Direct Cinema. And one brand-new model has arisen, perhaps due to reality shows. Director Morgan Spurlock told me: "Reality television has opened the door for audiences to get interested in the experiences of regular people. Viewers realize you don't have to be a star, or be bankable, to be watchable. It's a great thing for documentaries."

Spurlock laughingly says, of course, that his own show, *30 Days*, is his favorite reality show, but then goes on to praise *Top Chef*, citing the fact that his wife is a chef. "We enjoy watching that show. Also, I like the show where you watch people make clothes. It's creative. I'm a creative person. Some of them are a bit too much, of course, like the show about the sweet-sixteen birthday party [MTV's *My Super Sweet Sixteen*]." No slouch when it comes to mixing it up, Werner Herzog said in the spring of 2007 at both Goethe

House and the Film Forum that he had planned to "do something on *The Anna Nicole Show*, but she died before I had the chance."

And muckraking Michael Moore was clearly on to something when he interviewed the producer of *C.O.P.S.* in *Bowling for Columbine*. Though violence was the ostensible topic, *C.O.P.S.* was also a significant development in reality programming. It first aired in the spring of 1989, coming about partly due to the need for new programming during the five-month-long strike of the Writers Guild of America. It showed police officers on duty apprehending criminals; it introduced the camcorder look and cinéma vérité feel of documentaries to be imitated by much subsequent reality television.

Even a relative purist like Barbara Kopple is accepting the envelope-stretching quality of some of today's reality television. In *Documentary Filmmakers Speak*, she says, "There's reality shows with sort of manipulated reality. And as much as people might not like that, it's really opened up the whole world of nonfiction filmmaking to show people at networks and other places that they can be entertaining and exciting and interesting and that there are audiences for them."[7]

History Repeats Itself

What also makes reality television attractive to today's filmmakers and TV producers is economics. It costs $1 million to produce an hour-long reality television show, and $2-3 million to produce a regularly scheduled sitcom episode. One reason, of course, is that writers are not required. Or are they? Instead they take the title of executive producer, as some fess up to. It seems to be an open secret that the shows are set up in advance. And according to Ron Simon, the curator of television at New York City's Museum of Television and Radio, this is a trend that can be traced to the manipulation of contestants (and audiences) in television's earliest quiz show, *The $64,000 Question*.

The stunt aspect, taken from reality TV, was transferred successfully to the films of Spurlock, Moore, and others. So, too, the notion of the "fish out of water"—like *The Simple Life*, with Paris Hilton and Nicole Richie. That is, putting someone in a completely unfamiliar environment or situation and watching them squirm, then make the most of it or not. If the premise of some of these shows seems sadistic or Hobbesian, this is perhaps one reason why they are looked down on by snobs as well as much of the left-leaning press. Though perhaps not those who enjoy class interchanges, such as reversal shows that (temporarily) exchange and contrast wives or families in different social castes.

Alessandra Stanley, the television critic for the *New York Times*, finds other categories. In her think piece "The Classless Utopia of Reality TV," she focuses on other conventions of documentary film used in reality television. Two types she singles out are what she terms "the confessionals" and a "hybrid of semiprofessional personalities who play themselves on camera" (From an acting point of view, this might be seen as a potentially lucrative cottage industry):

> *The Hills*, like its forerunner, *Laguna Beach*, aims to be absorbed as drama. This crypto-scripted show dispenses with the so-called confessionals, a convention of the reality genre in which a protagonist breaks away to vent directly to the camera, and relies instead on evocative shots of skylines or highway traffic at dusk, lingering close-ups and moody pop music to underscore emotional highs and lows.
>
> The principals, whose romances and kitchen quarrels furnish plotlines, are not really actors, but neither are they ordinary people exactly; they are a new hybrid of semiprofessional personalities who play themselves on camera. Men and women recruited for their resemblance to *Us* magazine celebutantes are now featured players in *Us* magazine, and boast lifestyles as lavish, and socially restricted, as Paris Hilton.[8]

Such interchangeability owes a great deal to the new hybrid, which mixes fact and fiction and is categorized in the book *Faking It*.

> Another hybrid documentary form is Reality TV, which is distinctive because it pairs documentary traits with fictional aesthetic devices. … Reality TV, with its characteristically shaky hand-held camera, gives the impression of unmediated, spontaneous action, captured as it happens.(Dovey, 1995)…These new hybrid reality formats make careful attempts to 'establish their public service credentials' (Kilborn and Izod, 1997, 160) by claiming an educative role, and by arguing that such programs encourage viewers to help solve crimes. However, they owe more to tabloid sensationalism and similarly reflect the need to entertain and retain large audiences.… Docu-soap and Reality TV are connected to mock-documentary because they too have developed in the spaces between fact and fiction.[9]

Questioning the Form in the Womb

Pauline Kael wrote about some of these matters in her notorious piece on *Gimme Shelter*, and it is an article that posits that fooling with "reality" is bad, though Kael makes some allowances. Would that she were around to pillory reality television, but her thoughts on 1960s television documentaries will have to do, prescient as they were in capturing some coming areas of discussion: "With modern documentarians, as with many TV news cameramen, it's impossible to draw a clear line between catching actual events and arranging events to be caught. A documentarian may ask people to reenact events, while a TV journalist may argue that it was only by precipitating some events that he was able to clarify issues for the public—that is, that he needed to fake a little, but for justifiable reasons. There are no simple ethical standards to apply."[10]

Do ethics apply to shows like *American Gladiators* or *Dancing with the Stars*? Does the reality TV audience know or care that some of the content was planned in advance? At the moment, the slick and legitimate-looking surface of these shows, plus the immediate gratification of watching a winner, loser, or just "ejectee" seems to satisfy audiences that what they are looking at is for real, especially in shows such as *Big Brother, Supernanny, Wife Swap, The Biggest Loser, Celebrity Apprentice*. The immediate gratification of seeing a conclusion looks real enough.

These shows actually do not stray too far from their roots in sports events, especially television's "fake" wrestling, which began in the 1950s.

Richard and Lisa sweat it out the in the *Top Chef* season finale of 2008.

It was questioned, but not a lot, because it was fun. "Lucky Samanovitch" was one flamboyant and incredibly amusing wrestler, a bottle blond if there ever was one, and a great actor grimacing and grinning when he rubbed his opponents on the mats, or against the ropes. Then as now, we knew that it wasn't real, that it was a blast, and that it was a spoof on competition.

Today it may be a goof, but the competition is only too real. The most sobering part about today's reality television is not that it depends on documentary-type reality, or that hybrids of stars populate it, or that entertainment values have tainted its newscasters (an old complaint)—but that it is so serious.

You die if you lose in the new century, or you lose your fortune, or social caste. Wasn't it a lot more fun when only the game was up for grabs?

The Heisenberg Principle, As Done on TV

The first reality television show was about the Loud family. *An American Family*, the first truly invasive show about a family's private life, live on television, aired in the 1970s. It brought up many issues of privacy, the effect the camera had on the family, the subsequent notoriety of the Louds, and even whether the show contributed to the family's breakup. Here discussions about the loosely applied Heisenberg Principle (though not so formally referred to) dominated the media at the time. Would the Louds have gotten divorced if the show hadn't been made and highlighted some of their issues? Why did the Loud husband allow the discovery of his infidelities while cameras were in the room? How was Pat's, the wife's, reaction changed?

Should Pat Loud have announced her intent to divorce her husband on television? Could the marriage have been fixed and the divorce rescinded if it hadn't been publicly announced for all the world to see?

Lance may have been gay and that fact would not have been altered by his coming out on national TV, yet in this case the old-fashioned social intent of documentaries may have met a goal. A "progressive" issue was vetted and advanced in the popular consciousness.

Currently the form has some loyal if not unexpected promoters. Reality television can capture some of the high points of the spontaneous, creative signposts of documentary filmmaking according to television producer Michael Hirschorn. "The best moments found on reality TV are unscriptable, or beyond the grasp of most scriptwriters. It's no coincidence that 2006's best scripted dramas—*The Wire*, HBO's multiseason epic of inner-city Baltimore, and *Children of Men*, Alfonso Cuaron's futuristic thriller—were studies in meticulously crafted 'realness,' deploying naturalistic dialogue, decentered and chaotic action, stutter-step pacing, and a reporter's eye for the telling detail." Of course, the author then goes on to observe that Michael Moore was inspired by reality television in his "dropping the form's canonical insistence on pure observation."[11]

By those standards, Eisenstein, Vertov, and even the Lumiere Brothers would be taking a crack at reality TV.

The Web and Its Ways

And now, the new media. Web graphics, with their pop-ups, visual impositions, and frequent repeat images have certainly influenced the new doc's style. (Though no one yet has used the Web for marketing as successfully as the directors of *The Blair Witch Project*.)

Contemporary fascination with the doc also owes a debt to technology. Digital is cheap enough for many to try their hand at making a film, and the financial success of many of the docs make the form even more enticing.

And the most obvious, if saddest fact of all: documentaries are providing some of the few detailed images of our vanishing planet. For as wonderful as the series by David Attenborough may be and as we marvel at the technology, which can capture underwater as well as land plants and animals, part of our awe may have to do with our realization that these records may be needed to keep these images alive, for otherwise we will have no moving "hi def" representation remaining.

Still, we must face up to something about the form. Many of the most iconoclastic, genre-busting, and innovative documentary filmmakers are now middle-aged and beyond. Perhaps their generation just naturally gravitated to more expressionistic shapes. And a number of today's younger documentary filmmakers are returning to what they see as a more standard, straightforward format. This may be because they are from a more conservative time, or it may be the cyclical nature of how we view documentaries. Or it may be because the next (younger) generation always rejects what has gone before. Pragmatically, if self-servingly, and with neither gratitude nor guilt, some seem to adapt the breakthroughs of their immediate progenitors in whatever combination they require to make their points, and their films.

Did They Take It Too Far?

"The ghost of 9/11 did a lot of damage to documentaries," says Aaron Woolf, the previously mentioned director of *King Corn*. "Documentary filmmakers depend entirely on the trust of people who agree to take part in their films, and after Michael Moore and *Borat,* it's getting harder and harder to get access to executives, or to convince people you want to hear what they have to say and not misrepresent them. There's a huge wall to climb over now cause they've seen what it's like to deal with Michael Moore."

And while you hate to take one little white-haired gentleman as the center of a maelstrom about the contested documentary form, it does seem to be that sometimes Al Maysles finds or puts himself there. Not only with the contested *Blue Yonder* footage, and that he allegedly threatened to not turn up in Amsterdam if that personal and subjective film of his niece's, *Wild Blue Yonder*, were shown.

He often takes up central theories of the documentary, even in his personal life and press releases. For instance, Mark Wexler was pleased to tell me that he had gotten a "note from Al" saying he had very much enjoyed *Tell Them Who You Are*, the doc in which he was interviewed about his friend Haskell Wexler, Mark's father. Yet in my talk with Al he said he felt Mark had gone too far in the personal film (and subsequently Mark said he was surprised—and seemed a bit hurt—to hear this when I indiscreetly mentioned the comment). Of course, Maysles takes a position on the on-going dialogue about Michael Moore, and even about those who "correct" Moore.

In the film *Michael Moore Hates America*, director Michael Wilson tries to expose what he considers the deceptive and manipulative techniques of Michael Moore. One person he interviewed for the film was Maysles.

But after the film's release, Maysles said he had no idea he was actually going to be in the film, and that he only found out by reading the review in *Daily Variety*. He objected to the context in which the film's interview used his quote (that Moore is "tyrannized by his method, which is to simplify complex ideas"). Wilson countered that Maysles had given a "verbal release."

Of course, you have to wonder what Al thought the footage was going to be used for.

So far, Al (or more properly, Al's attorney and Al) has had the last word: "What irritates me so much is that it's so contrary to the way I work. The only other experience I've had like this was when Pauline Kael wrote a review of *Gimme Shelter* in which she assumed that we had staged everything," said Maysles. And Maysles's attorney concluded, "Mr. Maysles was misled into granting an initial interview based on the representation that the interview would be about Michael Moore's technique, not a personal attack on Michael Moore and his films."

"It's propaganda," Maysles ultimately decided about *Fahrenheit 9/11*. "I would clearly say that, but it's good when it's on your side."[12]

So he's taken a "little thing" like an interview in a relatively minor film, and used it to comment on reconstruction, propaganda, the purpose of docs, and more. Whether you agree with him or not, his energy is amazing.

Other Methods, Other (Editing) Rooms

Many, even Spike Lee, are making films that might have come out of the labs of Grierson or Maysles. Nick Broomfield, one of the first to use the inserted narrator in the contemporary age, and known for his subjective docs such as *Aileen: Life and Death of a Serial Killer* and *Biggie and Tupac*, has made a straightforward and highly praised documentary about the Iraq war, *Battle for Haditha*, lauded for its verisimilitude, a term one would hardly use for the boundary-breaking *Driving Me Crazy*.

Still other new docs have uniquely created a patchwork of techniques. For instance, some, like *Tell Them Who You Are* and *Sketches of Frank Gehry*, may seem to be based on the one-on-one or talking heads interviewing techniques of news journalism to investigate personal issues. But on closer examination, they have the stylistic intensity of an Errol Morris movie, and the manner of lingering long on their subjects and really looking as poetry is said to do, by making us slow down long enough to consider and re-consider. My doctoral dissertation director told me there once was a course at Harvard University, in the heyday of the "New Criticism" in English departments, called a "A Course in Slow Reading," and in many ways that's what documentary filmmakers are now enticing us to undertake: To examine images to see if "truth" lies within the image, or within the context (implying narrative, and a filmmaker's point of view). Morris emphasized this slowing down aspect when I spoke with him in the spring of 2008: "I like to use slow motion," he said, "because I'm telling a story around a still image. Photographs can reveal and conceal. Photographs both expose and cover up."

My own feeling is that there is enough here for everyone, practitioners of the neo-doc and traditional doc alike. Moreover, now that the cat of expressionism is out of the bag once again, it will not go back in.

Whether or not the more fanciful approach to filmmaking will be dominant, it is unarguable that the postmodern era seems to have brought a sense that images alone cannot define absolute truths. Filmmakers continue to seek out new ways to present a truthful view of reality and history; they employ a variety of strategies, including interviews, (some) re-creations, and fictionlike narratives, in an effort to choose among several relative truths, as they attempt to retrieve the truth of the past and of the present. And for even those cinematic neo-cons using nearly exclusively the older format, there seems to be a true quest for permanence in a scary world.

"The word 'documentary' used to make people shiver," said Kees Ryninks, cofounder of CinemaNet, a European organization based in Amsterdam devoted to promoting the best docs around. "But I credit films such as *March of the Penguins*, *Fahrenheit 9/11*, and *Super Size Me* for transforming conceptions about a boring genre into an exciting one."[13]

Robert Thompson, director of the Center for the Study of Popular Television at Syracuse University, takes it down to cases. "I like the idea that eight years from now there may be a half-dozen docs out there with wild and crazy axes to grind, battling it out at the cineplex. Part of our entertainment regimen might be watching these dueling ideologies. I think it's a fine use of movies and a healthy thing for the culture."

Perhaps predictably, when I repeated this comment to Morgan Spurlock, he lit up happily and said, "From your lips to God's ears."

• • • • • • • • •

Endnotes

1. See Carl Plantinga, "The Mirror Framed: A Case for Expression in Documentary," *Wide Angle* 13.2 (April 1991): 41–42, for a discussion of the "suppression of documentary expression" in not recognizing certain films. Plantinga says, "Perhaps the most obvious example of the suppression of documentary expression is the lack of recognition accorded certain recent documentaries by the Academy of Motion Picture Arts and Sciences. In its award nominations, the Academy has ignored many of the most important documentary films of the last decade. *Gates of Heaven* (1978), *Sherman's March* (1984), *The Thin Blue Line* (1988), and *Roger and Me* (1990), to name just a few, have all been neglected in the nominations for Best Feature Documentary. Ironically, these are also films which have played commercial theaters, drawn sizeable audiences and generated impressive media attention. ... [and] the official snubbing of these films is a symptom of widely held notions about the nature of documentary film. ... Thus, forty-five filmmakers, including Spike Lee, Pamela Yates and Louis Malle, signed an open letter to the film community last year, protesting the omission of *Roger and Me* from the Academy Award nominations for Best Feature Documentary."

According to Plantigna, the nominating committee "seems to have a very narrow-minded approach to what documentary films are. They can only be, quote unquote, 'objective reportage.'"

2. "Interview with Ira Wohl," *Soho Weekly News* (March 12, 1980).

3. Michael Koretsky, *Reverse Shot* (December 3, 2007).

4. Jeannette Catsoulis, "About a Boy, His Village, and Time in the Spotlight," *New York Times* (December 6, 2007).

5. Brian Winston, "North American Documentary in the 1960s," in *Contemporaruy American Cinema*, ed. Linda Ruth Williams and Michael Hammond, (Berkshire, England: McGraw-Hill, 2006), 78–79, 88.

6. G. Roy Levin, "Documentary Explorations," *Millimeter* (March 1976).

7. Liz Stubbs, *Documentary Filmmakers Speak* (New York: Allworth Press, 2000) 219.

8. Alessandra Stanley, "The Classless Utopia of Reality TV," *New York Times*, (December 2, 2007).

9. Jane Roscoe and Craig Hight, *Faking It: Mock-Documentary and the Subversion of Factuality* (Manchester and New York: Manchester University Press, 2001), 38–39.

10. Pauline Kael, "Beyond Pirandello," *The New Yorker* (December 19, 1970).

11. Michael Hirschorn, "The Case for Reality TV," *The Atlantic* (May 2007).

12. A fuller recounting is in "American Brouhaha" by Gabriel Snyder and Robert Koehler, *Variety* (October 14, 2004).

13. Ryninks quoted in "Compared with Their Filmmakers, the Penguins Have It Easy," *International Herald Tribune*, by Doreen Carvajal, reprinted in the *New York Times* (September 28, 2005).

TIPS AND TRICKS OF THE TRADE

On Writing

Davis Guggenheim: I don't write a script. I shoot and see where it takes me.

Werner Herzog: I was asked how much money I would need for a script, and I said $1.50 for a ream of paper. I don't do research. But I don't start the script until I have visualized the entire film. I ponder the idea for a while. Then I go for three or four days writing the script, making no corrections. Maybe I work this way because I see the whole movie in my mind. And maybe that's because I do not dream. I never have. [In press interviews in the 1970s, collected in the Herzog clippings file at Billy Rose Theatre collection at Lincoln Center, Herzog says he "rarely" dreams.]

Writers for Sacha Baron Cohen—Ant Hines, Dan Mazer, Peter Baynham

Ant Hines: We come in with a point of view. We wanted the film to say something. *Jackass* is hilarious, but it doesn't say anything. And *Borat*, even in the three-minute things—in the same way as *Da Ali G Show* and Bruno [another Cohen character]—they all say something.

Dan Mazer: We have a point of view; it's satirical and—hopefully—politically relevant. We've always wanted to do that.

Peter Baynham: Also, the story has, like everything else, got to be slave to the comedy in order to deliver eighty-five minutes or ninety minutes that you keep watching. And for you to stay interested, you must care about what's going to happen to Borat. We had versions of this where there was much more of Borat and Azamat and their relationship. Then you sit and you go, in the end people will [only] care about that relationship to a certain point. You want them to care about Borat and Azamat just enough so that when you get to the naked fight and it kicks off, you care.

Cohen: The objective of a film scene is twofold: first, be funny, and second, to have a plot point or beat. It's a constant struggle.

On Finding a Topic

Mark Wexler: When you make a documentary you have to pick subjects that you feel passionate about because you are not doing it for money. . . . I love New York and lived there for ten years when I was a magazine photographer. But even though now I'm in California, I don't think my subjects are limited in terms of the documentaries I'm making or want to make. Advances in equipment have made that possible.

Grace Lee: The beauty of documentaries is that you can be anywhere to make them as long as you have a compelling subject.

Roy Frumkes: I spend a lot of time riding the bus in New York City rather than the subway, which would be more time-efficient, because it allows me to be truly alone and meditate on ideas. Hard to do at home, when the phone is bound to ring.

Frederick Wiseman: Instead of making my subjects superstars, or picking superstars for subjects, I make the place a star.

Career Paths

Henry Corra: At this particular moment in time, I would say personalize your film, and pay attention to the aesthetics.

Jason Reitman (on making one's first film): My mom gave me the best advice: get your first shot in an hour and the crew will respect you. I did. And she was right.

Daniel Gordon: I wrote a couple books on sports topics—I've always been mad for sports—and one was nearly a best seller. When I was a teen, too, I had started publishing a kind of sports magazine. After the books came out I went to work as a producer for Sky Television. People say all kinds of things about Rupert Murdoch, but if I had been at the BBC I would never have risen so quickly. Then, after a while at Sky, I decided to go out on my own and formed my own film production company, VeryMuchSo Productions.

Overall Approach to Documentaries

Celia Maysles: Anyone can learn technique. But the kind of film I do is all about trust with the subject.

Kim Longinotto: I set about filming in as relaxed a way as possible so that people can express themselves freely. I think the brilliant thing about documentary is how you have to be incredibly flexible and quite humble, really, as the story takes on a life of its own, but at the same time be very clear about what you're trying to do. I like it when the experience of watching a documentary feels like fiction, in that it doesn't tell you what to think; you get caught up in the action and it's an emotional experience.

Errol Morris: I have this style of letting people talk, of not having a specific agenda, not knowing what you're going to hear. I was a Wall Street investigator for three years doing really, really huge cases. But when you clear aside all of the fancy frills about private investigators and private-detective work, it really comes down to people talking to each other and people being willing to give you information about themselves. Nothing really more than that. That's the essence of it.

Werner Herzog: To make films, you must be able to survive the humiliation, the stress. If you can't do that, you shouldn't be making films.

Kevin Macdonald: Making a film feature or documentary, I take each day new, without a grand master plan. That way you can be more spontaneous and respond to what is actually going on around you. I like to work in an atmosphere of controlled chaos.

Sara Lamm: I heard Albert Maysles speak so beautifully once about making a film with compassion, and it really resonated with me. And my friend the photographer Lloyd Ziff has said, "It's easy to take a mean photograph. It's hard to capture what's beautiful about someone." I thought about both of them while I was working on *Dr. Bronner's Magic Soapbox*. And, I watched *Crumb* like six times.

Frederick Wiseman: I recommend having complete editorial control. I have the right to turn down a broadcast, which is written in the contract, so the station can't split the film even if they want to [some of Wiseman's documentaries are up to three hours long]. That can really screw up a film.

Lauren Greenfield: Being accepted by these women at Renfrew [the Florida rehab center for anorexia] was a continual process, and something that we were constantly working on the whole time we were there. When I made *Thin*, I had a very small crew—all female. And we all had to get to know these women, and gain their trust. And it was a constant process.

Social Purpose of Documentaries (or Not)

Al Maysles: I don't go in with an overall specific social purpose. I let it evolve. For instance, the women in *Grey Gardens*. They weren't crazy, though the reviewer in the *New York Times* dismissed them that way. One could have been a very great singer. And yet there they are, women alone, clinging to each other, abandoned by their family. My brother was on a plane once and ran into Jackie O. She said, "I've got to go see the film. But I'll have to sneak in so the family doesn't find out I saw it." [Jacqueline Kennedy Onassis was the niece of "Big Edie" Beale.]

Mark Wexler: I made *Tell Them Your Name* because I thought it would be cheaper than therapy.

On the New Documentary Forms

Raoul Peck: The more films I make, the more blurred everything becomes. Reality is so much stranger than anything you can invent.

Jeremy Levine, the twenty-something writer-director of *Good Fortune*, a film about everyday Kenyans standing up for international efforts to alleviate poverty, in an impromptu interview at a Brooklyn Academy of Music event on doc films in 2007: While I appreciate the move away from objectivity and the acknowledgment of the filmmaker's position, I don't believe this new positioning needs to equate with an obsession of the filmmaker's role in the film.

Sydney Pollack: Since it's my first documentary [*Sketches of Frank Gehry*], it was completely different than any other experience I've had directing. When you work without a script, you are in a sense working in a much more improvisational way than when you are totally prepared.

Kevin Macdonald: The kind of documentaries I make are very narratively driven and adopt a lot of stylistic ideas from fiction into them. I'm not the kind of director who made sensitive, observational documentaries about children in Leeds or something. Ultimately, it all comes down to storytelling and it all comes down to having characters who are interesting and have depth and ambiguity, and aren't just obvious clichés. And the editing and the music is all part of the storytelling.

Errol Morris: I've heard complaints that my new film [*Standard Operating Procedure*] is too slick, too well made. As if that meant it was less truthful. I call it a nonfiction horror film.

Werner Herzog: I wanted to get shots of Pilgrims crawling around on the ice trying to catch a glimpse of the lost city, but as there were no pilgrims around I hired two drunks from the next town and put them on the ice. One of them has his face right on the ice and looks like he is in very deep meditation. The accountant's truth: he was completely drunk and fell asleep, and we had to wake him at the end of the take.

Schedules and Deadlines

Morgan Spurlock: I get up every day and try to exercise and clear my mind. I learned during a month's stay on a Navajo reservation to try to have an intent for every day. I work twelve- to sixteen-hour days; yes, I'm a workaholic. I grew up with a father who was one, and learned something both good and bad from that. For my new film, I have 900 hours of footage; we've been editing for fourteen months.

Werner Herzog: I shot *Grizzly Man* in nine days. I've never missed a deadline.

Frederick Wiseman: We get up at six or seven in the morning, shoot all day, drop stuff off at the lab, have a sandwich, and watch rushes until one or two in the morning. We are always talking about the film, reacting to it in some way, or telling stories about the shoot.

Training to Be a Documentary Filmmaker

Alan Berliner: The best training I got was learning about film's relationship to the other arts, and about other filmmakers, in the unique interdisciplinary program at SUNY Binghamton.

Werner Herzog: I never studied filmmaking. The only one who ever taught me anything about film was the actor Klaus Kinski. [Their filmmaking experiences are chronicled in the ironically titled *My Best Friend* (1999), where Herzog reminisces about the death threats he and Kinski exchanged during the making of *Aguirre: The Wrath of God* in the Peruvian jungle.]

Al Maysles: I don't think you have to go to school to learn to be a filmmaker. But for some people it's the right thing. I have a criticism of the way documentary is taught. They give kids a Bolex, it makes a lot of noise, and it only lasts for three minutes. It's the wrong kind of training, and sends people off in the wrong direction.

Barbara Kopple: New York has a wonderful and supportive filmmaking community, particularly for social issue documentaries. In my opinion, there is no better place to work. One really exciting thing about New York is that there is a whole host of new venues and festivals popping up every year, many of which are geared toward new filmmakers and innovative cinema. In addition, TV stations are starting to pick up more nonfiction, DVD distributors like the Criterion Collection are reaching new audiences and taking risks on classics and cutting-edge new works, and new technologies like podcasting and YouTube are redefining the way we think about distribution.

On Starring Yourself in Your Own Movie

Sacha Baron Cohen: You just have to be a believable character. The audience has to totally believe that you are who you say you are and like you enough to want to open up to you.

Kim Longinotto: I love the way Nick [Broomfield] appears in his films, but I don't want you to be thinking about me, or the camera or the filming, when you watch my films. I want you to feel that you're there, standing where I am and going through the emotional experience.

Money

Leon Gast: I worked on *When We Were Kings* for a very, very long time. When I started on it, my kids were in grade school. When it finally came out, I was a grandfather. After the first film [originally intended to be about the music festival accompanying the fight] fell through, I stayed in Africa and filmed the event with my own funds. But then when I came back to the US, I had to sue for the rights to the footage. I needed $100,000 to make the film. It seemed I was forever on the verge of making a deal. People would look at it and say it was great, then three months later it would fall through. Finally, after twenty-three years of living with footage in my apartment, my former lawyer came through and made a deal for me.

Morgan Spurlock: It's completely mind-blowing to me. We made *Super Size Me* for $60,000. It was upped to $65,000 when we got it into Sundance. Now it's the eighth highest grossing documentary of all time. To date it's made over $10 million.

Michael Moore: Every single film I've made has made lots of money [because] ultimately I won people over when they remember that the crazy guy in the baseball cap was one of the first to say that we're being led to war for fictitious reasons and that it wasn't going to work. Now, after all these years, people are seeing that's exactly what happened. So I turned out to sort of have my finger on the pulse that time. Maybe next time it might be worth listening to what I'm saying.

Al Maysles: For documentary, you're better off in New York. If you want something on HBO, for example. Sources for money are here. Public relations is here. The press is here.

Werner Herzog: Much of my creative life is spent trying to get money together. For instance, *Grizzly Man* financed *The Wild Blue Yonder*. But when you have a real strong project, the money falls into place.

Aaron Woolf: You can't imagine how difficult it is to go to people and try to get backing for a film when you say, 'It's a documentary about agricultural subsidies.'

Roy Frumkes: It's cheap today to commit yourself to an iffy form like the documentary. Really cheap. So cheap you could probably finance a feature doc entirely yourself and not break stride in terms of supporting yourself at the same time. So today, if you have a calling for it, how could you possibly not give it a shot?

Equipment and Crew

Frederick Wiseman: If I cannot raise the money to continue shooting in sixteen millimeter, I will have to go to one of the newer technologies. But I still edit on a Steenbeck; I don't use an Avid. I can't afford an Avid and also I don't need all the things that an Avid has because I don't do fades or dissolves. I don't mind taking the time to find material or rewind. I like handling the film, as it gives a chance to think about the material. I know guys who used to edit on Steenbecks or the 16 millimeter equivalent who switched to Avids, and some say it's great, and others, they don't like it. I am very loyal to DuArt Labs in New York City. I feel extremely obligated to Irwin Young of DuArt. He is the independent filmmaker's friend. He's genuinely interested in independents' work and has helped me out since 1966.

Sydney Pollack: If I were going to make a documentary now, I would probably do the entire doc with the lightweight, hi def digital cameras. There are certain sequences in a motion picture that I think can be done extremely well doing hi def digital. [But] I filmed all of the architecture [in *Sketches of Frank Gehry*] in Super 16 because I needed it to look as perfect as possible. In the interviews, particularly with Frank, I wanted him to be absolutely at ease and completely candid, so I could not use a crew or lights. I therefore did, in fact, shoot all of it with the Canon GL.

Al Maysles: I've switched completely to digital. I don't see that digital is so different from film. It's easier to handle, more economical. It's not that different and I don't see any aesthetic to say that it is. Whether it's Polaroid, digital, or film, you end up with the same picture.

Frederick Wiseman: Digital quality is not as good, but it means that a lot more people will have an opportunity to make films. But it remains to be seen if a lot more good films will be made, because the technical advances don't necessarily mean quality.

Werner Herzog: Digital is a file. Celluloid has its own life.

Aviva Slesin: I get tired of reading all these interviews with documentary filmmakers. They are repetitive, and they always forget to mention the important work of the cinematographers and editors of their movies. What about the cooperative nature of filmmaking?

Mark Wexler: I've never paid anyone to be in my films. As a rule I would not pay people; maybe a survival-type gift or something if someone is really destitute, of course.

On Publicity and Marketing

Morgan Spurlock: I learned how to market by working for two and a half years for the Sony Corporation. I learned all about branding from working with executives.

Film Festivals

Morgan Spurlock: South by Southwest is a rockin' festival. But Sundance is the quintessential film festival for independent filmmakers. When I got in and realized I might win, that all those years of film school and hard work and dreaming and being inspired by the win of *sex, lies, and videotape* in 1989 were going to pay off, there was a Cinderella moment. Cause there's always one little guy who comes out of nowhere and wins. And it's like, all of a sudden you realize, 'Oh my God. I am that guy.'

Roy Frumkes: Until recently I thought film festivals were, by and large, self-aggrandizing rip-offs. With the insane proliferation of feature docs and narratives due to the advent of professional-looking digital video equipment, my feelings have changed in that regard. More than 90 percent of indie features today will not be picked up through normal channels. But exposure at fests presents opportunities for critics and others with clout to see the film and say something about it, which then can become part of one's press kit. Fests are still self-aggrandizing rip-offs, but indie filmmakers can get something important out of them, too.

BRIEF LIST OF FILM FESTIVALS

· · · · · · · · · ·

Amsterdam International Documentary Film Festival
Kleine-Gartmanplantsoen 10, 1017 RR Amsterdam, Netherlands
Telephone: +31 20 627 3329
Fax: +31 20 638 5388

Aspen Film Festival
www.aspenfilm.org

Berlin International Film Festival
www.bertinale.de

Big Sky Documentary Film Festival
www.bigskyfilmfest.org

Boston Independent Film Festival
www.iffboston.org

Brooklyn Independent Cinema Series
www.brooklynindependent.com

Cannes Film Festival
www.festival-cannes.fr

CineRail Paris Festival
www.cinerail.fest.com

Cleveland International Film Festival
www.clevelandfilm.org

DokFest Munich, Germany
www.dokfest-muenchen.de

Durango International Film Festival
www.durangofilm.org

FirstGlance
www.firstglancefilms.com

GenArt Film Festival
www.genartfilmfestival.com

Hamptons International Film Festival
www.hamptonsfilmfest.org

Hot Docs Festival
www.hotdocs.ca

IFP Market [New York]
www.ifp.org
Director: Ally Derks
Email address: info@idfa.nl
Web site: *www.idfa.nl*

Margaret Mead Film Festival
www.amnh.org/mead

Mill Valley Film Festival
www.mvff.com

National Geographic Environmental Film Festival
www.nationalgeographic.com

Nantucket Film Festival
www.nantucketfilmfestival.org

New York Film Festival
www.filmlinc.com/nyff/nyff.htm

New Zealand International Film Festival
www.insidefilm.com/australia.html

Newport International Film Festival
www.newportfilmfestival.com

Oxdox International Documentary Film Festival
www.oxdox.com

Park City Film Festival
www.parkcityfilmmusicfestival.com

Princeton Documentary Festival
www.princeton.edu/spo/films

Provincetown Film Festival
www.ptownfilmfest.org

Red Shift Film Festival
www.rsfest.com

San Francisco Film Commission [complete listings of San Francisco film festivals]
www.sfgov.org/site

San Francisco Gay and Lesbian Film Festival
www.frameline.org

Sarasota Film Festival
www.sarasotafilmfestival.com

Silverdocs: AFI/Discovery Channel Documentary Festival
http://silverdocs.com

South by Southwest Film Festival
http://sxsw.com

Sundance Film Festival
www.sundance.org/festival

Sydney Film Festival, Sydney NSW
www.sydneyfilmfestival.org

T/F Film Fest [self-described as upstart Midwesterners hell-bent on showcasing all that is new, nontraditional, and genre-defying in nonfiction filmmaking]
http://truefalsefilmfest.blogspot.com

Telluride Film Festival
www.telluridefilmfestival.com

Toronto International Film Festival
www.tiff08.ca

Traverse City Film Festival [Michael Moore's film festival]
www.traversecityfilmfest.org/tixSYS/2006/festival

Tribeca Film Festival
www.tribecafilmfestival.org

Woods Hole Film Festival, Cape Cod
www.woodsholefilmfestival.org/2008

Woodstock Film Festival
www.woodstockfilmfestival.com

SELECTED BIBLIOGRAPHY

· · · · · · · · · ·

Alexander, William. *Film on the Left: American Documentary Film From 1931 to 1942*. Princeton, N.J.: Princeton University Press, 1981.

Arthur, Paul. "But Enough About You: First-Person Documentaries." *Film Comment* 42.4 (July/August 2006): 24–5.

——. "Essay Questions: From Alain Resnais to Michael Moore: Paul Arthur Gives a Crash Course in Nonfiction Cinema's Most Rapidly Evolving Genre." *Film Comment* 39.1 (January-February 2003): 58–62.

Arthur, Paul and Janet Cutler. "On the Rebound: Hoop Dreams and its Discontents." *Cineaste* 21.3 (1995).

Aufderheide, Patricia. "The Camera as Conscience: How Social Issues Inspire Moving Documentaries." *Chronicle of Higher Education* 45.9 (Oct 23, 1998).

——. "Public Intimacy: The Development of First-person Documentary." *Afterimage* 25.1 (July-August, 1997): 16–18.

Baker, Maxine. *Documentary in the Digital Age*. Burlington, MA: Focal Press, 2006.

Barnouw, Erik. *Documentary: A History of the Non-Fiction Film*, 2nd rev. ed. New York: Oxford University Press, 1993.

Barsam, Richard Meran. *Nonfiction Film: A Critical History*, Rev. and expanded. Bloomington: Indiana University Press, 1992.

——, ed. *Non-Fiction Film: Theory and Criticism*. New York: Dutton, 1976.

Beattie, Keith. *Documentary Screens: Non-Fiction Film and Television*. New York: Palgrave Macmillan, 2004.

Birri, Fernando. "The roots of documentary realism." *Argentine Cinema*, ed. Tim Barnard. Toronto: Nightwood Editions, 1986.

Bromley, Carl. "While the Academy Slept: The strange career of the documentary Oscar." *The Nation*, 272.13 (April 2, 2001): 40.

Brownlow, Kevin. *The War, The West and the Wilderness*. New York: Knopf, 1979.

Brunner, Edward. "Ersatz Truths: Variations on the Faux Documentary." *Postmodern Culture: An Electronic Journal of Interdisciplinary Criticism* 8.2 (January 1998).

Bruzzi, Stella. *New Documentary: A Critical Introduction*. London, New York: Routledge, 2006.

Bryant, Marsha. *Auden and Documentary in the 1930s*. Charlottesville: University Press of Virginia, 1997.

Carroll, Noel. "Nonfiction Film and Postmodernist Skepticism." *Post-Theory: Reconstructing Film Studies*, eds. David Bordwell and Noel Carroll. Madison: University of Wisconsin Press, 1996.

Casebier, Allan. "Idealist and Realist Theories of the Documentary." *Post Script: Essays in Film and the Humanities* 6.1 (Fall 1986): 66–75.

Chris, Cynthia. *Watching Wildlife*. Minneapolis: University of Minnesota Press, 2006.

Corless, K. "Documentaries: Thinking outside the box." [Includes an interview with Nick Broomfield]. *Sight & Sound* 17.1 (January 2007): 30–1.

Corrigan, Timothy, ed. *Werner Herzog: Between Mirage and History*. London: Routledge, 1987.

Corner, John. "'Documentary' in Dispute." *International Journal of Cultural Studies* 4.3 (September 2001): 352–59.

Cronin, Paul, ed. *Herzog on Herzog*. London, New York: Faber and Faber, 2002.

Crowdus, Gary. "Reflections on *Roger and Me*," *Cineaste* 17.4 (1990).

Culbert, David, ed. *Film and Propaganda in America: A Documentary History*.
Vol. I ed. Richard Wood, Vols. II and III by Culbert, Vol IV by Lawrence H. Suid. New York: Greenwood Press, 1990–1994.

Davidson, David. "Depression America and the Rise of the Social Documentary Film." *Chicago Review* 34.1 (Summer 1983): 69–88.

Dibbets, Karel and Bert Hogenkamp, eds. *Film and the First World War* Amsterdam: Amsterdam University Press, 1995. Series title: Film culture in transition.

Dorst, John D. "Which Came First, the Chicken Device of the Textual Egg? Documentary Film and the Limits of the Hybrid Metaphor." *Journal of American Folklore*. 112.445 (Summer 1999): 268–81.

Dovey, Jon. *Freakshow: First Person Media and Factual Television*. Sterling, Virginia: Pluto Press, 2000.

Druick, Zoe. "Documenting False History: Oliver Stone's Docudramas." *Studies in Documentary Film* 1.3 (December 2007).

Eaton, Michael. "Drawing it Out." [on Crumb] *Sight and Sound*, 5.7 (July 1995).

Eisner, Lotte H. *The Haunted Screen: Expressionism in the German Cinema and the Influence of Max Reinhardt*. Berkeley, Los Angeles: University of California Press, 1969.

Eitzen, Dirk. "When Is a Documentary? Documentary as a Mode of Reception." *Cinema Journal* 35.1 (Fall 1995): 81–102.

Ellis, Jack C. *The Documentary Idea: A Critical History of English-Language Documentary Film and Video*. Englewood Cliffs, N.J.; Prentice Hall, 1989.

Ellis, Jack C. and Betsy A. McLane. *A New History of Documentary Film*. New York: Continuum, 2005.

——. "American Documentary in the 1950s." *The Fifties: Transforming the Screen*, ed. Peter Lev. Berkeley, CA: University of California Press, 2006.

——. *The Documentary Idea: A Critical History of English-Language Documentary Film and Video*. Englewood Cliffs, New Jersey: Prentice Hall, 1989.

Feldman, Allen. "Faux Documentary and the Memory of Realism." *American Anthropologist* 100.2 (June, 1998): 494–503.

Fitzsimmons, Stephen J. and Hobart G. Osburn. "The Impact of Social Issues and Public Affairs Television Documentaries." *The Public Opinion Quarterly* 32.3 (Autumn 1968): 379–397.

Frumkes, Roy and Rocco Simonelli. *Shoot Me: Independent Filmmaking from Creative Concept to Rousing Release*. New York: Allworth Press, 2002.

Gaines, Jane M. and Michael Renov, eds. *Visible Evidence*. Minneapolis: University of Minnesota Press, 1999.

Gehring, Wes D. *Parody as Film Genre: "Never Give Saga an Even Break."* Westport, Conn.: Greenwood Press, 1999.

Godmilow, Jill. "How Real is the Reality in Documentary Film?" Interviewed by Ann-Lousie Shapiro. *History and Theory* 36.4 (Dec, 1997): 80.

Gouvaert, Charlotte. "How Reflexive Documentaries Engage Audiences in Issues of Representation: Apologia for a Reception Study." *Studies in Documentary Film* 1.3 (December 2007).

Grierson, John and Forsyth Hardy, ed. *Grierson on Documentary*. Revised ed. London: Faber, 1966.

Hockings, Paul and Yasuhiro Omori. *Cinematographic Theory and New Dimensions in Ethnographic Film*. Osaka: National Museum of Ethnology, 1988. Senri Ethnological Studies no. 24.

Hogue, Peter. "Genre-Busting: Documentaries as Movies." *Film Comment*, 32.4 (July-August 1996): 56(5).

Izod, John and Richard Kilborn, with Matthew Hibberd. *From Grierson to the Docu-Soap: Breaking the Boundaries*. Luton, Bedfordshire: University of Luton Press, 2000.

Jacobs, Lewis. *The Documentary Tradition, from Nanook to Woodstock*. New York: Hopkinson and Blake, 1971. 2nd ed. New York: W.W. Norton, 1979.

Jacobsen, Harlan. "Michel and Me." *Film Comment* 25.6 (Nov.–Dec. 1989).

Lane, Jim. *The Autobiographical Documentary in America*. Madison: University of Wisconsin Press, 2002.

Kael, Pauline. "Beyond Pirandello," *The New Yorker* (December 19, 1970).

Lay, Samantha. *British Social Realism: From Documentary to Brit-Grit*. London: Wallflower Press, 2002.

Loizes, Peter. *Innovation in Ethnographic Film: From Innocence to Self-Consciousness, 1955–85*. Chicago: University of Chicago Press, 1993.

Lovell, Alan and Jim Hillier. *Studies in Documentary*. London, Secker, and Warburg [for] the British Film Institute, 1972. Series title: Cinema One, 21.

Macdonald, Kevin and Mark Cousins, eds. *Imagining Reality: The Faber Book of Documentary*. London; Boston: Faber and Faber, 1996. *Author's Note: This is the same Kevin Macdonald who is the documentary filmmaker.*

MacDonald, Myra. "Performing memory on television: documentary and the 1960s." *Screen* 47.3 (Autumn 2006): 327–45.

Michelson, Annette, ed., *Kino-Eye: The Writings of Dziga Vertov*. Kevin O'Brien, trans. Berkeley, CA: University of California Press, 1984.

Milius, John Q & A with Ken Burns, "Reliving the War Between Brothers" *New York Times*, Sept. 16, 1990, an article published on the eve of the opening of *The Civil War*, which met in advance some academic historians' possible objections. Burns declares, "academia has taken away the idea that the word history is mostly made up of the word 'story.' And so one of the great faults is that we're not teaching history as a story. Historians traditionally were popularizers. People who were telling, singing, epic poems."

Miller, Mitchell. "Frame up." *Art Review* 3.11 (November/December 2005): 58–9.

Muir, John Kenneth. *Best in Show: The Films of Christopher Guest and Company*. New York: Applause Theatre & Cinema Books, 2004.

Nichols, Bill. *Blurred Boundaries: Questions of Meaning in Contemporary Culture*. Bloomington: Indiana University Press, 1994.

——. "Documentary Film and the Modernist Avant-Garde." *Critical Inquiry* 27.4 (Summer, 2001): 580–610.

——. "History, Myth, and Narrative in Documentary." *Film Quarterly* 41.1 (Autumn, 1987): 9–20.

———. *Representing Reality: Issues and Concepts in Documentary*. Bloomington: Indiana University Press, 1991.

O'Connor, John E., ed. *Image as Artifact: The Historical Analysis of Film and Television*. Malabar, Fla.: R.E. Krieger Pub. Co., 1990.

Plantinga, Carl. "The Mirror Framed: A Case for Expression in Documentary." *Wide Angle* 13.2 (April 1991).

Plasketes, George M. "Rock on Reel: The Rise and Fall of the Rock Culture in America Reflected in a Decade of Rockumentaries." *Qualitative Sociology* 12.1 (March 1989): 55–71.

Rabinowitz, Paula "Wreckage upon Wreckage: History, Documentary and the Ruins of Memory." *History and Theory* 32.2 (May, 1993): 119–137.

Renov, Michael, ed. *Theorizing Documentary*. New York: Routledge, 1993. Series title: AFI Film Readers.

Roscoe, Jan and Craig Hight. *Faking It: Mock-Documentary and the Subversion of Factuality*. Manchester; New York: Manchester University Press, 2001.

Rhodes, Gary D. and John Parris Springer. *Docufictions: Essays on the Intersection of Documentary and Fictional Filmmaking*. Jefferson, N.C.: McFarland & Co., 2006.

Rotha, Paul. *Documentary Film*. First published in London: Faber and Faber, 1935. Edition referred to in these pages is the third, revised and enlarged in 1952, R. MacLehose and Company,. The University Press Glasgow, reprinted by Communication Arts Books, Hastings House, New York. Ruoff, Jeffrey, ed. *Virtual voyages: Cinema and Travel*. Durham, NC: Duke University Press, 2006.

Sherman, Sharon R. *Documenting Ourselves: Film, Video, and Culture*. Lexington, KY: University Press of Kentucky, 1998.

Slide, Anthony. *Before Video: A History of the Nontheatrical Film*. New York: Greenwood Press, 1992. Series title: Contributions to the study of mass media and communications no. 35.

Spottiswoode, Raymond. *Film and its Techniques*. Illus. by Jean-Paul Ladouceur. Berkeley, CA: University of California Press, 1951.

Steven, Peter, ed. *Jump Cut: Hollywood, Politics, and Counter Cinema*. Toronto, Canada: Between The Lines Press, 1985.

Strauss, Neil, "The Man Behind the Mustache," *Rolling Stone* (November 14, 2006).

Stott, William. *Documentary Expression and Thirties America*. New York: Oxford University Press, 1973.

Stubbs, Liz. *Documentary Filmmakers Speak*. New York: Allworth Press, 2002.

Sturken, Marita. "Reenactment, Fantasy, and the Paranoia of History: Oliver Stone's Docudramas." *History and Theory* 36.4 (December, 1997): 64.

Trinh T. Minh-Ha "Documentary Is/Not a Name." *October* 52 (Spring 1990): 76–98.

Warren, Charles, ed. *Beyond Document: Essays on Nonfiction Film*. Hanover, NH: University Press of New England, 1996.

Wells, Paul. "The documentary form: personal and social 'realities,'" In: *An Introduction to Film Studies*, edited by Jill Nelmes. 2nd ed. London, New York: Routledge, 1999.

Winston, Brian. "Documentary and history on film: Brian Winston looks back at some of the ways in which history has been presented on the screen, and sees the documentary based on archival footage as intrinsic to its success." *History Today* 56.1 (Jan 2006): 29(5).

Wolfe, Charles "Straight Shots and Crooked Plots: Social Documentary and the Avant-Garde in the 1930s." *Lovers of Cinema: The First American Film Avant-Garde, 1919–1945*, ed. Jan-Christopher Horak. Madison: University of Wisconsin Press, 1995, 234–66.

INDEX

Books from Allworth Press

Allworth Press is an imprint of Allworth Communications, Inc. Selected titles are listed below.

Documentary Filmmakers Speak
by Liz Stubbs (6 × 9, 240 pages, paperback, $19.95)

Get the Picture? The Movie Lover's Guide to Watching Films, Second Edition
by Jim Piper (6 × 9, 304 pages, 130 illustrations, paperback, $24.95)

Making Independent Films: Advice from the Filmmakers
by Liz Stubbs (6 × 9, 224 pages, 42 b&w illustrations, paperback, $16.95)

Making Short Films
by Jim Piper (7 3/4 × 9 3/8, 288 pages, 325 b&w illustrations, includes DVD, paperback, $24.95)

The Art of Motion Picture Editing
by Vincent LoBrutto (6 × 9, 240 pages, 50 b&w illustrations, paperback, $19.95)

Splatter Flicks: How to Make Low-Budget Horror Films
by Sara Caldwell (6 × 9, 224 pages, 22 b&w illustrations, paperback, $19.95)

Screenplay Story Analysis: The Art and Business
by Asher Garfinkel (5 1/2 × 8 1/2, 208 pages, paperback, $16.95)

The Perfect Screenplay: Writing It and Selling It
by Katherine Atwell Herbert (6 × 9, 224 pages, paperback, $16.95)

Jumpstart Your Awesome Film Production Company
by Sara Caldwell (6 × 9, 208 pages, paperback, $19.95)

Producing for Hollywood, Second Edition
by Paul Mason and Don Gold (6 × 9, 256 pages, paperback, $19.95)

Hollywood Dealmaking: Negotiating Talent Agreements
by Dina Appleton and Daniel Yankelevits (6 × 9, 256 pages, paperback, $19.95)

The Filmmaker's Guide to Production Design
by Vincent LoBrutto (6 × 9, 240 pages, paperback, 15 b&w illustrations, $19.95)

To request a free catalog or order books by credit card, call 1-800-491-2808. To see our complete catalog on the World Wide Web, or to order online for a 20 percent discount, you can find us at ***www.allworth.com.***